Jordanna -

Thank you so muc[h]

for coming! I am s[o]

grateful for the support!

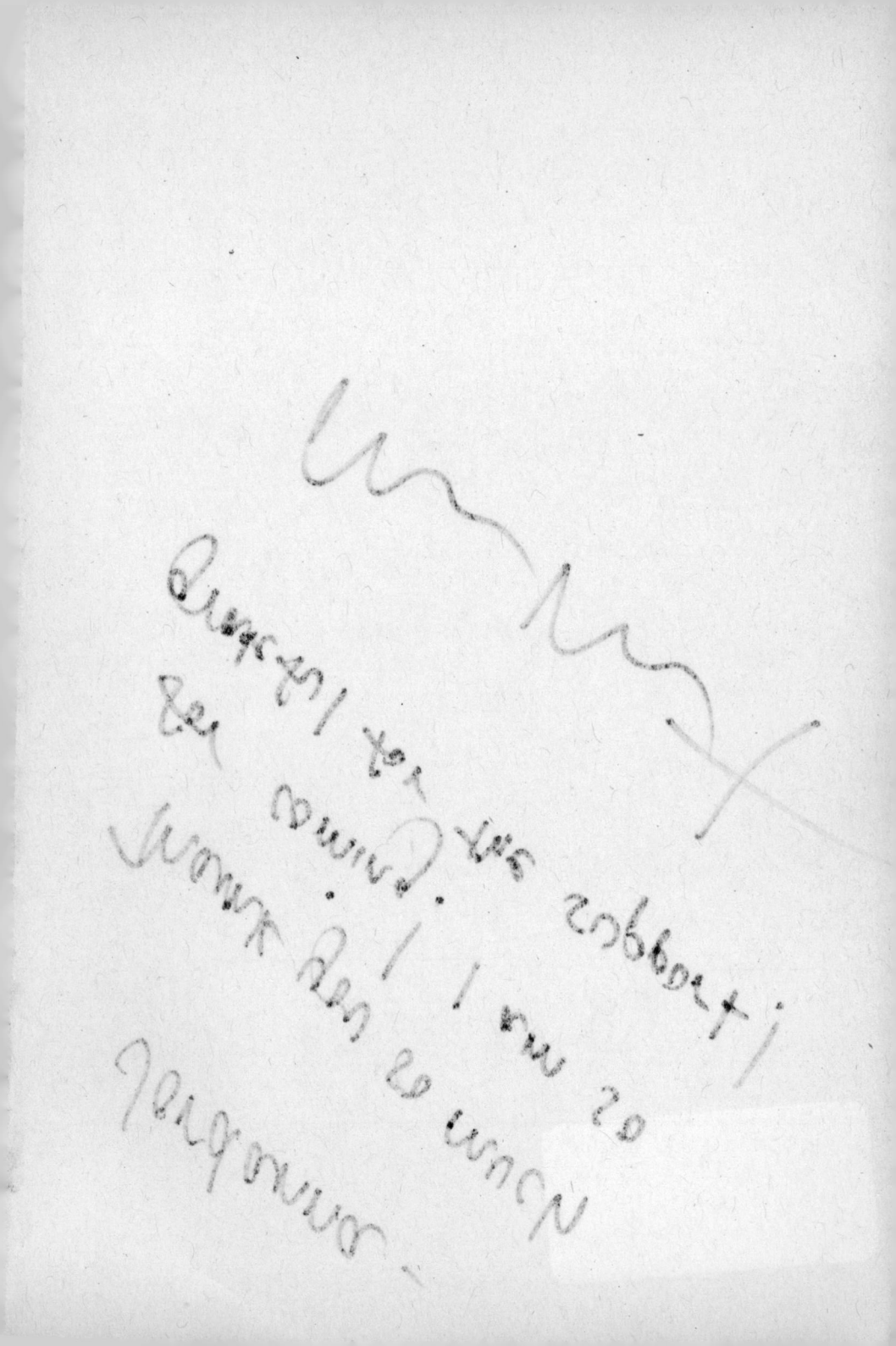

She's Got

GAME

She's Got GAME

The Woman's Guide to Loving Sports

(or Just How to Fake It!)

Melissa Malamut

ST. MARTIN'S GRIFFIN
New York

Author's Notes: Some names and event details have been
changed in the personal stories to protect the formerly
sports-clueless. At the time of this book's writing,
all player, team, and league information is current,
but since sports changes as often as the weather,
check some of the resources listed in the back of the book
for the most up-to-date information.

Illustrations copyright © 2010 by Leonard Camacho

Book design by Nicola Ferguson

www.stmartins.com

Library of Congress Cataloging-in-Publication Data

Malamut, Melissa.
    She's got game : the woman's guide to loving sports
(or just how to fake it!) / Melissa Malamut. — 1st ed.
      p. cm.
    ISBN 978-0-312-59896-9
    1. Sports—Miscellanea.   2. Sports—Terminology.
I. Title.
    GV707.M24 2010
    796—dc22

                            2009046947

First Edition: June 2010

10 9 8 7 6 5 4 3 2 1

In memory of my father, Robert Malamut, who
taught me a love of sports.

In memory of my nana, Sally Baler, who taught me
a love of writing.

CONTENTS

CONTENTS

CONTENTS

CONTENTS

Introduction

The Girlie Girl's Guide to the Games

I have definitely been called high-maintenance before. Not in the "you must eat at a nice restaurant" way, but in the "you take an hour and a half to get ready" way. On the other hand, I know more about sports than half of your guy friends. I have always wondered why more women don't love sports. I mean, competition is drama. And what woman doesn't love a little drama? And the people providing the drama? Just the most gorgeous, chiseled-bodied, athletic specimens in the country. Watching good-looking men flex their muscles, sweat, rage, and ooze testosterone is enough to get me hooked for a few hours. Never mind that the games themselves are actually pretty cool too.

Now, don't get me wrong, I don't sit and watch every game on television at all times. In fact, I can't stand watching games that my teams are not playing in. I can think of a hundred things I'd rather do than watch a game between two teams that I couldn't care less about. But if one of my teams is playing, that's a different story. In most cases I will not watch my team at a sports bar, because I end up missing all the action. At a bar I get too distracted socializing. I prefer to watch my team at a house party on a comfortable couch in front of a big-screen television. But if one of my teams is in a big game like a playoff or championship, then I need to be in front of my own television so I can hear every play and every bit of commentary. Obsessive and superstitious? Absolutely.

She's Got Game: The Woman's Guide to Loving Sports (or Just How to Fake It!) is a hip, humorous, and—most important—smart guide to all things sports, fashion, and beauty. It's not campy or gimmicky; it's an educated and knowledgeable introduction to the rules of the games. But there's more to it than rules—I also talk about history, superstitions, miracles, and the drama that has caused passion, heartache, and intrigue for millions of fans. Detailed drawings help explain the text, and beautiful illustrations show what going to a game can be like.

Additionally, sports slang, definitions, and abbreviations are explored and explained in overanalyzed laywoman's terms, with advice about the best time to go to the bathroom during the game and how to find your car after the game. I'll make sure you know things like how to pronounce players' names correctly, when the lines will be shortest at the concession stands, and where to sit for the best views. The basic rules are infused with funny accounts, quick tips, and a few "don't let this happen to you" horror stories.

But that's only the beginning. *She's Got Game* is not just about the games themselves; it is also a detailed and well-researched guide on what to wear when you go to a game. When attending a sporting event, whether for the first or the 50th time (or in my case, the 500th time), a big problem for women is what to wear. It can be more difficult to dress for than a first date, and what if the first date *is* a sporting event? How can we get away with heels when climbing narrow steps and navigating even narrower seating rows? Obviously jeans and sneakers are a comfortable option, but they're not always the most flattering.

Take going to a party, for example. If the man in your life says that you two are going to a friend's party tonight, that tiny bit of information is most likely enough for him to go about his day and be ready in five minutes. However for women it's "Well, whose party is it? Who is going to be there? Is it indoors or outdoors? What kind of flooring? Is it grass, tile, brick, or (worse) cobblestone?" If you are like me, you overanalyze everything and try to be prepared for all of the elements. Obsessing about these details can be mind-numbing, but in most cases it's necessary.

My motivation for this book was to gather all of the information that I had been accumulating for years about the best way to attend a game and really enjoy it, by covering all the bases (pun intended). It all began more than ten years ago, when my friends and I were discussing how to get away with wearing heels to a baseball game.

The fashion and beauty tips cover all different areas of the country because obviously dressing in winter in Minnesota is much different than in South Florida. *She's Got Game* is filled with extensive interviews with fashion and beauty editors from around the country. They give detailed tips on what to wear from clothing to makeup to accessories. Questions like "How do I get away with wearing heels?" and "What if I'm coming straight from work?" are answered. *She's Got Game* stays away from trends to ensure that your look remains classic and timeless. Interviews with female sportswriters and sports front-office professionals give a behind-the-scenes look at the games and share the intimate details that a fan can get only from someone on the inside.

I wasn't always a girlie girl. In fact, growing up, I was a tomboy to the core, a girl whose heart bled for the Red Sox and whose knees bled from sliding into home plate. I played on boys' Little League baseball teams and quit cheerleading because it conflicted with soccer season. My father's passion for the games was instilled in me at a very young age not only through his stories of sports lore, but through season tickets to ten different pro and college teams. This was in two different states and covered three climate zones. I thought that every kid grew up like me. My family wasn't rich. My father just loved sports. Most parents took their children out of school early for doctor's appointments or family emergencies; mine took me out for baseball's Opening Day (almost always a day game).

When I was a little girl, my mom would tell me stories about how she played on the boys' teams. This came from one of the most feminine women I'd ever seen. So it was normal for me to follow in her footsteps by playing every sport imaginable. Besides playing sports, my other main after-school activity was dance. I loved the makeup and hair and costumes that we got to wear for recitals. On Saturday I'd be a made-up ballerina, and on Sunday I'd be in my baseball uniform.

My father wasn't just an average sports fan. He was hardcore. He would travel to see big games. I remember being extremely jealous, sitting in my living room on a cold December Sunday in Massachusetts looking for my father in the stands

at the 1985 AFC Championship when the Patriots were playing the Dolphins in Miami in eighty-five-degree weather.

I remember how my father would doze off while watching
extra innings on television during the dog days of summer. I
remember how he scoured the *Boston Globe* sports section re-
ligiously. The look on his face when we entered a ballpark
or stadium is mirrored on my face when I enter a game today.
And although for me these emotions were inherited, I know
that they can also be learned and, as this book will show,
taught.

We took family vacations every summer, and no trip was
complete without visiting that destination's sports facilities,
like Dodger Stadium in Southern California, RFK Stadium
in Washington, D.C., or Madison Square Garden in New York
City. We had season tickets to the Red Sox, Celtics, Bruins,
and Patriots. We also lived across the street from some Boston
College football players and attended their games as well.
When we moved to Florida it was baseball's spring training
and Miami Heat, Florida Panthers, Florida Marlins, and Miami
Hurricanes games.

It was only natural that I would end up with a career in
sports, and I have had a variety of sports-related jobs while
simultaneously writing and editing beauty, lifestyle, and fashion articles. Whether I was working in public relations for the
NHL (pro hockey) or the PGA (golf), writing my own weekly
newspaper sports column or researching for *ESPN The Magazine,* I seamlessly switched from lip gloss to grand slams (a
baseball *and* tennis term).

My father was in a tragic accident in late 1997. He was jog-
ging and was hit by a car driven by a speeding and distracted
teenager. My father spent two years in the hospital paralyzed

from the neck down before he passed away. Sports still kept us going. I remember watching the NCAA March Madness selection show in the hospital room and reading the newspaper sports pages out loud to keep him filled in while passing the time.

My father wouldn't ever say which sport was his favorite, but I believe it was baseball. He taught my brother and me everything we knew about the game, but most important, he taught us passion for the sport. The strange thing is that the last sports game that my father saw (in person) was a Game 7 extra-inning World Series win for the Marlins. My father's accident was two weeks later.

After my father's death, my brother and I continued our family's sports traditions. Sports became more than just a game; for me, they became my last connection to my dad and a way to keep his memory alive.

I learned most of my sports knowledge and fan behavior from my father, but I have also picked up a few of my own traits along the way. My number-one rule is to be a good fan. Class and tact are traits that cannot be bought. My second rule is that I don't boo my own team. People will argue with this one, but it's just something I don't do. And rule number three is don't be a groupie. There is a repulsive "in the business" name for groupies: "road beef."

If you are reading this book to learn about sports to be closer to a man, that is just fine, but tread with caution. Some men will appreciate a woman who knows a thing or two about sports, but in my experience, being "one of the guys" doesn't always translate into becoming "one of the guy's girlfriends."

My focus in this book has nothing to do with a man. It's about learning and developing passion for the games *for you.*

There was an interesting article on ESPN.com years ago that I've never been able to get out of my head. It was written by a female sportswriter on the subject of how men don't really want to watch sports with you, no matter how educated you are on the subject. The male brain is different from the female brain, and even the way we watch sports is different. In the article, the men interviewed said that they wanted a woman to let them watch; she might make a great comment about a play and possibly bring them some food, but that was about it. They didn't necessarily want to watch *with* her. They wanted that separate part of their lives where she was not a participant. A beer-drinking, burping, just-one-of-the-guys girl is not sexy for all men.

Some women out there might think this book is a bunch of high-maintenance mumbo jumbo. They will throw on an oversized sweatshirt, ill-fitting jeans, and a pair of old sneakers and go to the game. And that is just fine; good for them. But for the rest of us it's good to know that sports aren't just for the guys or for the tomboys of the world. Sports can be all about the girlie girl. And after reading this book you will be well versed in any possible scenario that could come up during a game.

Of course, my deepest wish is that you fall in love with at least one team, sport, or player. But this book will also teach you how to be yourself and still look like a woman while eating a hot dog, drinking a beer, and booing the other team.

While you can certainly use this book to help you look the part of a sports fan, I think you'll have much more fun if you remain true to yourself. Even if that self is, well, high-maintenance. And that's okay, because sports fans in general are very high-maintenance. They demand the best in gear, food, and tickets. Have you seen a football game on television lately? Some men at the game will have their bodies painted from head to toe. I can guarantee you that those men took longer to get ready for the game than I did.

She's Got
GAME

1

The Best White After Labor Day (Home Whites): Major League Baseball (MLB)

It was a chilly April morning when I was in the fifth grade that I first realized I was sports spoiled. Just a few hours into the school day there was a knock at the classroom door and my father walked in and interrupted our English lesson. My classmates turned to me and asked, "Are you going to the doctor?" and "Are you in trouble?"

Most parents would take their kids out of school for only those kinds of reasons. My family, however, was a bit different.

"No," I said. "I'm going to Opening Day."

The smell of the grass still gets me just as excited as it did when I was that wide-eyed fifth-grader heading to the ballpark with my father. The feeling I get when I walk into a ballpark, any ballpark, is magical. I just feel at peace. If I ever won the lottery I'd take a summerlong trip to see every professional park in the country.

My passion for baseball is so extreme that on two separate occasions while I was sitting in the stands teaching a friend about the game, a stranger turned to me and asked if I worked for the team.

Every ballpark around the country is different. Some are right in the middle of the city, built into the landscape among the skyscrapers and condos. Some are in more rural areas with huge parking lots and lots of space. Some are old, some are new, and some are new but built to look old.

Because of this, the experience of attending a game is different in every city. Some parks have lots of fanfare and are surrounded by bars, restaurants, and fans that fill the streets before the game. Others are in more suburban areas with lots of cars in big parking lots where people tailgate and play catch.

Because baseball has so much rich history, the fans are very particular and educated about the game. Most take what happens on the field personally, as if their family members were playing the game. This is the same game, same team most likely, that their parents watched, and their parents' parents. And although it is just a game, to the men and women who spend their hard-earned paychecks to go watch it, it is more than a game. To some of us, it's a connection with loved ones who have passed away, a place where childhood memories come back to life, and a brief escape back to a time when things were easy and carefree.

In Major League Baseball (MLB) there are two leagues: the National League (NL) and the American League (AL).

NATIONAL LEAGUE

NL EAST
Atlanta Braves
Florida Marlins
New York Mets
Philadelphia Phillies
Washington (D.C.) Nationals

NL CENTRAL
Chicago Cubs
Cincinnati Reds
Houston Astros
Milwaukee Brewers
Pittsburgh Pirates
St. Louis Cardinals

NL WEST
Arizona Diamondbacks
Colorado Rockies
Los Angeles Dodgers
San Francisco Giants
San Diego Padres

AMERICAN LEAGUE

AL EAST
Baltimore Orioles
Boston Red Sox
New York Yankees
Tampa Bay Rays
Toronto Blue Jays

AL CENTRAL
Chicago White Sox
Cleveland Indians
Detroit Tigers
Kansas City Royals
Minnesota Twins

AL WEST
Los Angeles Angels of Anaheim
Oakland Athletics
Seattle Mariners
Texas Rangers

THE GAME

Three basics to keep in mind before game time:

1. There is no time clock in baseball.
2. Unlike in most other major sports, once a player is taken

out of the game (for any reason), he is out for the rest of the game.

3. The batting order (**lineup**), which is the sequence that the players will bat in, is brought to the umpires before the game starts. This order is done strategically. Usually a speedy player bats first and the power hitter (home run hitter) bats fourth. This way the bases may be full of runners for the possible home run.

Batting Practice

Before the game begins, the players take batting practice in order to warm up. The ballpark will usually let fans in to see batting practice, although it's always important to check in advance. Watching batting practice is basically just watching the hitters take practice swings and most likely hitting balls out to the outfield or even out of the ballpark. It's also an opportunity for fans to get into the front rows even if their tickets for the actual game are all the way in the back. These seats are commonly referred to as nosebleeds, located so far away or so high up that a nosebleed could theoretically occur from altitude.

Ceremonial First Pitch

It is long-established tradition at most games to have a ceremonial first pitch. A lucky person or lucky people get to stand on the pitcher's mound and throw a pitch to home plate. In the past, some first pitches were thrown from the stands—by President Woodrow Wilson in 1916 and President John F. Kennedy in 1961. Most recently, President Barack Obama threw out the first pitch (from the mound) at the 2009 All-Star Game, the first president to do so at the All-Star Game since Gerald Ford in 1976.

This pitch in no way counts toward any part of the game; it's just a fun pregame activity and tradition in most parts. Many presidents, politicians, dignitaries, military personnel, former ballplayers, athletes from other sports, celebrities, contest winners, children, sponsors, and others have had the opportunity to take part in this pregame ritual.

Please Rise and Remove Your Caps

Before the game starts it's customary at all ballparks to sing the national anthem. For the girlie girl who chooses to wear a baseball cap as a cute accessory, be advised that you will have to remove it for the national anthem. So wearing a cap to cover a bad-hair day is not a good idea.

Immediately After the National Anthem

"Play ball!" The phrase is heard from the loudspeakers and from most fans. Sometimes it's just an ump saying the phrase; other times it will be a child or contest winner. It officially marks the beginning of the game.

Take Me Out to the Ball Game: The Seventh-Inning Stretch

The time between the halves of the seventh inning is what is known as the "seventh-inning stretch." It's traditionally a time to stand and stretch your legs. At all stadiums the fans sing "Take Me Out to the Ball Game." The song's lyrics were jotted on scrap paper in 1908 by songwriter Jack Norworth while riding a train to Manhattan. The chorus and part that's sung at the ballparks is:

Take me out to the ball game;
Take me out with the crowd.
Buy me some peanuts and Cracker Jacks,
I don't care if I never get back.
Let me root, root, root for the home team,
If they don't win, it's a shame.
For it's one, two, three strikes, you're out,
at the old ball game.

I have always sung the fifth line as "So let's root..." instead of the proper "Let me root...," which means I've been singing it wrong for decades. Also, at Marlins games in Miami the concessions at one time did not provide Cracker Jacks, instead, they offered Crunch 'n Munch (this was also the case at one time with the New York Yankees). We substituted the latter into the song ("Buy me some peanuts and Crunch 'n Munch"), usually gaining much laughter from the crowd.

There are a few urban legends out there about who or what really created the seventh-inning stretch, because it was not a part of the baseball rule book. One of the most widely circulated is the popular story of William Howard Taft, the twenty-seventh president of the United States. He was growing restless at a ball game, and his six-foot-two,

BONUS POINTS: THE NAME GAME

Impress *and correct* friends and boyfriends (and TV broadcasters!) with proper pronunciation of some of the hardest-to-say names in the game.

MARK TEIXEIRA
(New York Yankees, 2009)
(Teh-SHARE-ah)

ASDRUBAL CABRERA
(Cleveland Indians, 2009)
(As-DREW-bull)

DAISUKE MATSUZAKA
(Boston Red Sox, 2009)
(DICE-kay Mahz-sue-ZAH-kah: in Boston, they just call him Dice-K)

JARROD SALTALAMACCHIA
(Texas Rangers, 2009)
(Sal-tah-lah-MAH-kee-ah)

KOSUKE FUKUDOME
(Chicago Cubs, 2009)
(KOH-skay Foo-koo-DOUGH-may)

AKINORI IWAMURA
(Tampa Bay Rays, 2009)
(AH-kee-nor-ee EE wah moo-rah)

WILLY AND ERICK AYBAR
(Tampa Bay Rays and Los Angeles Angels of Anaheim, 2009)
(EYE-bar)

300-pound body could no longer sit comfortably. By the middle of the seventh inning he couldn't take it anymore and stood up to stretch his aching legs. The patrons in the ballpark all stood up out of respect for the president, and the seventh-inning stretch was born.

Another story, less romantic but possibly more accurate, is that in 2003 historians found a note dated 1869 from Harry Wright of baseball's first pro team, the Cincinnati Red Stockings. It describes fan behavior at the ballpark. He wrote, "The spectators all arise between halves of the seventh inning, extend their legs and arms and sometimes walk about. In so doing they enjoy the relief afforded by relaxation from a long posture upon hard benches." This makes it seem that it was the fans who actually started the tradition, merely out of necessity to keep circulation flowing in their legs!

The song "Take Me Out to the Ball Game" was a Top 10 hit in 1908. For years it was spontaneously sung by fans at ballparks during the games, but it wasn't until the 1980s that the whole country got into the act. Famed Chicago Cubs broadcaster Harry Caray began leading the crowd at Wrigley Field in the tune during the seventh-inning stretch in the early 1980s. (He started the tradition with the Chicago White Sox a few years earlier.) The Cubs played on cable television, which at that time was a relatively new technology. For the first time, baseball fans could see a team from another city because the games were broadcast throughout the country. This helped make the ritual national, and soon after, other teams adopted the tradition.

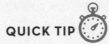

QUICK TIP

The two oldest ballparks still in use today are **Fenway Park**, home of the Boston Red Sox, which opened in 1912, and **Wrigley Field**, home of the Chicago Cubs, built in 1914. These two parks are considered the cathedrals of baseball, and the rich history of each club is deeply embedded in its city's history and culture. Both parks offer tours during non-game days and in the off-season. No trip to Boston or Chicago is complete without visiting these storied landmarks.

THE SEASON

Spring Training

Players report to spring training in mid-February and stay through late March for practices, exhibition games, and workouts, and to get reacclimated to the game after the off-season. Hall of Fame manager Sparky Anderson, who is fifth all-time in wins, says that there are two major reasons for camp: to get in top physical condition for the long season ahead, and to drill the fundamentals of the game into the players' heads. Anderson also says that it's a learning process and a way for a manager to see what a player can do. "I never cared if we won a single game during spring training," Anderson says. "My whole focus was on preparation for the regular season."

Spring training is entertaining and highly enjoyable with lots of fanfare. The players are accessible, and the ballparks are much smaller than during the regular season, so the atmosphere is filled with smiling kids with painted faces running around and showing off the latest autograph on their jersey or glove. Typically spring training draws crowds of people from the North who escape the cold winter and travel to warmer climates to see their team get ready for the season.

All MLB teams attend spring training in either Florida, known as the Grapefruit League, or Arizona, nicknamed the Cactus League. Because both of these destinations are filled with transplants from the North, spring training can be the only time these fans get to see the team they grew up with, so games can get crowded. Teams that train in Florida play other teams training in the state, and Arizona-training teams play

TO SOME PEOPLE, DH IS A FOUR-LETTER WORD: THE DESIGNATED-HITTER RULE

I thought it was important to bring up this highly controversial rule very early, not only to get it out of the way but to minimize the confusion and questions that will arise when reading this chapter. The designated-hitter (DH) rule is like math, meaning that there's no point in asking why. It just is.

The DH is a roster player who only bats. The spot is for big power hitters who usually lead the team in home runs. The DH replaces the pitcher in the batting order.

Baseball purists believe that there should be no DH, and for good reason: Use of the DH eliminates strategic complexities. Without a DH, managers have to make hard decisions like taking out a pitcher to get a better bat. The game was originally played without a DH, and the pitchers always batted. Declining ticket sales in the early 1970s had owners searching for ways to boost profits. They reasoned that a game with more hitting and home runs would be more interesting to fans. In 1973 the leagues were given the option to adopt the DH rule. Only the American League said yes.

The National League still plays without a DH. Generally pitchers will bat last in the lineup because they aren't very good hitters. There are some exceptions to the rule, most notably Babe Ruth, who was one of the best ballplayers of all time.

There's no clear answer to why pitchers are usually poor hitters, but it makes sense since pitchers spend all their time practicing

one another. Teams that train in Arizona do not play teams that train in Florida during spring training.

There are many different kinds of spring training games. Besides regular games against other teams training in the area, some teams will play a college or two, so the University pitching, there's little or no time for hitting. Another explanation is that power pitchers use their leg strength to throw, usually resulting in a lack of upper-body strength. Also, if an organization has a young pitcher coming up in the system, would it really want to risk that prospect getting hit by a 95-mph fastball? I think not.

When a pitcher is at bat with runners on base, his goal is merely to move the runners over. That's called playing small ball. **Small ball** is done by bunting, hitting a sacrifice fly, or intentionally grounding out. The batter sacrifices himself for the good of the team. Small ball is intentional and systematic. It's not just the pitcher who does this. Every guy on an NL team at one point takes one for the team.

The National League plays a lot of small ball, and most NL teams seem to be made up of scrappier guys who are fast and light on their feet. It also makes the NL, in my opinion, a far more difficult league in which to be a manager. When a manager wants to pinch-hit for a better bat, he has to look at bringing in a different pitcher.

In the American League, on the other hand, the pitcher does not bat, and a DH is in the lineup for every game. The DH spot in the lineup cannot change during the game; the player can, but the batting order remains the same. The DH does not play the field; his only purpose is to bat. Some DHs are experienced at field positions, but they rarely play them. The DH rule also gives older players the chance to extend their career by allowing them to continue playing even after their body is too beat up to play the field.

It doesn't seem fair, but that's just the way it is.

of Miami may take on the Florida Marlins, or the University of Michigan may battle the New York Mets. There are also split-squads games, where the team is scheduled to play two games against two different teams on the same day. The ball club splits its roster into two teams and plays both games that day, usually at the same time. Some ball clubs will take on minor league teams, and others will play intrasquad games, where members of the same team play one another.

QUICK TIP

For spring training, flip-flops, shorts, and tank tops are what everyone will be wearing. Most people are on vacation or retired, so comfortable and casual is the way to go.

Check out your team's Web site for location information.

The major league season is an exhausting 162 games, played from early spring through sometimes late fall. In 1997 the major leagues started **interleague** play. Up until 1997, teams never played teams from the other league in games that counted (they did play in the All-Star Game and sometimes in spring training) until the World Series, where the winner of the NL plays the winner of the AL. Now they play interleague games for a special few weeks during the season, usually around June. When the teams are in an AL park, the DH rule is implemented; in an NL park, it isn't. So when the AL team is the visitor in an NL park, the AL pitchers have to bat. It's sometimes quite comical to see the AL pitchers take an at bat. This rule is also in effect for the All-Star Game and World Series play.

The **All-Star break** is the midway point in the season. The fans choose the All-Star players by ballot at the ballpark or online. The managers of the All-Star teams are the two managers of the World Series teams from the previous season, the winners of the AL and NL pennants. The managers choose the pitchers. Pitchers tend to pitch only an inning or two because this is not a regular-season game and teams don't want to tire out their pitchers. The game could see more than six pitchers on each team.

The winning league of the All-Star Game gets home-field advantage in the World Series. This rule was adopted starting with the 2003 season because of the infamous 7–7 tie in eleven innings at the 2002 All-Star Game in Milwaukee. The teams ended up running out of pitchers. Commissioner Bud Selig had no choice but to call the game a draw, amid a sea of boos from the crowd.

All-Star weekend is filled with fanfare and activities, but the most popular event besides the actual game is the **Home Run Derby**. The nationally televised event is usually held the night before the All-Star Game. The popular contest is open to the best home run hitters in each league. Eight players participate in the event, and each player is given ten "outs" per round. Any swing that is not a home run is considered an out in this contest. The four players with the most home runs advance to the semifinals, where they again are given ten outs. Their previous round's total carries over to this round. The top two players advance to the finals, where the home run numbers are reset to zero and they go again for ten outs. The player with the most home runs at the end of this final round wins and is dubbed the Home Run Derby champion.

For the players not elected to the All-Star teams or participating in any of the other weekend activities, the long weekend is a welcome midseason break to rest and visit with family before the dog days of summer and postseason fever take over.

The Postseason

After the 162-game regular season is completed, the teams with the best records and winning percentages in each division, plus a **"wild card,"** the next best team in any of the three divisions

(East, West, and Central), make the playoffs. The four teams compete in the first round of postseason play. Both the AL and NL follow the same format to whittle down the teams to their representative in the World Series.

The first round is called the Division Series and consists of the American League Division Series (**ALDS**) and the National League Division Series (**NLDS**). These are best-of-five-game series (meaning the first team to win three games wins it all).

The two winners then play in the Championship Series—the **ALCS** and the **NLCS**. These are best-of-seven series (the first to win four games wins it all). The two series champions then play each other in the **World Series**.

The Dance

The World Series is the climactic event in baseball. The whole season comes down to this series. The weather is chilly, the leaves have turned colors, and two lucky teams get to battle it out to reign supreme in baseball. The World Series is a best-of-seven series pitting the American League pennant winner against the National League pennant winner. (The **pennant** is a baseball term for winning a division or league.) The home team is determined from the winning league of that year's All-Star Game.

THE TEAMS

In the System: A Look at the Minor Leagues

Making it to the show (the majors) in baseball is one of the toughest accomplishments in all sports. The minor leagues are a very large system, with more than 245 teams (190 that play in the U.S.) and more than eight thousand players scattered across the globe. With only an approximate one in one hundred minor leaguers making it to the big leagues, baseball can be brutal on young players. The system is set up to help develop the young players into major leaguers, but with so many people and teams it's easy to get lost in the system and become a "career minor leaguer." Each major league team has agreements with one AAA team, one AA team, at least two at level A, and at least one in a U.S.-based Rookie League.

Single A: These clubs are usually located in suburbs or small cities like Asheville, North Carolina. The lowest clubs in a "farm system," Single A ball clubs can also be split into High-A and Low-A teams (think A+ or A-). Most players in these leagues have signed straight from high school or college. The High-A leagues are the Carolina League, the California League, and the Florida State League. The Low-A leagues are the Midwest League and the South Atlantic League.

Double A (AA): These teams are more advanced and have quick turnaround because the league consists of top prospects and promoted players. Some players will jump straight from AA to the majors. These teams are usually located in midsize cities like Corpus Christi, Texas.

Triple A (AAA): The highest of the minors, these clubs are for talented players, and for some players they are just stopping grounds or "parking lots," as some baseball enthusiasts call them. Most team in the majors "call up" from their AAA affiliates, especially after September 1, when the clubs expand their rosters. Many of the players in AAA have been in the minors for at least a few years and can play at the major league level when a team needs them due to injury or suspension of players in the majors. Many of the players get an invite to the major league affiliate's spring training camp to try to earn a spot on the team. Teams in AAA are usually located in large cities without a major league club like Sacramento, California, or Columbus, Ohio.

Rosters

Every major league team has two rosters, the twenty-five-man roster and the forty-man roster. The twenty-five-man roster is the main team throughout the season, and these twenty-five players are eligible to play in games. The forty-man roster consists of the twenty-five-man roster plus an additional fifteen players who are either on the disabled list (see below) or in the minor leagues.

On September 1, teams get to expand to their forty-man rosters for the rest of the regular season, what is commonly called **September call-ups**. Many minor leaguers use this time to play in their first big-league games.

Disabled List

The **disabled list** (DL) is a list that injured players are placed on in order to make room on the roster for other players. There are two DLs, the fifteen-day and the sixty-day. Players are put on one based on either how serious an injury is or how long their recovery will take. When a player is put on the DL it opens up a roster spot for the club to fill with a minor leaguer.

QUICK TIP:
BEST TIME TO LEAVE THE SEATS

We are all used to waiting in line for the bathroom, and a baseball game is no exception. The bad news is that the bathroom line won't be the only line. Concessions and merchandise shops can get crowded, especially since everyone seems to go at the same time. In order to skip this hassle, go to the bathroom when your team is *batting*. Yes, it can be disappointing missing your boys' at bat—especially when you get back and everyone's talking about the great moon shot (a well-hit home run that looks like it could hit the moon) that you just missed—but since most people want to see the offense, the lines will be much shorter or even non-existent. This really works, even at large sold-out ballparks like Yankee Stadium.

GAME STRUCTURE

The game is split into nine **innings**. Each inning has a top half and a bottom half. The visiting team always bats in the top half, and the home team bats in the bottom half of the inning. That leaves the home team with the final chance to score runs if it needs to in order to win the game (they have "last ups"). The teams are either **at bat** (offense) or **in the field** (defense) in each half-inning, so while one bats, the other fields.

This seems like a simple concept. But it does get a bit trickier, even at this basic stage of the game. If the home team is winning in the top of the ninth, and the top half of the ninth inning finishes with that lead still intact, then the home team wins the game and doesn't need its **last ups**. When this is the case (it happens a lot, due to home-field advantage), then the game isn't exactly a full nine innings, but ends up finishing with only eight and a half innings played. That is, of course, unless the score is tied.

Extra innings—or as my dad liked to call them, "free baseball!"—are a splendid part of the game (unless you have an early morning the next day). Extra innings could really go on until the wee hours of the next morning. This is because there's no time clock in baseball, and the only official tie on record in the new age was at that 2002 All-Star Game. It is possible that a game could go on for days. The two longest major league games on record (by innings) are:

- National League: In 1920 the Brooklyn (now Los Angeles) Dodgers played the Boston (now Atlanta) Braves in Boston to a twenty-six-inning tie. There are no longer ties in baseball.
- American League: In 1984 the Chicago White Sox defeated the Milwaukee Brewers 7–6 in a remarkable twenty-five innings. This game was shut down at one A.M. (no new inning can start after one A.M.) and was continued the next day.

Extra innings are played in the same manner as the rest of the game. There are no special shoot-outs or sudden-death overtimes like in other sports. It is just a continuation of the same game you've been watching. The game is not over until a team has scored and a full inning is completed. If the visiting team scores in the top half of the inning, the home team has its last ups to try to either tie it back up or win it all. If the home team ties it back up again, the extra innings continue; if it doesn't and three outs are recorded, the game is over.

If the home team scores, that is usually called a **walk-off**, meaning the teams walk off the field immediately after the run is scored. Once the home team is up, there's no need to finish the game and record three outs. Walk-off is a term heard when the home team wins it in the ninth inning, extra innings, or any other game-ending situation.

Rain, Rain, Go Away

Baseball is not a sport that is played in all weather. If a light rain is sprinkling the field the game will continue, but a heavy storm or one bit of lightning will cause the game to be delayed.

A rain delay can take place before a game starts or any time during the game. If the weather gets bad, the grounds crew will put a tarp over the infield to protect it and leave only the outfield grass exposed to the elements. Actually, watching the grounds crew get the tarp on the field is a fun and sometimes hilarious sight on its own.

If the game hasn't started yet and the weather is not improving, the game will be **called** (as in called off, canceled), and it's a rainout for that day. Look at your ticket for information on getting a rain check. The game must be made up, so the team's Web site will have information on when that game is, and usually you can enter with your old ticket from the rained-out game. Most likely, the game will be part of a doubleheader the next day, so be prepared.

If the game is delayed after it has already begun, then there are a few options. If fewer than four and a half innings have been played, the game can be called and no game technically took place. If five innings have been completed and the home team is ahead, the game can be called and the game counts.

Sometimes, though, you must be prepared to wait it out. I

remember one game in Boston in the summer of 2004 when the Red Sox were down by a run in the seventh inning and it started pouring. At least three hours passed and most people went home, but since the home team was down, the Red Sox had the option of waiting and seeing what would happen. There's no way the home team is going to call a loss for itself. So after a few hours the game finally resumed. With three-fourths of the fans gone and a nasty mist in the air, I got to sit in the front row right behind home plate, which, even soaking wet and cold, was so great I'd do it all over again!

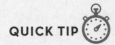

QUICK TIP

If rain is in the forecast or it just cleared up, grab paper towels from the bathroom and put them in your handbag to wipe up the seat. In some luxury seats an attendant will do it for you, but most of the time, you're on your own. I can't count the number of times people have seen me do it and then run to the bathroom for their own.

Don't Let This Happen to You: Respect the Game

I had been to games alone before, but this time I thought I was going with nine other people.

Five things to know about me and baseball:

1. I refuse to miss the first pitch.
2. I don't leave early.
3. I'm a sucker for a hot dog in the third inning and an ice cream in the seventh. Peanuts all game.
4. I have been to many games alone. (I lived across the

street from Fenway Park and could hear the crowd
from my roof deck. Give me a break.)
5. I watch the game and occasionally keep score. (Yes, I
do sometimes get distracted by the tens of thousands of
people around the ballpark, but I'm mostly focused on
the game.)

Brittany is a gorgeous, hip, and incredibly stylish friend of
mine. Even in sweatpants, she's one of those hated ladies who
always look put together. If Brittany and five other women all
wore the same dress, she'd look the best in it. Yes, she's *that* girl.
She lives in Boston, where sports rule and there are more female fans per capita than in any other city in the U.S. Her
sports knowledge is enough to get by. She loves the Red Sox and
whatever else is going on in town but doesn't care passionately
about the games. If the Sox win, drinks for all! If they lose, it's
just a game. Although this may describe many fans, Brittany's
a little more extreme in the happy-go-lucky department.

A very popular game in Boston is the annual Patriots' Day
game, played the same day as the Boston Marathon is run. It
has an unusually early start time (around eleven A.M.) because
of the marathon; not to take anything away from Opening
Day, but this game is like an unofficial kickoff to the season.
The weather has warmed a bit and spring fever fills the air,
which adds to the excitement and hope of a new beginning. The
trees are budding, the cherry blossoms are sprouting, and fans
fill Lansdowne Street and Yawkey Way in a colorful collage
of red and white that forms into a single object like a classic
Georges Seurat painting.

One year, Brittany decided to be the ringleader and purchased a whole row—that's ten tickets—to this highly overpriced

game ($75 each for bleacher seats). This eclectic bunch of friends—guys and girls of different ages, styles, and living locations—were bound to have problems. I immediately predicted what might occur with so many people all going together and insisted on picking up my ticket early. I lived within walking distance of Fenway Park and knew the others were coming from all different directions. This looked like a prime third-inning-arrival disaster waiting to happen. I didn't want to miss that much of the game.

Much is the understatement of the year.

Everything was all set in the morning. It was about a seven-minute walk (door to gate) to Fenway from my apartment. We were all supposed to meet at a bar across the street from the park at ten A.M. I waited at the bar and checked my phone until about 10:45 A.M. before heading into the park alone because I didn't want to miss the first pitch.

I sat in the aisle seat and stared at the completely empty row. The park was sold out. I got a few looks from passersby making their way to seats farther up in the nosebleeds but made friends with the boys behind me and the girls in front of me. I kept getting texts from Brittany: "We'll be there soon!"

Brittany and company finally arrived just one out before the *seventh-inning stretch*. I was terribly embarrassed when nine drunk and loud people made their way through the row to their seats.

The Red Sox ended up winning in walk-off fashion and sent Fenway into euphoria.

Brittany and company immediately got on their phones to figure out which bar we were going to to see the marathon runners finish the race. And they couldn't wait to talk about the great game they had just *watched*.

Moral of the story:

Why would you pay $75 for bad seats to see less than three innings of baseball? The cost skyrockets once you factor in the pregame (and in their case, *during-game*) bar tab. Save your money for something else you'd obviously like better. At ballparks like Fenway Park, where every game is sold out, those tickets could have gone to people who really wanted to be there to watch the game, not just say they *went* to the game.

If you do choose to go to a game, try to arrive on time. Obviously, things can happen, like when you are dashing across town from work in traffic, but try to be there before the third inning at the latest. It will keep the jeers from other fans away. It will also prevent having to tell the people that have already been in your seats for half the game to get up, while the fans in the rows behind you are yelling at you to sit down. The common phrase you will hear is "Down in front!" It's not fun. Some fans can be nasty. Save yourself the trouble. And money.

BALLS AND STRIKES

The strike zone, the area over home plate, between the knees and the chest, is supposed to be univer- sal, but really depends on the height of the hitter. It's also up to the discretion of the umpire and his vision, which to fans, most of the time, is not very good. It's not unusual to hear people in the crowd calling the umps "bum" or "blind" and shouting various obscenities.

A strike is called if the hitter swings his bat and misses the ball, or if he is "caught looking"—when the ball passes through the strike zone and the player just stands there and doesn't

BEST BASEBALL MOVIES

These baseball movies are more than just great; they help teach the game of baseball, including the passion and folklore behind the game that's been around longer than most pop icons in American history. Here's my list of "must-see" baseball movies:

Field of Dreams (1989). This is one of my favorite movies of all time. There is something about the combination of baseball, a father-son relationship, and James Earl Jones's acting chops that makes this movie magical. I've seen this movie a hundred times yet I still cry at the end. Every time. It has a great grasp of the folklore and mystery that surround the game, and although the movie is a fantasy, Jones's famed monologue toward the end is Hall of Fame worthy . . . and said to be the reason he took the role in the first place.

Bull Durham (1988). Another Kevin Costner film (he's also in *Field of Dreams*), but this movie takes an R rating, while *Field of Dreams* is PG family fun. It's sex and baseball, all taking place in a minor league town. The movie is a great lesson on a baseball player's mentality to get to "the show," and if you don't know what that means yet, it also will help with definitions and lingo.

swing. A swinging strike is when the player swings and misses the ball (called a whiff) or swings and hits it foul (only for the first two strikes).

Hitters will sometimes just check their swing. A **check swing** is when the bat is swung, but just a little. The bat does not swing all the way around. If a player can hold up his swing to make it only a check, it means he successfully laid off the pitch.

Susan Sarandon and Tim Robbins met on this movie, and this film is what started their longtime real-life love affair. Sarandon's character, Annie (named after "baseball Annies," a.k.a. "groupies") worships in the "Church of Baseball." The movie also has a 100 percent rating on Rotten Tomatoes, the movie critics' Web site, making it one of the highest-rated and most critically acclaimed movies of all time.

The Sandlot (1993). This is a kids' movie, basically, but magical nonetheless. The movie brought me back to my childhood, when I first discovered a love of the game, and can do the same for its viewers. It's a family film and discusses the legends, like Babe Ruth, who make the game great.

Major League (1989). A young and good-looking Charlie Sheen, Tom Berenger as an aging ballplayer looking for one last bit of glory, and an almost unrecognizable Wesley Snipes make this movie a classic. It's slapstick but hilarious with a big heart. The classic "Wild Thing" scene near the end of the movie still puts a smile on my face every time I watch it.

Note: These are my favorite baseball movies. Many people may disagree, and other titles will come up, including the fantastic *Eight Men Out*, *The Natural*, *The Rookie*, and *61**.

If the pitch is out of the strike zone and the player check-swings, it will be a ball. If the pitch ends up in the strike zone anyway, it will be a strike.

If four **balls** (pitches out of the strike zone) are called before three strikes or before the ball is put in play, the player walks. A **walk** is a free ride to first base. There is another way to get to first base without hitting or walking. If a player is **hit by a**

pitch (HBP), he is granted first base automatically. Sometimes, a player may try to take one for the team and lean into the ball or get lucky and have it touch only his jersey but still get the call. The downside is that if it's purely an accident and a player is struck by a pitch, a 90-mph fastball is going to hurt and can cause serious injury. Also, if a player gets HBP, the next time that team is in the field, that team's pitcher will sometimes hit a member of the other team on purpose in order to protect his teammates. This usually can cause warnings from the ump or even get the pitcher thrown out of the game. Boys will be boys.

A player cannot be called out on a strike three if the third strike is a foul ball (a ball that is not hit into the area of play, usually to the immediate left or right of the batter, determined by the foul lines on this field—see figure on page 39). A **foul ball** is considered a strike but only for the first two strikes. Once the batter has two strikes against him, hitting a foul ball is simply another do-over. Having a long at bat with a lot of foul balls can really tire out a pitcher and is seen as a good at bat for the offense regardless of the outcome. Theoretically, if a player has two strikes and keeps hitting foul balls the at bat could go on forever.

There is no record for the longest at bat. Neither MLB, the National Baseball Hall of Fame, nor even the Elias Sports Bureau—the statisticians for MLB—has an answer for this question. Apparently such things were never considered important until the age of televised games and restricted pitch counts (the number of pitches thrown by a pitcher in a game before he is taken out for health and productivity reasons). These two factors have significantly sped up the game. *Baseball Digest* seems to have the most accurate account. It reported that in 1940, Chicago White Sox Hall of Famer Luke Appling fouled off twenty-four pitches in one at bat before ultimately drawing a walk. The opposing pitcher, Red Ruffing of the New York Yankees, was said to be barely able to lift his arm afterward and so was taken out of the inning, cursing the whole walk to the dugout.

In today's game, that number is unheard of. Nowadays, at bats with seventeen foul balls seem extraordinary. I would estimate that an at bat with twenty-four pitches fouled off, plus the four balls to walk the batter, could take upwards of twenty minutes. In today's game, twenty minutes can be a whole inning. I imagine that TV networks sigh with relief that something like that hasn't happened recently.

CHICKS DIG THE LONG BALL: HITTING

When a team is at bat, there are three recognized positions: the player **at bat,** the player who's scheduled to hit after him, said to be **on deck**; and the one after him, who is **in the hole.**

The player at bat must step into the **batter's box** to begin his plate appearance. Hitters bat right- or left-handed. Some players, who are lucky to be baseball ambidextrous, can hit from both sides of the plate and are called switch-hitters. This can be a major advantage against pitchers.

A hitter's main goal is to get a hit by putting the ball in play. A single is when the player hits the ball and makes it to first base. This is also called a **base hit**. A double is when he gets to second base, also called an **extra-base hit**, and a triple is when he makes it to third.

A home run is when the ball is hit in fair territory and the batter makes it all the way around the bases. Usually the home run ball sails out of the park or stays in the park, by going over the home run line (usually yellow) and bouncing back in. A player can also hit a home run by getting an **inside-the-park home run**. This is a rare feat, usually the result of a speedy runner and the ball taking a bad hop in the outfield.

Always a spectacle and fan favorite, a **grand slam** is when the bases are loaded with runners and a home run is hit, earning the lucky team four runs.

The Basic Ways to Get on Base

SAFE

1. Hitting a fair ball that is not caught by a fielder before it touches the ground.
2. Hitting a fair ball that touches the ground before a fielder gets to it and the runner makes it to first base before the ball does. ("Safe!")
3. Walking on four balls.
4. Getting hit by a pitch.
5. Hitting a homer.
6. Someone in the field making an error (dropping the ball, making an erratic throw, or some other mishap).
7. Bonus points: The third-strike rule is when the pitcher throws strike three, but the catcher drops the ball and the batter makes it to first base before the ball does.

The Basic Ways to Be Called Out

OUT

1. Pop fly (a ball hit in the air, usually still in the infield, and caught).
2. Foul out (a pop fly hit in foul territory and caught).
3. Fly out (ball caught by an outfielder).
4. Strikeout (three strikes).
5. Ground out (hitting the ball on the ground or bouncing it to a fielder who catches it and throws the batter out at the base; the ball either gets to the base before the batter or the batter is tagged out while running to a base).
6. When a ball is bunted or lightly hit and touches the bat for a second time while in fair territory.
7. Bonus points: The hitter hits a foul tip (a ball just clipping the bat), and the catcher catches it on the fly for strike three.

RBIs

Perhaps the most important stat in baseball, a player's runs batted in **(RBIs)** really determine what kind of season he had. A player is awarded an RBI when his at bat results in a run being scored by his team. A player who can drive in runs is very valuable to a team.

Making Sacrifices for the Greater Good

Sacrificing is an art form (in today's power game, a dying art form). Used mostly in NL games, sacrificing is a fundamental way to play small ball. When a batter sacrifices an at bat for the team, it is not counted toward the batter's average. That way, there is no penalty; it's as if the at bat never happened. There are three main ways to make a sacrifice for the team:

- Bunt: When a batter holds the bat in front of him, usually he is trying to bunt. The point is to hit the ball softly in an effort to advance base runners while giving up the chance to take a good swing at the ball. A bunt often rolls barely past the pitcher's mound, and a fielder picks it up and throws to first for an easy out. In the meantime the base runner or runners have advanced a base.
- Sacrifice fly: A batter can hit a sacrifice fly by hitting a fly ball to the outfield with fewer than two outs so that the runner, can tag up and advance to the next base or score (see "Baserunning," page 32). The sac fly is not counted as an at bat, and if a runner scores, the batter is awarded an RBI.
- The hitter can hit a strategically placed ground ball so that the fielder throws out the batter but not the runner advancing to second or third base.

QUICK TIP: BEST SEATS IN THE HOUSE

At perpetually sold-out ballparks, like Fenway Park in Boston, just getting a seat, any seat, is a feat in itself; but at many other parks, fans get to choose their seating area. It's really just a matter of taste. I suggest sitting in a different area of the field each game you attend until you get a feel for what you like and dislike. Obviously, infield box seats will always have a better view than the bleachers. But some may want the bleachers because they always have the most rowdy and social atmosphere. Most teams' Web sites now have photos to show the view from a particular seating section.

Seats behind home plate are universally considered the gold standard, providing the best complete view of the field. But even sitting in seats costing $1,000 or more, some people just can't stand watching through the foul ball net. It takes an inning or two (at least for my eyes) to get used to it. Other fans want the opportunity to catch foul balls. Left field will have the most foul balls because most hitters are right-handed and that's the way their fouls fly most of the time. The infield grandstands and infield upper deck on the first- and third-base lines are the best places for foul balls in general. The upper deck also has much cheaper seats, and you get a bird's-eye view of the field.

A Great Hitter Spreads the Ball Around the Field

When a hitter comes up to the plate, there are usually two ways he can stand (stances): open and closed. An open stance is when the batter almost faces the pitcher. His body is open to the pitcher and the ball. A closed stance is when the batter is at almost a full 90-degree angle to the pitcher, if not more. His body is closed off to the ball and pitcher. There are advantages and disadvantages to both stances, and players will determine their stance based on their strengths and weakness when hitting.

Hitters can **pull** the ball or hit it to the **opposite field**. Pulling the ball means that the batter hits the ball early or hits the ball in front of him. Right-handers pull to the left side of the field; left-handers pull to the right. Typically, the more closed the batter's stance, the more he'll pull the ball.

A more open stance allows for more pitches hit to straight-away center field (the back center of the outfield and the longest distance from the plate) or the opposite field.

BASERUNNING

There are a few key fundamentals of playing the game that coaches instill in players from their first Little League game through their time in the pros: "Keep your eye on the ball!" "Catch with two hands!" and "Run hard to first!"

The second there is contact with the ball, even if it's a foul or an easy out, a hitter should run hard to first base. First base is the only base that a player can overrun (step over) and not be called out.

Seven Ways to Be Called Out as a Baserunner

1. Being tagged out: The ball is in the fielder's glove or hand and he tags the runner out if the runner is not on a base and the ball is still in play.
2. Being forced out: A force play is when the runner on base must run to the next base to make room for the player behind him. In this case, the fielder with the ball only has to step on the bag that the runner is heading for to get the runner out. Example: If there is a runner on first base, when the batter hits the ball on the ground, the runner must advance. But if there's a

player on second base and no one on first, the runner doesn't have to run if the batter hits a ground ball. Instead, he can wait to see what the ball does.

3. Failing to tag up: **Tagging up** is when the batter hits the ball (fair or foul) in the air, usually to the outfield, so the runner on base has the option to move ahead to the next base. But this is only if the runner waits for the catch, then touches his own base, and then proceeds to the next base. Failure to wait for the catch before you tag your own base is considered an out. If a ball is dropped the play goes on as if it were a base hit.

4. Missing a base: The bases must be touched in order. Sometimes a player gets too excited when running and can miss the base, which results in an out.

5. Running outside the base path: When running to a base and trying to avoid a tag, a runner can only move within three feet of the base path.

6. Being touched by a batted ball: If a runner is hit by the ball before it passes a fielder, the runner is out. If the ball passes a fielder and then hits a runner, the play continues as if nothing happened.

7. Interference: When a runner or batter gets in the way of a fielder who is trying to make a play, it's called interference. There are many ways for this to occur. One of the most memorable examples occurred in Game 6 of the 2004 ALCS. The Yankees third baseman, Alex Rodriguez, was running hard to first and intentionally swung his arm like a tomahawk chop and swatted the ball out of then Red Sox pitcher Bronson Arroyo's glove. The first-base ump did not see the play clearly because the Red Sox first baseman was in his way, and the ump called A-Rod safe. But the home-plate ump,

who had a clear view, disagreed. After a lengthy umpire huddle, they got it right and called A-Rod out due to intentional interference.

QUICK TIP: FAN INTERFERENCE

We'd all love to catch a foul ball, but not at the expense of our team winning the game. Fan interference is when a fan hinders and/or changes the course of a play. It happens all the time and can hurt your team in many ways. A highly publicized case of fan interference left one fan facing death threats. For one lonely fall season, passionate Chicago Cubs fan Steve Bartman was the most hated man on the North Side of Chicago even though it's still unclear if he really did anything wrong. In 2003, with the Cubs trying to go to their first World Series in fifty-eight years (at that time), a fly ball was hit into the first few rows of the stands. Cubs fielder Moises Alou thought he had a shot at the ball, but the excited Bartman also tried to catch the ball, hindering Alou from making the play. Replays show that the ball was clearly in the stands, and fan interference was not called by the umpire, but Cubs fans across the world still feel that it ruined their chances of winning the game. If, however, the visiting team had been in the field, and Bartman had hindered their chances of catching the ball, he'd be a hero.

Moral of the story: If you are sitting close to the field, please keep your hands to yourself.

Take the Lead

Once a player is on base, he usually will take a **lead**. The runner will be a step or two *or three* off of the bag toward the next base. This is legal and often necessary to get safely to the next base. But it's not all good for the runner. If the pitcher or catcher notices that a runner has a very big lead and thinks he can get the runner out, before or after the pitch he can throw to the fielder guarding the base that the runner is on; if the runner is tagged while off the base, he is out.

If the pitcher or catcher throws to the next base (the base where the runner is trying to go and hence taking such a large lead), the runner can end up in a **pickle**. A pickle is when the runner is caught between two bases and the fielders are throwing the ball back and forth in an effort to get the runner out. Ninety percent of the time, a runner caught in a pickle ends up being out.

Getting Dirty

Players with dirty uniforms are my favorites. They're not merely playing the game; by the evidence of their uniforms, they are seriously invested in the outcome. The quickest way to get dirty is to slide. Sliding—usually into a base—helps runners reach the base more efficiently and effectively. The television show *MythBusters* on the Discovery Channel tested sliding and found that there was a small time advantage—a matter of milliseconds. Also, having the body low to the ground makes it easier to sneak into the bag. Sliding is not easy and has to be practiced frequently, especially early in a baseball player's development. Another advantage of sliding is that it can also throw the fielder off, testing his balance, timing, and other vital skills, considering the fact that the runner is about to crash into him.

First base can be overrun. Second and third bases cannot. If a player overruns second or third base, they can be tagged out.

Stealing Is Encouraged!

If a player can get away with stealing without getting caught then he should steal! This runner doesn't even have to wait for a hit, walk, or other way to advance. He takes it upon himself (well, usually only if the manager says it's okay and/or tells him to do it) to advance to the next base completely on his own ability. Usually fast players steal, but occasionally a slow runner will get a good jump on lackadaisical infielders. While the pitcher makes his pitch, the runner is leading off the bag, and then he runs to the next base in the hopes of getting there before the catcher throws him out.

Stealing is risky because even if a player is speedy, the velocity of a pitch can determine how the play ends. The catcher can also have a good arm (throws hard, fast, and accurately). If the player is tagged before he touches the base, he is out. The runner can also be picked off at first. When the runner takes his lead, an alert pitcher can throw to first to try to catch the runner off guard. If the first baseman catches the ball and tags the runner before he gets back to the bag, he is out.

Infield Fly Rule—Still Confusing After All These Years

The infield fly rule was first introduced in 1895, but was modified to the way we use it today in 1901. The rule came about to prevent unfair gamesmanship by fielders, who started using reality show–esque backhanded tactics to win games. The rule tries to protect the integrity of the game.

There are a lot of ifs regarding this rule, but it does happen regularly enough to explain it:

If there's zero or one out . . .

If there are base runners on first and second or the bases are loaded . . .

If a fair fly ball is hit where, in the umpire's judgment, it can be caught with ordinary effort by an infielder, then . . .

TALKING TRASH

I don't know any women who don't like to talk. Fortunately, it's okay to talk at a baseball game, even shout and raise your voice when appropriate, and not just for cheering. Try to stay away from using expletives when shouting. It's not very ladylike, and if you have decent seats there will probably be a lot of kids around. When I trash-talk I tend to direct it at the other team. Don't boo your own team. Have respect. Sometimes you'll hear an older fan calling a player a "bum," but that term isn't as common as it used to be. Here are some phrases you can shout out loud.

"You blind, ump?" When a call doesn't go your way.

"Two hands!" This is for your own team. One of your outfielders makes a catch but doesn't use his bare hand to secure the ball. Catching with two hands is a fundamental you learn in Little League. Even though the outfielder may make the catch, I still shout it and get lots of laughs.

"Filthy" or "Nasty." Usually used in reference to the pitcher, for whom it's a *good* thing to have his game called filthy. If you hear someone saying, "That pitch/pitcher was filthy," it means the pitch or the pitcher was exceptionally good.

"Infield fly, batter's out!" the ump says, while raising one arm straight up to signal that the rule is in effect. The batter is automatically out and the inning continues.

This is all because the devious infielders in the late 1800s, who were put in this game situation, started using unsportsmanlike tactics to get easy outs. They would drop the easy catch *on purpose* in order to get a double or triple play. What happens is the ball looks like an easy out, so the runners won't try to advance, even in a force-out situation. So if the crafty infielder drops the easy catch, then the force-out rule comes into effect, which means the runners have to advance to the next base. Then the fielder can easily just pick the ball up and get the quick and easy outs.

QUICK TIP: DON'T BOO YOUR OWN TEAM

"I've never heard a crowd boo a homer but I've heard plenty of boos after a strikeout." —Babe Ruth

It's just tacky to boo your own team, no matter whom you root for. Some people will disagree with me, and that's fine, but I boo only the *other* team. Occasionally if there's a player on the opposing team that I think is classy and talented, I might give him a short applause the first time he's up, but that's as nice as I get with the opposing team.

PLAYING THE FIELD

Screwing Up-E for Error

Everyone makes mistakes in life, and in baseball it's no different. Even the best players in the game make errors; it's only natural. Errors are mistakes like fumbling a grounder, drop-

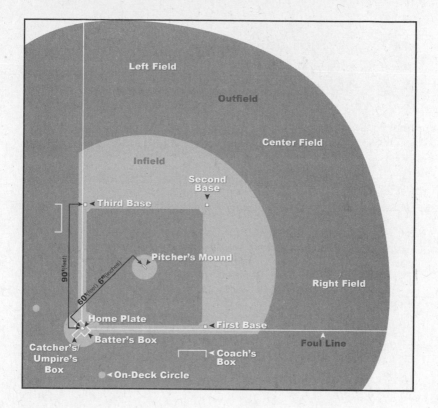

ping a fly ball, booting a line drive, making a bad throw, and so on. Errors can result in runs for the other team or can have no consequence at all, but they're never a good thing.

Fielder's Choice (FC)

A fielder's choice play is when the fielder succeeds in throwing out the lead runner and not the batter-runner. This does not count as a hit, even though the batter was safe at first. Because the lead runner was out, it is not considered a sacrifice (see "Making Sacrifices for the Greater Good," page 30).

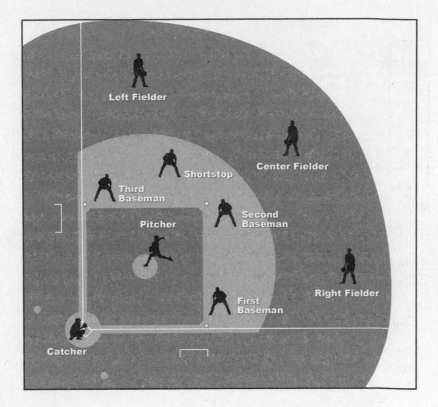

The 6-4-3 Double Play (DP)

Double plays occur most often because of baserunning rules. Due to the force-out, if a ball is grounded to an infielder, he can try to get two outs on one play by throwing to one base and having that fielder step on the bag and then throw to another base. The most commonly heard double-play call is the 6-4-3 double play. The position 6 (shortstop) picks up the ball and throws to 4 (second baseman), who then steps on the base and throws to 3 (first baseman), who then steps on his base. The end result is two runners are out.

Official scorers use shorthand to keep an accurate score throughout the game. This was created many years before technology made digital scoring possible. Field positions are numbered to make things easier.

1. Pitcher
2. Catcher
3. First Baseman
4. Second Baseman
5. Third Baseman
6. Shortstop
7. Left Fielder
8. Center Fielder
9. Right Fielder

The numbers are used in the scorecards and managers lineups so that positions don't have to be written every time. The numbers are also helpful for recording how a ball was fielded.

Putting on the Shift

A manager can tell his infield and/or outfield players to "shift" their regular positions to the left or right, depending on the batter. Some hitters (even great hitters) tend to hit the ball to one side of the field. The shift anticipates this, and the fielders all move over to cover where they think the batted ball will travel. Some of the greatest players in history have had a shift named after them. Even though they always tended to hit to one side, they were still outstanding hitters. Most notable was Hall of Famer Ted Williams, for whom managers devised the "Ted Williams Shift." Teddy Ballgame, as the baseball and war hero was known, would hit to the shifted fielders *on purpose* to try to get the ball past them and into the outfield for a hit. It was almost like a game within a game for Williams. Even after his passing, he is still considered one of the greatest hitters of all time by colleagues and fans.

PITCHING

The pitcher is like the quarterback (for the football fans out there), and pitching is usually what will make or break a team's season. It is impossible to win a lot of games without excellent pitching. The game rests almost entirely on what kind of performance a pitcher has. There are many different kinds of pitchers.

- The **starting rotation** pitchers start the game and can ultimately end the game as well if they have an excellent outing. Generally, teams hope their starter can go at least six innings. If a pitcher has a great game, he can go all nine innings and close out the game himself.
- The bullpen consists of relief pitchers, who come into the game when the starting pitcher is taken out. There are long relievers—guys who can pitch a few innings of relief. These pitchers are especially useful if the starter comes out of the game fairly early, meaning after only a few innings. The **setup man** is the reliever who pitches an inning or two in order to bring the game to the **closer**. The closer finishes the game, usually being asked to pitch only the ninth inning and "close out" the game.

The closer's goal is to enter the game and finish it quickly and efficiently. If this happens, then he can record a **save**. A pitcher records a save if he is brought in during a save situation. The most common save situation is when a pitcher enters a game when his team is ahead by no more than three runs and he pitches at least one complete inning to close the game.

According to the MLB rules, pitchers can throw from only two positions: the **windup** and the **set;** throwing from the latter is also known as pitching from the **stretch**. In the windup position, a pitcher is usually facing straight at home plate, and it is most commonly used when the bases are empty; the set is used when there are runners on base. In the set position, the pitcher faces first base or third, depending on whether the pitcher is left- or right-handed. A pitcher usually switches to the set position or pitching from the stretch when there is a baserunner because pitching this way shortens the time it takes for the pitcher to deliver the ball. This lessens the chance the baserunner will steal a base.

When it looks like the starting pitcher needs to come out of the game, the manager will call the bullpen—he literally makes a telephone call to the bullpen (which is usually on the other side of the field) and tells the coaches there to get a specific pitcher ready.

Once a relief pitcher enters a game, he gets only one minute and/or eight pitches to warm up. During this time, play is suspended. One exception to this rule is when a player gets injured and the pitcher didn't know he was going to be entering the game. Then he is allowed as much time as he needs to warm up.

When a pitcher throws a pitch to the catcher during a game,

the catcher must throw back to the pitcher within twenty seconds. There are also a lot of minor movements that a pitcher can make and be reprimanded for. When there are runners on base and the pitcher goes into his motion, he must continue the movement and deliver a pitch to home plate.

A **balk** occurs when the pitcher tries to catch a runner with a big lead after the pitcher has already begun his delivery. It's very easy to miss when watching a game. The pitcher can't pick up either foot unless he is making a pitch. The exception is if the pitcher is in his set position. Then no balk is recorded.

Bonus Points: "Weapons in the Arsenal"

A pitcher's "weapons" are what he throws. If he can bring **heat** he's got a pretty good weapon. "Heat" is a fastball in the mid-90-mph range or higher. But bringing heat is hardly the most important weapon in the arsenal. Being able to throw **offspeed** pitches is equally important in order to throw off batters. And a great curveball doesn't hurt either. Some of the greatest pitchers around can't throw harder than 88 mph. These are called finesse pitchers. Here are the pitches to expect during a game:

Four-seam fastball: A basic fastball. The index and middle fingers are both across the wide part of the seam, touching two seams each. This makes the pitch straight, relying on speed alone to get past the hitter.

Two-seam fastball: A fastball that is gripped with the index and middle fingers right across the narrow part of the seam, causing a sinking action when the ball reaches the plate area. This pitch relies on both speed and sinking to get the hitter out.

Split-finger fastball: A fastball that sinks even more than a two-seamer, dropping to the batter's knees or even to the ground. The index and middle fingers are on different sides of the ball, "splitting" them.

Curveball: A pitch where the ball is thrown in such a way that it has spin and so breaks sharply, or curves, on the way to home plate. The hitter thinks the ball is coming at him in one direction and then it curves in the other. It's easy to see why the term is used in everyday life; when something was not expected, you were thrown a curveball. A curveball pitcher uses finesse rather than speed to get a batter out.

Slider: Another finesse pitch, halfway between a fastball and a curveball. It breaks but not as much as a curveball; it's faster than a curveball but slower than a fastball. Curveballs and sliders are also called breaking balls.

Change-up: A change-up is sometimes called an off-speed pitch, although any pitch besides a fastball can be called that. The pitch is thrown in the same manner as a fastball, but with less velocity. The hitter thinks he is getting a fastball but ends up with a much slower pitch. This is another finesse pitch to throw off the hitter.

Knuckleball: Baseball broadcasting legend Bob Uecker (Yoo-ker) says it best: "How do you catch a knuckleball? You wait until it stops rolling, and then go pick it up." The knuckleball is said to "dance." The pitch is thrown with the fingertips, and has very little if any spin. The pitch is erratic and unpredictable and as hard to catch as it is to hit. It takes a real specialist behind the plate and on the mound to control. Knuckleballers tend to have their best games in cooler weather. This is because air density affects the ball's spin. The colder the temperature, the denser the air, and therefore less spin.

Visiting the Mound

Throughout the game, it's common to see the manager or the pitching coach walk out to the mound for a "conference," a little chitchat with the pitcher. There aren't any microphones on the coaches, so it's impossible to know exactly what they are saying. When the pitching coach comes out to talk to a pitcher, the pitcher is usually in a jam and not pitching well. If the manager comes out to the mound, it is usually to take the pitcher out of the game and bring in another pitcher. Sometimes, a mound visit will also be just to give the pitcher warming up in the bullpen a little more time to get ready.

Only one mound visit by a coach or manager is allowed per pitcher. If a second visit occurs, the pitcher must be taken out of the game. The only exception is for an injury to the pitcher. The manager or coach may talk to both the departing pitcher and the newly brought in pitcher and it counts for only one mound visit.

Best Friends: Pitchers and Catchers

Pitchers and catchers have a special relationship. They are so tight that they even have their own sign language to communicate so that no one else understands. Some pitchers have their own personal catchers, guys who are familiar with their style of pitching and can specialize in catching a certain uncontrollable pitch, like a knuckleball. Before each pitch, after the catcher crouches into his position, he lowers his hand and starts flashing the signs: moving his fingers around in a way only his team understands. He will also use a knee to block

WILD PITCHES VERSUS PASSED BALLS

A **wild pitch** is when a pitch is so far out of the way that a catcher cannot get it with ordinary effort. It can be deadly because runners will advance, and if there's a runner on third he will almost certainly score a run. A wild pitch is not counted as an error, and runs scored because of it count toward earned runs.

A **passed ball,** on the other hand, is a pitch that could have been caught with ordinary effort but was misplayed. It counts as an error on the catcher. Deciding which way to rule on these pitches is at the discretion of that game's official scorer. It's been said that the catcher is usually given the benefit of the doubt, and that's why we see more wild pitches than passed balls in the game.

the opposing team's base coaches from stealing signs. If a runner is on second, he has a front-row seat to see what the catcher is signing to the pitcher. Measures are taken to block this as well. This pattern of signs lets the pitcher know what the catcher thinks he should pitch. Sometimes the pitcher will **shake off** the catcher because he has his own idea of what will work. But a successful pitcher usually listens to his catcher.

Rare Treats and Feats

If you ever get to see any of the following feats live, know that you have just witnessed something special. Many baseball fans have never seen the majority of feats on this list, even on television (where they are still extraordinary to see).

Walk-off: When a member of the home team ends the game by knocking in a run in the bottom of the ninth inning or in extras. The name comes from the team walking off the field because the game is over.

Shutout: When a team doesn't score a run the whole game, the pitcher or pitchers who kept the team from getting any runs records a shutout. If a pitcher goes the whole game, it's a complete-game shutout. If he goes seven innings, he pitched seven shutout innings. For a shutout, there can be hits and walks and plenty of base runners, but if no runs score, it is a shutout.

No-no's: Shh! Don't talk about it! When a team doesn't get any hits, and the pitcher goes the whole (complete) game, he records a no-hitter. There have been only 263 no-nos in MLB history (as of 2009). They are very rare and usually happen only once or twice a season. If you are watching a game where a no-hitter seems possible, please don't talk about it. It's superstitious, yes, but we don't mention what is happening, in order to preserve it. Although there are no hits in a no-hitter, there can be walks and errors. This means there can be base runners and runs, but the game can still be a no-hitter.

Perfect game: A true rarity, a perfect game is when a pitcher shuts down the opposing team completely and nobody gets on base, *at all*. No walks, hits, or errors: twenty-seven players up, twenty-seven players down. There have been only sixteen official perfect games in major league history (since 1900), with the last thrown by Mark Buehrle in 2009.

Bench-clearing brawl: Okay, so this isn't hockey, and fighting isn't expected or allowed, but it can and does happen. The name comes from the players clearing the benches in the dugouts and the bullpen. Sometimes even coaches get in on the action. The end result is usually suspensions with managers and players kicked out of the game.

Grand slam: Probably the most common feat on this list, a grand slam happens when the bases are loaded and a player hits a home run, resulting in four runs and four RBIs.

Inside-the-park home run: When a player hits a home run but the ball stays in play, it is an inside-the-park home run. This cannot be because of an error, or it will be scored a double or triple. It usually occurs due to a bad bounce and speedy legs. Roberto Clemente, the first Latin American Hall of Famer, is the only player in baseball history to hit a walk-off grand slam inside-the-park homer.

Hitting for the cycle: When a player hits a single, a double, a triple, and a home run in one game he has hit for the cycle. It does not have to be in that order, but if it is it's called a natural cycle, which is even rarer. There have been only 276 occurrences of hitting for a cycle in MLB history, with two or three usually occurring per season.

Back to back to back . . . to back? In early 2007 the Boston Red Sox had four players hit home runs one after the other. It's rare to see three in a row, but four is magical and unusual to see, even in a lifetime.

Triple play: When three outs are recorded with just one batter, it's a triple play. Since 1876 there have been 672 triple plays recorded. The odds of seeing it happen are a little more than one in 10,000 games. The unassisted triple play (when one fielder makes all three outs himself) is even more extraordinary and has happened only fifteen times in MLB history, with the most recent occurring late in the 2009 season by Eric Bruntlett of the Philadelphia Phillies.

Stealing home: A rare stolen base when a player takes a huge lead off third base and somehow runs and slides into home plate before the pitcher and catcher realize what's going on.

My Dad's Passion

For my family, summer meant the Red Sox. We had left-field season tickets at Fenway Park. They were box seats between the Green Monster and third base. In the 1980s this seating section was home to foul balls, the Green Monster, and Hall of Famer Jim Rice. My father, brother, and I would drive the short trip to Boston from the southern suburbs and park down in a "secret" spot my father had found to avoid rising parking-lot fees and traffic.

Every game we'd all have the same argument before getting out of the car. My father would insist that we bring our gloves to catch foul balls. My brother and I would complain about having to lug our gloves to and from the game, because we knew the chances of catching a foul ball were slim, even in our seats, which were foul-ball heaven. But we did it anyway to appease Dad.

One game against the Detroit Tigers, we really put up a fight, but my father was not budging. In the top of the third inning, I was about to ask to be walked to the bathroom when my father, straight-faced, leaned over and whispered, "You see this guy at bat? He is going to hit one right to us."

"Yeah, right!" my brother and I responded, and rolled our eyes.

"No, really, watch him. Watch his stance. He is hitting one right to us." My dad was in a zone.

"Whatever, Dad!"

Then came the pitch, and a loud crack of the bat that sent the ball sailing in our direction. As it floated toward us with an almost slow-motion effect, my mesmerized eyes couldn't look away. A man about ten rows in front of us stuck up his hand and gently nipped the ball, pushing it up, back, and right into my father's glove. There was a slight struggle with the man next to him, but my dad was victorious. Not only did he catch a foul ball, but he had predicted catching it.

I can't pinpoint the day I fell in love with the game but that day was as good as any to stake its claim. We never complained about bringing our gloves again. And most of the time, I still do.

HISTORY, DRAMA, CURSES, AND LEGENDS

History

The origins of baseball can be traced back to games like rounders and cricket. But exactly how the modern game came to be has been debated for more than a century. In 1905 a commission was created to uncover who invented baseball. The conclusion was that in 1839, a man named Abner Doubleday invented the game in a cow pasture in Cooperstown, New York. However, backroom politics were involved, and the commission constructed an answer that suited many of the involved parties. Its "findings" are now known to be a myth and have been debunked by baseball historians. Doubleday, it seems, was just a piece in a puzzle used to make baseball more popular and bring fame to Cooperstown. Most sources involved with the commission have been discredited, and Doubleday, a West Point graduate and decorated war hero, left an astounding sixty-seven diaries, found after his death, and not one mentions baseball. Adding to the myth, all remaining documents were destroyed in a fire in 1911.

The first documented rules for a professional adult league similar to the modern game as we know it today were written by Alexander Cartwright. He drew up the first field diagram and rules that are the basis for today's game in New York City in 1845. The original Cartwright rules debuted with his New York Knickerbockers team the next year. Since then there have been numerous changes to the original Cartwright rules. These include the number of players and innings, field dimensions, the addition of a pitcher's mound, banning spitballs (when saliva, petroleum jelly, or other substances are put on the ball to alter the way the ball moves), and counting foul balls as strikes. The premise is still the same, and the game is based on the innovative rules that Cartwright, the real "father of baseball," created.

There are many early references to baseball, dating back more than fifty years before Cartwright or Doubleday were even mentioned. In Pittsfield, Massachusetts, historians found a bylaw, dated 1791, that "bans the playing of baseball within eighty yards of the town meeting house." We can only assume that quite a few windows were broken before this law came to be. In Jane Austen's novel *Northanger Abbey,* penned in 1798 in England, the book's young heroine enjoys "cricket, baseball, riding on horseback and running about the country." Due to the continual discovery of new facts like these and the decades of debate over evidence that doesn't point in any one direction, Jeff Idelson, vice president of the National Baseball Hall of Fame and Museum, has stated that, in truth, "baseball wasn't really born anywhere."

The National Baseball Hall of Fame and Museum

There is no greater honor in the game of baseball than to be elected to the Hall of Fame. It's also quite difficult to achieve, as good players are rarely elected; only great players get to hang their hat in the hall of immortality. It's where the elite are enshrined forever, adding to the history and folklore that surround the game. The first five superstars elected to the Hall of Fame were the class of 1936: Babe Ruth, Ty Cobb, Honus Wagner, Christy Mathewson, and Walter Johnson. Players, coaches, executives, and other personnel can all be elected to the hall.

The process of electing players is painstaking for both the players who wish to enter and the members of the Baseball Writers' Association of America (BBWAA) who vote for the nominated. A player is eligible five years after he retires if he has ten years of service in Major League Baseball. A ballot goes out to the BBWAA with that year's class of eligible hopefuls. In order to be elected, a player must get more than 75 percent of the vote, meaning that player must be voted for on 75 percent of the ballots. If a player gets more than 5 percent of the ballot each year, but not enough to be elected, he can remain on the ballot for fifteen years. If not elected after that, he still has a shot from the Veterans Committee (which has a whole other set of rules).

The hall is located in Cooperstown, New York. The hall and museum are about a four-hour drive from New York City through the rolling hills of upstate New York. The hall is as magical today as it was at its opening in 1939. I remember visiting as a child, driving through the quiet countryside, passing livestock and barns, and eagerly awaiting our arrival. I know the first time I went there as a kid was in 1987 because I couldn't leave empty-handed and made my dad buy me the entire 1987 Topps baseball card collection. As soon as I got home I went through the cards, organized them by team, and wrapped each one in plastic wrap. They are still collecting dust in my closet somewhere.

For baseball and history enthusiasts like me, visiting the museum is like finding the holy grail. It's the greatest collection of baseball memorabilia in the world and houses the most priceless baseball artifacts of all time. A visit here could be a whole weekend affair, but it can also be a day trip. More than 250,000 baseball fans visit the hall every year.

Visit www.baseballhall.org for more information.

Diamonds in the Rough: Japanese Baseball

Further adding to the controversy over the origin of the game is the influence of the Japanese in baseball. Before Hideo Nomo first put on Dodger blue and long before Ichiro mania hit Seattle, on the other side of the world, as early as the nineteenth century, the Japanese had significant influence on the game of baseball. Documentation dates back to the early 1800s, according to the traveling museum exhibit from the National Japanese Historical Society and the Nisei Baseball Research Project. "Diamonds in the Rough: Japanese-Americans in Baseball" examines the rich history of baseball and Japanese culture. After the turn of the century, those Japanese who immigrated to the U.S. from Japan moved to the Western states. At that time there was no baseball west of the Mississippi River, so the Japanese immigrants created their own "farm teams" in their backyards amid their crops and animals. Baseball was a way for the American-born children to connect with their Japanese-born parents, and at the same time it was a way for the kids to assimilate into American society.

During World War II, when Japanese Americans were forced into detention camps, they used baseball as a coping mechanism. The portion of the exhibit called "Baseball Behind Barbed Wire" gives a fascinating glimpse into the spirit of humanity and how a sport can touch so many people of different cultures and generations. The Japanese Americans built full-scale baseball diamonds in the camps, and were allowed to play ball and travel to other holding camps with fields. These "diamonds in the rough" helped hone the skills of some very talented baseball players.

The Negro Leagues

While African Americans were playing baseball on amateur and even some pro teams in the late nineteenth century, baseball drew a color line. By 1899 owners had unofficially banned them from the game. (The owners had never acknowledged publicly the African Americans' presence.) But African Americans continued to play on independent teams, and in 1920 Rube Foster created the Negro National League.

The early years were a struggle for the league, as interest was lacking, but the late 1920s and early 1930s brought an influx of talented players, like pitcher Satchel Paige and catcher Josh Gibson, who are considered two of the best ballplayers of all time—in any league. Paige was a showman and a huge talent. He was the Negro Leagues' biggest drawing card, as fans of all colors lined up hours in advance to see him pitch. It is estimated that he won more than six hundred games during his thirty-year career.

Gibson, nicknamed "the black Babe Ruth," is considered one of the greatest all-around catchers, playing defense behind the plate with such ease that players said "he may as well been in a rocking chair." He was also a power hitter, topping seventy-five home runs in some seasons and consistently hitting .350 or higher.

World War II changed baseball's landscape considerably when many major league players (and stars) left baseball to enlist. While many Negro League players also left for the war, the majors were in much worse shape. During this time, the Negro Leagues thrived, with black Americans working in higher-paying war-related jobs and packing into ballparks to see their new heroes.

In the mid-1940s integration of pro teams was on the minds of a few forward-thinking executives. While the sport still had plenty of white-only supporters, some progressive owners started scouting the U.S., Mexico, and Puerto Rico for black talent. Whom they found, among others, was Jackie Robinson.

Hall of Fame infielder Jackie Robinson was the first African American player to take the field in the modern major leagues. His appearance in 1947 for the Brooklyn Dodgers single-handedly changed the game of baseball forever and made it the great game that it is today.

Although it took many more years for all of baseball to accept integration, the Negro Leagues declined as integration got more popular. By the end of the 1950s, many of the Negro League stars and top prospects had joined the majors. The Negro Leagues became an afterthought and eventually folded.

Negro League star Satchel Paige got to play in the majors

late in his career, at the age of forty-two. He shined for the Cleveland Indians when he debuted in 1948 during the post-season. He didn't fully retire until 1965 and was the first member of the Negro Leagues elected to the Hall of Fame. Star catcher Josh Gibson, however, was not as fortunate. Just three months before Jackie Robinson broke the color barrier, Gibson died of a stroke, after living with a brain tumor for four years. Gibson was thirty-five years old and would surely have made the transition to the majors during integration. He was elected to the Hall in 1972, one year after Satchel Paige.

There's No Crying in Baseball: All-American Girls Professional Baseball League (AAGPBL)

The 1992 Golden Globe–nominated movie *A League of Their Own,* starring Geena Davis, Tom Hanks, and Madonna, was fiction, but it is a good representation of the real league that was formed and thrived during and after World War II.

When Philip Wrigley, the chewing-gum magnate and owner of the Chicago Cubs, noticed that the minor league system was in shambles because the young talent was leaving for the war, he feared the majors would soon follow. Wrigley, along with other successful Midwestern businessmen, created the AAGPBL in 1943. The league had many name changes, but the Hall of Fame recognizes this name and abbreviation.

The women ballplayers had to take on an all-American, girl-next-door image; they took etiquette classes, learned makeup application, and were tutored in how to walk and speak. Most recruited women were playing in softball or baseball leagues and had to learn the new "men's" rules and then seamlessly switch to their baking class. The 1940s was an interesting time in women's history, between the women's suffrage movement of the 1910s and the women's liberation movement on the horizon in the '60s and '70s. Women were in a middle ground, torn between work and home, and it showed. The owners and managers told players to slide into second base without scratching their legs, yet the women athletes were forced to play in skirts. They were told to put their most aggressive work into the game, but to do it with a smile, and not to forget to have dinner ready by 6:30 P.M. But these women would take what they could get. With the men away at war, women were working in the factories, and playing baseball in front of crowds (and being paid for it) was better than working at the local cannery.

The league operated at first almost as a sideshow, where the novelty was watching women in skirts try to play baseball. But after the first season or so, the real novelty was the caliber of play that these women were producing. The league operated from 1943 to 1954. What's interesting is that the most successful seasons were in the late 1940s, after the war had ended and the men were back at home and in baseball uniforms. This showed the quality of baseball that these women played.

What They Wear

Since 1876 there have been more than four thousand different styles of uniforms worn in professional baseball. From the late 1800s to the 1940s players sweated it out in heavy flannel uniforms made of wool. The modern uniform (what they wear now) is a double-knit, synthetic-blend fabric that was developed to keep players cool and comfortable. It's a polyester-cotton mix that still seems heavy (if you have ever worn a replica jersey and sweated through a day game you know what I mean), but so far it's the best fabric possible for the elements the players face.

The National Baseball Hall of Fame and Museum has a fantastic exhibit available online only with time lines and photos of every type of uniform worn in the game since 1900. The exhibit is called "Dressed to the Nines" and is available at http://exhibits.baseballhalloffame.org/dressed_to_the_nines.

Tops: Jerseys have changed through the years, from lace-ups to pullovers to button-downs. Most teams have names and numbers on the back although names are not required (the Boston Red Sox have names on the back of only their road jerseys, and the tradition-minded New York Yankees still do not have names on their home or road jerseys). Fans can purchase replica and authentic jerseys at their local merchandise store.

Bottoms: Pants have gone from wool and long, to padded, to knickers. They've been worn belted, shortened, elongated, tight, and baggy. Some players still wear them shortened with socks and stirrups, but the modern-day trend is toward long and loose-fitting pants.

Undergarments: The big bulge you see is most likely a cup worn for protection. Jockstraps are also common, as are sliding shorts (compression shorts).

Accessories: The most common "accessory" or equipment piece is a glove. Caps are a must in the field. Jewelry has caused quite the debate over the years. MLB has rules and regulations banning excessive jewelry. But nowadays more players are seen wearing a $25 titanium-coated nylon necklace than the bling of years past. Titanium is said to give a player more energy, improve circulation, and reduce muscle stress.

Footwear: Baseball shoes were originally canvas and wore down so often that new shoes were needed weekly. According to the Hall of Fame exhibit, the first known leather baseball sneaker was made by Spalding in 1882 and was made of calfskin. The company introduced an all-kangaroo (said to be more durable) leather sneaker with metal spikes in the late 1880s. It was popular for many years. When artificial turf was introduced in the mid-1960s, it changed not only how the ball took a hop, but baseball fashion as well. Players were seen filing down their spikes, so rubber cleats were introduced in the late 1970s; the present-day plastic cleats made their debut in the early 1980s. The cleats provide better traction and balance when running and work on all surfaces.

Drama

Baseball is America's oldest professional game, and it has produced some of the fiercest rivalries in all of sports. The most notorious, the Boston Red Sox versus the New York Yankees, dates back more than a hundred years and is considered the greatest, most bitter, and longest rivalry in professional American sports. Most teams have a rival or two in the same division, the same state, or even the same town. Here's a look at the most legendary.

Boston Red Sox Versus New York Yankees

It could be the close geographic location (about a three-and-a-half-hour drive) or the fact that these two have been battling it out in the same division for a century, but regardless of why, fans of these two teams simply hate each other. The players may be friends (although a bench-clearing brawl in 2004 may have put those rumors to rest), but the fans' abhorrence for each other is as obvious as the Yankees' twenty-seven World Series titles.

It can be said that the rivalry started way back before either city had a team, when the people of Boston were fighting for a revolution and the city of New York was under British control and wanted to remain that way. After the manufacturing and population booms in the early nineteenth century, New York succeeded Boston as the most productive and financially profitable city in America, something Bostonians may never get over.

Most baseball historians agree that the real Red Sox/Yankee rivalry began when Babe Ruth was sold to the Yankees (see "The Curse of the Bambino," page 64), and it has continued through the Ted Williams and Joe DiMaggio days and on to the present day. For many years, the rivalry was quite one-sided, as the Yankees steamrolled and the Red Sox broke hearts, but every season there seems to be magic in the air when these two teams play each other. The rivalry may never end, as both teams consistently have high payrolls and prospect-rich farm systems.

Los Angeles Dodgers Versus San Francisco Giants

Another time-tested and lengthy rivalry, between the Dodgers and the Giants, started when both teams played in New York City (until 1957). Unlike the Red Sox and Yankees, this rivalry is much more balanced. Since 1901 the Dodgers and Giants have played each other more times than any other two teams. There's been plenty of postseason drama between these two, but the most notable (and cringe-worthy for Dodgers fans) was in the 1951 season, when the Giants pulled off an amazing comeback to win the pennant (winning the league championship and advancing to the World Series). It turns out, though, that the Giants had an elaborate sign-stealing system in place at their home field, the Polo Grounds in upper Manhattan. How elaborate could it have been be in the early '50s, without today's technology? The Giants' clubhouse was conveniently located just outside of center field, and coach Herman Franks would sit in the clubhouse and use a telescope to read the catcher's signs. He'd then set off a buzzer or bell in the bull-pen to identify a pitch, and a relay man would send it in to the batter. Smart, yes, but very unsportsmanlike. Dodger fans can only wonder what could have been. In the late 1950s, both teams moved to California, but the hatred continues.

Chicago Cubs Versus St. Louis Cardinals

With only a three-hundred-mile journey on Interstate 55 sep-arating these two historic teams, a rivalry has been in place since the late 1800s. Fans living midway between the two cities have been making a gut-wrenching decision for decades over what team to root for, sometimes alienating friends and neigh-bors. This rivalry was originally about territory and broadcast rights between radio and then TV stations, because most people in the area would receive both broadcasts. Although the rivalry has been on for more than a century, it really picked up steam in 1998 during the home run race between Sammy Sosa (Cubs) and Mark McGwire (Cardinals). The record-breaking compe-tition to be that season's home run king (McGwire won) was great for baseball: The strike of 1994–95 had turned away many fans, and this historic battle helped bring the fans back to baseball. The two teams play each other about eighteen times during the season; with that many games played, every season brings new drama and heartache.

Superstitions

Baseball is the most superstitious sport in the world; its players, coaches, and fans all have some sort of interesting quirk when it comes to how they play or watch the game. This is not a new phenomenon; documented superstitions go back more than a hundred years. For example: The entire 1894 Baltimore Orioles team drank glasses of turkey gravy before each batting practice. Also, Hall of Fame third baseman Wade Boggs famously ate fried chicken before each game. Here's a look at some of the more common player and fan superstitions.

- Some players will spit into their hands before stepping into the batter's box.
- Some will chew the same piece of gum all game.
- Some won't step on the foul lines or baselines when entering or leaving the field.
- Some believe it is good luck to step on a base before running off the field at the end of an inning.
- Some guys believe that lending a bat or other equipment to a teammate is bad luck.
- Some refuse to wash clothing while a streak is going on.
- Some players shave all their hair while others will grow it long during a streak.
- Many players wear an article of good-luck clothing under their uniforms.
- If a no-hitter looks possible, do not mention it . . . at all. Players will ignore the pitcher in the dugout.
- When getting ready to step to the plate, players can be seen adjusting and readjusting their batting gloves or armbands.

- Some players won't clean a helmet or bat covered with pine tar for the whole season. (Pine tar is the sticky substance applied to a bat to improve grip, and it ends up all over the batting helmet as well.)

Curses

Perhaps the biggest superstitions in the game of baseball are the "curses" that have plagued championship-hungry teams for decades. As a former believer myself, seeing two of the three major curses broken in consecutive seasons (2004 and 2005) was magical. The curse broken in 2004 (the Curse of the Bambino) was very close to my heart, and when the Red Sox won their first World Series in eighty-six years, I didn't know what to do. I was living in New York City, and I walked out of my apartment and looked up at the sky. I don't know what I was looking for. Flying pigs? Maybe an asteroid plummeting to the earth? Seeing a curse break before your eyes is seeing history. Here's a look at the most famous curses to grace the bases.

The Curse of the Bambino (1920–2004)–From Babe to Buckminster to Bucky to Buckner to Boone and Back to the Babe

The "Curse of the Bambino" gained national recognition as a phrase back in 1986, after another nail-biting postseason that once again ended in heartache and tears for all of New England. A sportswriter for *The New York Times* wrote a detailed story on the pitfalls of the Red Sox and the strange happenings after the sale of Babe Ruth on January 3, 1920. The article, written following the dreadful 1986 World Series, gained the interest of the nation. Then in 1990, legendary *Boston Globe* columnist Dan Shaughnessy wrote the book *The Curse of the Bambino,* which led the whole world to weigh in on whether or not the curse was real.

It all started in 1920 after then–Red Sox owner Harry Frazee sold star player Babe Ruth to the Yankees for $125,000 and other incentives to help pay his mortgage on Fenway Park and to finance a Broadway show, *No, No, Nanette.* Prior to the sale, the Red Sox had won five of the first fifteen World Series, including the first one, played in 1903. The Red Sox were feared and hated because they were the best team in baseball. The last World Series win for the Red Sox with Ruth was in 1918, and at this time, Ruth's power hitting was becoming so important that the Red Sox had their star pitcher switch to the outfield and first base to concentrate on hitting. After being sold to the Yankees in the Roarin' '20s, Ruth became larger than life. He was the first ballplayer to transcend baseball and become a celebrity superstar in his own right. If Ruth were around today, he'd be gracing the covers of the tabloids on a regular basis. He notoriously loved food, cigars, and women. But his prolific numbers were so amazing that nothing mattered except what he did on the field. What did he do exactly? He only became the greatest ballplayer of all time, breaking numerous records and practically inventing the "power game." He led the once fledging Yankees franchise to its first World Series win in 1923; that same year, when Yankee Stadium opened it was referred to as "the House That Ruth Built." The Yankees switched places with Boston: In the eighty-four years after the sale, the Yankees went to thirty-nine World Series and won twenty-six of them (the most championships won by one team in *any* sport), becoming the greatest team in MLB history. As for the Red Sox, once Ruth was sold, their fortunes reversed, and through 2003, they went to only four World Series, losing each of them in seven heartbreaking games.

Throughout the eighty-six-year drought, the Curse took on a life of its own. The Red Sox were expected to choke—big time—right when they needed a win. The more people started to connect the dots, the more supernatural the Curse became. I call it the five Bs, and all these oddities seem to have come from a higher power.

- First, the **B**abe was known to stay in a hotel (that is still open for business) across the street from Fenway called the **B**uckminster Hotel. This hotel is also famous for the Curse of the Black Sox (see below). Eerily, for decades, people would see a light on in "Ruth's old room" over-looking Fenway Park, as if the Great Bambino himself were watching Red Sox games. Hotel management said no light was ever on in the room and no one was staying in it. The mystery was finally solved when it was proven that the lights of Fenway reflect off one window, mak-ing it look like the light is on.
- In 1978 the Red Sox held a one-game playoff against the Yankees for the right to go to the postseason. **B**ucky "Bleeping" Dent hit a home run in the seventh inning, giving the Yankees the victory.
- In 1986 the Red Sox were one out away from winning the World Series in Game 6 against the New York Mets when a routine ground ball hit to Red Sox first baseman Bill **B**uckner was misplayed and went right through his legs, letting the Mets win that game and then the next game and the Series.
- In 2003 the Red Sox and Yankees were playing an epic battle in Game 7 of the ALCS to decide which team

would go to the World Series. In extra innings, Aaron Boone hit a walk-off homer to win the game and once again reduce the Red Sox faithful to tears.

For years, various methods were used to try and break the curse. There were exorcisms performed at Fenway Park. Divers searched a Sudbury, Massachusetts, pond for a piano Ruth supposedly drowned on the grounds of his farm, Home Plate Farm. And a "Reverse Curve" sign on Storrow Drive in Boston was vandalized into "Reverse the Curse" (no one knows when exactly), and city officials left it in place. Nothing seemed to work.

Some say the curse was broken August 31, 2004, when the blood of a young boy was spilled on Fenway Park. Former Red Sox great Manny Ramirez hit a hard foul ball and struck then-sixteen-year-old Lee Gavin in the mouth and knocked out his two front teeth. Strangely enough, Gavin actually lived in Babe Ruth's former residence, Home Plate Farm, at the time of the accident.

I believe the curse was finally broken during the 2004 ALCS playoff series. The Yankees had a 3–0 series lead, and the Red Sox amazingly came back and won four games in a row to beat the Yankees, and end the curse. This is considered the greatest comeback (or greatest choke, depending how you look at it) in sports history, as no team had ever come back from being down 3–0 in a series.

On October 27, 2004, during a full moon and a lunar eclipse (would Red Sox fans have it any other way?), the Red Sox beat the St. Louis Cardinals, a team they had lost the World Series to in 1946 and 1967, in a four-game sweep to end the eighty-six-year drought.

The Curse of the Black Sox (1919–2005)

Also known as the "Curse of Shoeless Joe" (see "The Soap Operas" below), this curse stems from the "Black Sox Scandal," where eight members of the Chicago White Sox were banned from baseball for intentionally throwing (losing) the 1919 World Series and handing the victory to the Cincinnati Reds. That Chicago team came to be known as the Black Sox because of the scandal. The "curse" was almost seen as retribution for what the ballplayers had done, and it seemed destined to haunt the White Sox forever.

The conspiracy started in Boston's Buckminster Hotel, where White Sox first baseman Arnold Gandil and a professional gambler connected to the Chicago mob came up with the original idea. Gandil recruited his teammates to purposely lose the World Series, and the participating members were promised a split of $80,000 to $100,000, according to reports from the time. After the White Sox lost the World Series, evidence and testimony mysteriously went missing, and all were acquitted of any wrongdoing in court, but not by MLB. Baseball's first commissioner, Kenesaw Mountain Landis, banned eight members of the White Sox team from baseball—for life.

The eight banned members of the White Sox were:

- Eddie Cicotte, pitcher
- Oscar Felsch, center fielder
- Arnold Gandil, first baseman
- "Shoeless" Joe Jackson, outfielder
- Fred McMullin, utility infielder
- Charles Risberg, shortstop

- George Weaver, third baseman
- Claude "Lefty" Williams, pitcher

The curse was broken in 2005 when the White Sox won their first World Series in eighty-eight years. The scandal is embedded in American history through Eliot Asinof's book *Eight Men Out*, published in 1963, which was adapted into a classic baseball movie in 1988.

The Curse of the Billy Goat (1945–Present)

The only curse still surviving as of the 2010 season opener is the Curse of the Billy Goat. Less passionate and romantic than the Bambino and Black Sox curses, the Billy Goat seems more like an excuse than a real curse. This is because the curse started in 1945 and the Cubs haven't won a World Series since 1908. So what "other" curse is responsible for the thirty-seven-year drought prior to this one? However, the Cubs haven't been to a World Series since 1945, so maybe there is something there.

It all started in 1945 when Greek immigrant Billy Sianis, who owned a nearby bar, the now-famous Billy Goat Tavern, had two tickets to watch the Cubs play the Detroit Tigers. He brought his goat with him to the game and at first the goat was allowed in. Management let the goat walk around the field wearing a blanket and sign that read, "We Got Detroit's Goat!" But after a rainstorm, security kicked Sianis and the goat out because the goat smelled really bad wet and people were complaining.

Sianis was outraged and placed a curse on the Cubs that they would never win a pennant or World Series again. The entire story sounds ludicrous, and it would be laughed off had the Cubs actually won something. But because they haven't, the curse seems more and more likely to be real.

There have been multiple attempts to break the curse, including the horrific (a slaughtered goat hanging from the famed Chicago broadcaster Harry Caray's statue) and the absurd (Sam Sianis, Billy Sianis's nephew-in-law, says that the curse can be broken only if the Cubs' owners let a goat into the park because they like goats, and not just for publicity). But as ridiculous as this all sounds, it is the only major curse still holding strong, so maybe the Cubs' owners should invite all the goats near Chicago to come graze in center field at beautiful Wrigley.

QUICK TIP:
WHICH GAME(S) SHOULD I GO TO?

The cheapest way to see a game in the best seats possible is to go to a weekday daytime game against a not-so-hyped team. If a weekday game is just impossible to attend, the next best thing is an early-in-the-week night game against the same kind of (not-so-popular) team. These games will be less crowded (again, with the exception of the ballparks that always sell out), and it will be easier to get the best seats for your money. Remember that night games against highly marketed teams, nationally televised games, and of course the playoffs will have higher ticket prices, larger crowds, and an exceptionally social atmosphere.

MLB teams are courting women and have made it easier than ever to attend a game and even get some free swag. The Florida Marlins, Toronto Blue Jays, and Los Angeles Angels of Anaheim all hold ladies' nights and events where women get free bags or T-shirts, info, autograph sessions, and discounted tickets. Many teams now offer these kinds of perks. Visit your team's Web site for more information.

WHO TO KNOW IN HISTORY: THE BEST OF THE BEST

Must-Know Position Players

Hank Aaron ("Hammerin' Hank" or "The Hammer") is second all time in home runs. The Hall of Fame outfielder broke Babe Ruth's record of 714 in 1974 amid fanfare and racist hatred. His record of 755 home runs stood for thirty-three years until Barry Bonds broke it in 2007. The twenty-one-time All-Star is number one all time in RBIs, total bases, and extra-base hits.

Ty Cobb ("The Georgia Peach") was notoriously disliked by many players for his aggressive behavior on and off the field. He was a well-known racist and instigator, but, in a straight baseball sense, he was a huge talent. The Hall of Fame outfielder is known as the best ballplayer of the dead ball era (from 1903 to 1920, a time when pitchers ruled and run scoring was very low), and amazingly, although he retired in 1928, he still holds the records for career batting average (.367), career steals of home base (54), and career batting titles (12).

Roberto Clemente was a twelve-time All-Star and four-time batting champion, and won twelve Gold Gloves. The Hall of Fame outfielder was known for more than just his amazing on-the-field abilities. He was a huge philanthropist and tragically died in a plane crash while trying to bring aid to earthquake victims in Nicaragua. He was the first Latin American voted into the Hall of Fame and the only ballplayer to have the five-year waiting period waived before induction. The Roberto Clemente Award is given annually to the player deemed to have done the best humanitarian work.

Joe DiMaggio ("Joltin' Joe" or "The Yankee Clipper") was a three-time MVP and thirteen-time All-Star who played his whole career with the New York Yankees. He famously married Marilyn Monroe just after his retirement, and even though their Hollywood marriage ended in a Hollywood divorce only 274 days later, they remained very close and were rumored to have been together romantically just before her tragic death. He is the player with the longest hitting streak (hitting safely in fifty-six games in a row), a record that has very little chance of being broken. Joltin' Joe helped the Yankees to win nine World Series in thirteen years.

Mickey Mantle played his entire eighteen-year Hall of Fame career with the New York Yankees. The sixteen-time All-Star and three-time MVP led his Yankees to seven World Series titles. Mantle was a Triple Crown winner (at the end of the season, the Triple Crown winner leads the league in the major offensive categories—batting average, home runs, and RBIs—a rare feat that has not been accomplished since 1967); but he was also famous for his off-the-field battle with alcoholism. His legendary career has caused Mantle merchandise to be among the most sought-after and traded memorabilia in baseball.

Willie Mays ("The Say Hey Kid") is fourth all time in home runs (660) and a record twenty-four-time All-Star. He also won eleven Gold Gloves and was inducted into the Hall of Fame in his first year of eligibility. Mays is most famous for "The Catch" during the 1954 World Series, the same year he won the batting crown. The amazing over-the-shoulder basket catch on the warning track is considered one of the top fielding plays of all time.

Cal Ripken Jr. ("The Iron Man") is the "newest" name to this legends list because he didn't retire from baseball until 2001. He was a nineteen-time All-Star and the 1982 Rookie of the

Year. The Hall of Fame shortstop/third baseman is best known for breaking and holding the record for the most consecutive games played with 2,632. The record was (and still is) deemed unbreakable in the modern era. The two-time American League MVP played his entire career with the Baltimore Orioles.

Jackie Robinson was the first African American to take the field in the modern game. It had been fifty-seven years of segregated baseball before Robinson broke the color barrier. He was a six-time All-Star, and his sensational ten-year award-winning career and unprecedented impact on the game led Major League Baseball to retire his number (42) in 1997 for all teams, the first and only time that has been done.

George Herman Ruth ("the Babe," "the Great Bambino," or "the Sultan of Swat") played between 1914 and 1935 and is known as the greatest ballplayer of all time. The Hall of Fame pitcher and outfielder was the first player to hit thirty, forty, fifty, and sixty home runs in a season. The record of sixty held for thirty-four years, and his all-time home run record of 714 held for thirty-nine years. He won seven World Series in his career, and legend has it that in the 1932 World Series against the Chicago Cubs, he "called" one of his home runs by pointing his bat to center field to predict where he'd hit it. It worked, and the ball sailed out in deep center. This moment is part of the legend and folklore that made him the Babe.

Ted Williams ("The Kid," "Teddy Ballgame," or "The Splendid Splinter") was the last player to hit higher than .400 in a season (.406 in 1941). The Hall of Fame left fielder for the Boston Red Sox left baseball twice to join his fellow Marines in war. He had a nineteen-year career and is recognized as one of the greatest hitters of all time. His book, *The Science of Hitting,* written in 1970 and revised in 1986, is a must-read for all young ballplayers. Williams was a war hero, a baseball hero, and a fishing legend. A member of the prestigious five-hundred-home-run club, Williams won the MVP twice and the Triple Crown twice, led the league in batting average six times, and was a seventeen-time All-Star.

Must-Know Pitchers

Roger Clemens won eleven Cy Young Awards and was an eleven-time All-Star. He is seen as one of the greatest pitchers of all time and the first to throw twenty strikeouts in one game, an honor he tied himself and now shares with two other pitchers.

Bob Gibson is a Hall of Fame pitcher who played his whole career with the St. Louis Cardinals. The eight-time All-Star won two Cy Young Awards and two World Series. He was the first pitcher in the National League to strike out three thousand batters, and his ERA in 1968 (1.12) is the second lowest of all time.

Sandy Koufax played his whole career with the Brooklyn/Los Angeles Dodgers. He was the youngest player ever elected to the Hall of Fame and the second Jewish player elected (the first was Tigers great Hank Greenberg). Koufax has a lifetime ERA of 2.76, second only to Tom Seaver's 2.73. The fire-throwing southpaw won three Cy Young Awards and two World Series MVPs.

Nolan Ryan pitched for a record twenty-seven seasons, earning eight All-Star selections. He currently holds the record for most strikeouts all time (5,714) and most no-hitters (7). Currently serving as president of the Texas Rangers (Ryan pitched his final five seasons for the Rangers), he was elected to the Hall of Fame on his first try in 1999.

Cy Young played twenty-two seasons from 1890 to 1911,

and the Cy Young Award, given annually to the best pitcher from each league, is named for him. Although he played so long ago, he still holds the records for most wins (511), complete games (749), and innings pitched (7,354).

The Soap Operas

These two notorious baseball players are legends, but for all the wrong reasons.

Pete Rose ("Charlie Hustle") is baseball's all-time hits leader with 4,256. He won three World Series and three batting titles, and was elected to seventeen All-Star teams. The switch-hitting superstar played for twenty-three seasons and managed for five. His nickname, Charlie Hustle, came from his heroic efforts on the field. When he was walked, he'd still run to first base. He was well known for his signature (and dangerous) headfirst slide. He was also instrumental in the Big Red Machine's (the Cincinnati Rods) domination of the National League from 1970 to 1976. Rose would have been a shoo-in for the Hall of Fame, but in 1989, three years after his retirement, Rose agreed to permanent ineligibility amid numerous allegations that he bet on baseball. This means he is banned from playing, coaching, managing, or being a part of MLB for any reason, including being inducted into the Hall. He did get to participate, controversially however, when he was voted a member of the All-Century Team, and during the on-the-field festivities prior to Game 2 of the 1999 World Series, when Rose was announced he received a loud standing ovation. He continually denied any wrongdoing even with overwhelming evidence to the contrary.

Finally in 2004, Rose admitted to betting on baseball, but

♔ BASEBALL AWARDS

Most Valuable Player (MVP): Awarded to the, well, *most valuable player* in each league. The MVP is seen as the highest honor a player can receive in a season, although the players will tell you they'll take a World Series win over anything.

Cy Young Award: Given to the best pitcher in each league, named after Hall of Fame pitcher Cy Young, who died in 1955. Young is seen as one of the greatest pitchers of all time, if not *the* greatest. He recorded five thirty-win seasons and ten twenty-win seasons, both unheard of in today's game (in 2007 there was only one twenty-game-winning pitcher in all of baseball). He also pitched the first "perfect game" in modern baseball.

Rookie of the Year Award: Given to the best first-year player in each league. Only one Rookie of the Year winner has ever won the Cy Young Award the same year, former Los Angeles Dodgers pitcher Fernando Valenzuela in 1981. Only two Rookie of the Year winners have won the MVP in the same season: Fred Lynn in 1975 and Ichiro Suzuki in 2001.

Gold Glove Award: In recognition of his defense, one player is awarded the Gold Glove at each position in each league (so eigh-

not against his teams, and he said he never threw any games. He only bet in favor of his bunch. Still, after years of applying for reinstatement, each application has been denied. There is always talk of "should he or shouldn't he be in the Hall," a teen are awarded annually) for displaying a superior individual performance at his position.

Silver Bat Award: Given to the batting champion (the highest batting average) in each league.

Hank Aaron Award: Introduced in 1999 to celebrate the twenty-fifth anniversary of Hank Aaron breaking Babe Ruth's home run record, the award is given to the player in each league who has the best offensive performance for the season. It measures hits, home runs, and RBIs to decide the winners.

Roberto Clemente Award: Given to just one player a season for his charitable work and contributions to in the community. The award is named after Hall of Fame outfielder Roberto Clemente, who died in a plane crash in 1972 while delivering supplies to earthquake victims in Nicaragua.

Silver Slugger Award: Given to the best offensive player in each league at each position. The award is similar to the Gold Glove but recognizes offense instead of defense.

Relief Man of the Year Award: Introduced in 1976, it honors the best relief pitcher in each league in a season.

Manager of the Year Award: Recognized by MLB in 1983, the award is given annually to the best managers in each league.

debate that will continue for years to come. Personally, I'd like to see Rose in the Hall of Fame, but I won't hold my breath.

"Shoeless" Joe Jackson was the best-known member of the Chicago Black Sox that notoriously threw the 1919 World

Series, and eight members of the team were banned from baseball for life. Jackson got his nickname during a minor league game when his new spikes gave him blisters. In pain, he took off his shoes and played the game in only his stockings. The nickname stuck throughout his career.

Jackson's participation in the Black Sox scandal is highly controversial and debated among baseball enthusiasts. He hit .375 (which is fantastic) and committed no errors in games he was supposedly trying to throw. Furthermore, Jackson was illiterate and may not have fully understood what the terms of the shady deal were. Also, in true conspiracy style, rumors circulated that Jackson's family was threatened if he did not participate. The most damning evidence against him is that Jackson did accept $5,000 from the gamblers, and on his lawyer's advice he pled guilty. The world will never know exactly what happened or what was going through Jackson's head, but he is idolized in the movies *Eight Men Out* and *Field of Dreams*. On his deathbed, Jackson is widely reported to have said, "I'm about to face the greatest umpire of all, and he knows I'm innocent."

STITCHES AND SEAMS: BASEBALL FASHION

It's baseball! It's summer! So who cares, right? For girlie girls everywhere, baseball can actually be the hardest sport to dress for. This is because most games are played in the hot summer months (the "dog days")—the time of year when it's especially easy to get in a fashion rut. Summer can mean flip-flops every day, casual clothing, and carefree fashion. For those of us that still want to be stylish, short lightweight dresses and flats may be cute outfits for everyday wear, but they're not good for a baseball game. Unless, that is, you prefer your thighs touching and sweating on the wood or plastic seats. Believe me, it is not a good way to enjoy the game.

If the game is at an outdoor park, it's a sunny, sweltering 90-degree day, and there's no overhead covering, the question of what to wear is really ridiculous. I have worn everything that I don't recommend: flip-flops (yes, your feet will get dirty, and yes, it's gross), a white cotton tank top (white shows less sweat and reflects light), and short shorts (bring a towel to place on the seat to combat the sweaty-thigh syndrome). I was a miserable ball of sweat, along with everyone else, but at least I was showing less of it by wearing a white top. Sometimes that's just the way it is. But if you are dripping sweat, most likely everyone else is too, so hydrate and enjoy the game.

But most of the time, weather permitting, I want to look good and still be comfortable.

My rules:

1. I try to never wear light-colored pants or shorts. At most parks, between the mishaps that can happen with the seats, bathrooms, food, drinks, and the unpredictable summer rainstorm, it's almost always a bad idea.
2. I try not to wear flip-flops. The floors are usually covered with litter, spilled drinks, mud, sand, and grass from the parking-lot area, and probably a few disgusting unknown substances. Oh, and I can't forget the peanut shells that are guaranteed to stick to even the most minimally sweaty feet.
3. I'm short and always prefer to wear some sort of heels, but when I'm at a game, I don't usually want to *look* like I'm wearing them.

OH NO SHE DIDN'T!
BASEBALL FASHION FAUX PAS

"I think what shocks me the most is the women who show up wearing little miniskirts or shorts with their butts hanging out or teeny tiny tank tops with their boobs popping out and/or their tummies exposed. It looks so trashy. I'm still shocked women think this is what's sexy."

—Heather Eubanks, *San Diego* magazine

"Unless it's your team's adorned logo, skip the rhinestones and glitz. It's a baseball game, not a nightclub."

—Stacy Burton, St. Louis fashion stylist

"Absolute don'ts: anything silk, nice pants, stilettos of any kind, and nothing uncomfortable or too tight. You don't want to be the bitch that everyone is annoyed with because you can't stop complaining."

—Danielle Goldman, New York City fashion stylist

"Too much makeup for a day game will make you look like a drag queen."

—Lori Haney, Phoenix fashion stylist

"Unless you are in high school or younger, it's best to skip the face paint and team-logo temp tattoos."

—Stephanie Shanahan, Dallas-area fashion stylist

Because the baseball season starts in early April and ends in October, the weather plays a huge part in deciding what to wear to a game. April and October in Chicago feel a lot different than they do in Los Angeles.

Definitely use the Internet to check weather conditions, and use each team's interactive Web site to map your seats in the ballpark. You can figure out east and west and see what kind of sun you will be dealing with throughout the game and see if you will have overhead covering. You can also mark the closest entrances and exits.

Unfortunately for women who must wear dressy business attire or suits to work, for baseball games a change of clothes or a swap of a few key items is almost always necessary. There are exceptions if you're sitting in a luxury box or club section. Luxury boxes are definitely dressier and have amenities like air-conditioning, indoor concessions, newer and cleaner bathrooms, and concourses that can look like luxury hotels. Also, a lot of men will be in suits in this seating area. Most people in these sections come straight from work. The view is nice (both of the field and of the people watching), but it's still baseball, and it's still summer, so channel your inner Coco Chanel and take off at least one accessory before arrival.

"On days when I have to transition from cubicle to skybox, I wear a turtleneck and slacks (in colder weather) and high-heeled pumps to work, and I only freshen up my makeup. I don't change my clothes, because most people will be in work attire anyway," says West Coast fashion stylist Stephanie Simons. "To be honest, I've never really felt relaxed at those games."

For those of us who won't be in a luxury box, there is plenty of women's apparel like caps, tank tops, and fitted tees that are now available on team Web sites and at stores. Even team-logo thong underwear is available. Also, actress and baseball fan

Alyssa Milano, fed up with jerseys hanging down to her knees, launched her own line of baseball fan wear with MLB called Touch by Alyssa Milano, offering highly stylized and form-fitting tanks, tees, hoodies, and crystal-emblazoned logos.

For years, I ordered vintage kids' jerseys on eBay to find the right fit, but now MLB also offers women's jerseys that are replicas of the real thing but shrunk to a flattering size.

Although it is not necessary to buy any merchandise to look feminine and appropriate at a game, big-time fans should take advantage of these offerings. I usually will wear some sort of team jersey or T-shirt. I am an überfan, though, so I usually go way above and beyond and look for vintage or retro T-shirts online.

Some women, however, wouldn't wear those items to a game. "Once upon a time, I used to dress for a baseball game in official team wear. Then one day, it hit me," says Boston fashion editor Rachel Solar. "Just because I'm at a baseball game, do I have to lose my sense of style? Upon entering the ballpark, do I suddenly cease to be a woman? I think not."

If choosing from the closet sounds better than buying something, remember that it's hot outside, so showing some skin can still be classy in this kind of environment. As with any event, there's a fine line between sexy and trashy. "My rule of thumb is that I don't wear anything to a game I wouldn't want to run into my ex-boyfriend in," Solar says.

Hope Misterek, a Seattle-based fashion stylist, says that she doesn't wear team-oriented clothes but will sometimes wear a team-colored tee or hoodie. "My favorite thing to wear to a game is my skinny jeans with layered tee, depending on the weather, and sometimes I'll wear team colors. I love my Converse sneakers and a cropped jacket with some femininity to it if it's chilly."

Tissue-weight tees and tanks are perfect for a baseball game because you can layer depending on the weather, and the shirts are thin enough to put in your bag if you get too hot. "I love the slim-fit lightweight tees that are all over the place now. They are sexy and body-hugging, but lightweight enough to keep you cool in the hot summer months," says L.A. fashion stylist Shannon Lee. "When paired with jeans the tops make jeans and a tee so much sexier than it sounds. Yet, you're still just wearing jeans and a tee."

Jeans are the best bottoms to wear no matter what climate you are in. In the South you may get hot at day games, but I choose that over my legs sticking to the seat. Capris are also popular and comfortable, in a cargo style or a dark-colored cotton or linen.

"Jeans are always the best choice," says fashion stylist Hope Misterek. Consider the length of your pants or jeans as well. "The bathrooms at baseball games are usually horrific and if your jeans or pants skim the floor, they will be skimming the unmentionable wetness that accumulates in there as well. Keep this in mind when choosing shoes too."

For skirts, skip the minis unless you want everyone to see . . . well, more than they should. If a dress or skirt is preferred, try to keep it no shorter than just slightly above the knee. Between standing to cheer, walking through the row to get to your seat, and other normal activities, you will be exposed if it's any shorter.

Location, Location, Location

For women who live in a city with a team lucky enough to have a retractable roof, you really get the best of both worlds. If the weather is bad, the roof closes and you're shielded from rain and cold. If it's a glorious day, you are sitting outdoors, watching baseball as it should be watched. It's simply brilliant. This is a fairly recent technology, so most retractable-roof stadiums are somewhat new.

Beautiful Safeco Field in Seattle has a retractable roof and is an excellent example of how different locations can mean different clothing choices. Former *Seattle Times* columnist and Mariners fan Pamela Sitt says that Safeco is perfect for beginner fans and expert fans alike.

"Safeco is a great field because whether you are into baseball or not, it's a fun time," Sitt says. "It's really shiny and new and clean! There's a ton of food options and not just typical ballpark fare. You can get sushi and salads and even salmon. It's a fun place for people watching, and on Friday and Saturday nights it's a 'meat-market' environment, and the twenty- and thirty-somethings make an effort to look cute. Those nights are definitely dressier, but casual cute, not going-to-a-club cute."

A domed baseball stadium is also perfect for girlie girls. A climate-controlled 72-degree indoor ballpark makes it easy to dress because there are no weather issues, including humidity and wind. On the flip side, watching a baseball game in a dome, in my opinion, is a bit daunting. It gives the game a different and almost surreal feel. It just doesn't seem natural to me. At a recent Tampa Bay Rays game at the domed, mall-like Tropicana Field (they have great museums in there too!), I wore a nice fitted pair of boot-cut jeans, wedges with a two-inch heel, and a team jersey. I looked great and felt comfortable, and although being in a dome for baseball was a bit weird, the fashion options were limitless.

I prefer a large handbag for most occasions. Living and

working in a city means fewer opportunities to run home to change, so I usually have my whole life in my handbag. City living also means not having a car and taking public transportation to the game. For a baseball game, a big bag adds convenience and the knowledge that I have everything I could possibly need. It does pose problems because the seats in most stadiums are small and I have serious issues with placing my two-weeks'-salary handbag on the floor. And even though stuffing it behind me or placing it on my lap can be annoying when I want to stand and cheer, the positives outweigh the negatives.

Chelsea Greenwood, former managing editor at *Boca* magazine, says that a handbag has become a focal point of fashion, and she won't deny herself this luxury. "Plus it needs to carry my phone, wallet, sunglasses and case, brush, makeup, camera, keys, and still have room for souvenirs!"

If I'm going to a casual day game, I usually bring a casual messenger-style, cross-body flat bag or something smaller. But for night games and those when I'm coming from work, it's always a bigger bag.

The West Coast's more laid-back style is apparent right off the bat (pun intended). Opposite coasts, in this case, equal opposite handbag choices.

Heather Eubanks, former fashion and beauty director at *San Diego* magazine, suggests a small bag, assuming, of course, that you can't shove what you need in your boyfriend's pockets. "I bring a small canvas bag to Padres games," she explains. "The fabric makes it washable and it also allows you to squish it in the seat to be more comfortable than holding it on your lap."

For accessories, keep it simple, with one item like simple hoop earrings or a single long necklace. Studs, rings, bracelets, necklaces, belts, scarves, and oversized sunglasses all can have a place at a baseball game, but only in moderation. "Wear just one item like a long necklace and put the large hoops or whatever else you like to wear in a handbag if the day or evening isn't over when the game is," says Eubanks. "It's important to keep it simple."

The best footwear is obviously flats. They will be the most comfortable, and with the amazing selections around today it can be easy to wear flats and still have major style. Tennis shoes, sandals, and ballet flats all work too.

If you must wear a heel make sure it has a casual look to it. A wedge or espadrille with a sturdy heel (that can be covered with long jeans or pants so that it doesn't look like you are wearing a heel) is perfect. Trickery aside, I find this to be the *only* acceptable way of wearing a heel to a baseball game.

There is always the luxury-box exception, but for the rest of us, this is the rule. For early-spring and late-fall games, if a height boost is necessary, then heeled boots with pants or jeans are perfect. I prefer a somewhat thick heel, not too chunky but sturdy enough to be able to tackle narrow seating rows, narrower stairways, and crowded walkways with unpredictable obstacles along the way, like other people's feet.

My advice isn't about judging as much as it is about looking out for your style and comfort, and the best way to *enjoy* a game. Truth is, I love wearing four-inch stilettos and even higher, but not to a baseball game. The girl in the four-inch stilettos is probably wearing other dare I say inappropriate items (I guess I am judging!), and the bottom line is that she is most likely *not* there to watch, learn, and enjoy the game, because if she were, she would know better. My judgment aside, there are some girls who just don't care about other people snickering and the possibility of falling and breaking an ankle. And for other women, there's simply no choice. Maybe you have other plans later than evening, or you forgot to bring a change of shoes or clothes to work. But if you do have a choice, skip the stilettos.

"A couple of years ago at a Marlins game, a girl sitting two rows in front of me was being ogled by every man in sight. She was a very pretty girl, but she was wearing four- or five-inch cork platform sandals with short shorts and a tube top, filled out with the classic South Florida fake boobs," Greenwood says. "The steps became too much to handle. With a full tray of nachos in one hand, and a beer in the other, her foot slid out from under her and she fell on her butt, skidding down a few steps. She had nacho cheese all over her and other people sitting in the aisle seats. She got a lot of attention after that. But not the good kind."

Don't Let This Happen to You

Olivia is a gorgeous sometimes blonde, sometimes brunette who looks great no matter what her hair color du jour may be. She always seems to be on the forefront of fashion and reminds me of Gwen Stefani, with similar fashion and style, and the personality to match. She's rocker chic with a girlie twist. She is the most photogenic girl I've ever met and always carries herself perfectly.

Although Olivia isn't really into sports, she never passes up a fun day in an exciting environment. I had an extra ticket for Game 3 of the National League Championship Series (NLCS) at Sun Life Stadium (called Pro Player Stadium then), where the Florida Marlins were playing the Chicago Cubs to see who would go to the World Series. We had a beer or two (or three) in the parking lot while tailgating with the rambunctious crowd awaiting the game.

The stadium was sold out and everyone was given a little white towel to wave during the game. The stadium was a sea of white. The Marlins were in desperate need of a win, so the air was thick with excitement and passion, never mind super-thick from the South Florida humidity. It was hot. Brutally hot. And sunset was no relief, with temps hovering in the mid-90s and the humidity near 100 percent.

Late in the game the home team was down but rallying and the crowd was on its feet, with towels waving and everyone screaming; it was quite the scene. The roar was so loud that it was impossible to hear anyone; even my brother's screaming in my ear sounded like a faint ringing.

Most people had basically stripped down to the bare minimum clothing thanks to the sweat and stickiness covering everyone in the stadium. My hair was soaking wet from sweat, and I was waving my towel in a frenzy. It was so crazy there that I had hot chills and a big permasmile, and was dizzy with exhilaration. Right in the middle of all the excitement, I felt a tap on my shoulder, and the man behind me pointed to my friend sitting next to me.

Olivia was passed out, with peanut shells stuck to her sweaty skin.

Moral of the story: Do I even have to say it? If you are of age and you choose to drink alcohol, please do so in moderation. Gauge the other factors, like heat, crowds, sun, and your limit. Don't drink too much. It's not classy or attractive in any setting. Nor is it fun for your friends to have to carry you to the car after the game.

Makeup

For day games, remember, less is more. Day makeup and night makeup should always be different. For a hot day game, I recommend a tinted moisturizer with SPF 30. Tinted moisturizers work double time to moisturize and cover, but they do it sheerly, so your face isn't melting off by the third inning.

"Some people don't get this, but there is such a thing as daytime makeup and evening makeup," says Eubanks. "A sheer, tinted moisturizer with sunscreen is best for day, with a neutral gloss and mascara. For night games, you can vamp it up a bit by applying a darker lipstick, some liner, and eye shadow. If you go dark on your lips, offset it by going lighter on your eyes or vice versa."

I prefer to keep daytime makeup simple, but my staples are mascara and lip gloss. Baseball games can run anywhere from three to four hours, if not longer sometimes for nationally televised games, so if you like to reapply like I do, bring blotting sheets or powder and a small cream blush to rub on for a quick flush.

For lips, stick with sheer glosses, or if you must wear lipstick, stick to lighter shades. Between the eating and drinking, a dark-colored lipstick will most certainly end up all over your face, and with all the handsome men that attend baseball games, maybe someone else's.

Fashion for the Big Games and the Playoffs

If your home team is lucky enough to make the playoffs, I still don't recommend stilettos, but this is the only time casual baseball can be a bit dressier. The playoffs will be sold out. That's more than 35,000 people in most cases, plus millions on national television and thousands more crowding into the bars and restaurants surrounding the ballpark.

Some night games toward the end of the season can also be a "playoff atmosphere" when the home team is battling for a chance at the postseason. Just like for the playoffs, for these games I wear a little more makeup and wear my hair down, and although I still wear a jersey or T-shirt, I make sure it is fitted with nice tailored jeans and heeled boots, cute flats, or a wedge covered by a long jean. The playoffs and most big games happen in September and October, when it is getting chilly enough for boots and a sweater.

QUICK TIP

Always, always, always write down (that means bring a pen and paper in your handbag) exactly where you parked. Some larger stadiums and ballparks have color-coded signs to help ease confusion, but when there are forty thousand cars in a huge lot and everything looks the same, even the most avid fan can get lost. After years of having season tickets and attending countless games at Sun Life Stadium for baseball and football, even my father and brother (two macho men) would get lost, and we'd all wander aimlessly through the parking lot.

DO THE MATH

Baseball is a game of numbers, statistics, and percentages. Teams are run using these statistics to see which players to spend money on and who to let go. It's a puzzle. Strangely, though I'm someone who just doesn't have the math part of her brain, baseball is my favorite sport. You can love the game and hate numbers like I do. It's never necessary to do the math yourself, but if you ever wanted to (why on earth would you?), here's how.

Batting average (AVG): Measures a hitter's ability by dividing the number of hits by the number of at bats. If a player has 500 at bats and 170 hits, his batting average would be .340 (170/500). That would be a fantastic average to have at the end of the season in today's game. An average of more than .300 for the season is considered having a great season. Hitting .400 or higher seems unfeasible; the last player to do so was Ted Williams, who hit .406 in 1941 and won the batting crown that year. Modern-day players have flirted with that number but no one has achieved it since Williams.

Earned Run Average (ERA): Measures a pitcher's performance by multiplying the total number of earned runs by nine, and dividing the result by the total innings pitched. For pitchers, the lower the ERA they have, the better. Pitchers who accumulate an ERA under 3.00 have had an excellent season. If Johan Santana allows 52 earned runs in 200 innings, multiply 52 by 9: $52 \times 9 = 468$. Divide 468 by 200 (his innings pitched): $468/200 = 2.34$. Santana's ERA is 2.34.

Slugging Percentage (SLG): Measures a hitter's power. Divide the number of total bases—meaning how many bases the player has touched from all of his hits—by the number of times at bat. Players who hit a lot of home runs usually have higher slugging percentages. If David Ortiz has 291 total bases and 460 at bats, then divide 291 by 460 to get his slugging percentage: $291/460 = .632$.

On-Base Percentage (OBP): Commonly used with the SLG

above; the two combined can give teams a good measure of a player's overall production on offense. The OBP determines how often the player is on base. To calculate, add the total number of hits, walks, and times hit by a pitch (HBP) and then divide by the number of the player's at bats, walks, HBPs, and sacrifice flies. If Cleveland Indians center fielder Grady Sizemore has 434 at bats, 152 hits, and 59 walks, has been hit by nine pitches, and has hit six sacrifice flies, then his OBP is .433. Basically almost half of the time he's up, he gets on-base: $(152+59+9)/(434+59+9+6)=220/508=.433$. That's an excellent number.

Fielding Average or Percentage: Measures a fielder's performance. Divide the total number of putouts (getting a man out) and assists (helping on a play) by the total number of putouts, assists, and errors. If Derek Jeter has 223 putouts and 294 assists, while committing only three errors, his fielding percentage is $(223+294)/(223+294+3)=517/520=.994$.

Magic Number: If you're lucky enough to be tabulating your team's magic number, then the playoffs are within reach and every game counts. Take the number of games still to be played, add one, and then subtract the number of games the team is ahead in the loss column of the standings from the closest opponent. If the Brewers are three games ahead in the standings, with ten games remaining, their magic number would be eight.

Games remaining $(10)+1=11. 11-3$ (games up)$=8$.

The other popular method is to take the total number of games in a season (162) and add one (163) and then subtract your team's wins and then subtract the next team's losses. $162+1-\text{WINS}-\text{second-place team's losses}=\text{magic number}$.

THE GIRLIE GIRL'S BASEBALL GLOSSARY

Ace: A team's best starting pitcher.

Alley: The section of the outfield between the outfielders. Also **gap.**

Around the horn: A double play starting from third base then to second and finally to first.

Backdoor slider: A pitch that appears to be out of the strike zone but then breaks back over the plate for a strike.

Bag: A base.

Bang-bang play: A play in which the base runner hits the bag a split second before the ball arrives or vice versa.

Basket catch: When a fielder catches a ball with his glove near belt level.

Brushback: A pitch that nearly hits a batter, as if to "brush" him off the plate.

Can of corn: An easy catch by a fielder.

Caught looking: When a batter is called out on strikes without swinging.

Cellar: Last place.

Cheese: A good fastball.

Chin music: A pitch that is high and inside, appearing to almost brush the chin.

Closer: A relief pitcher that finishes the game.

Cycle: When a batter hits a single, double, triple, and home run in the same game.

Dinger: A home run.

Gap: See **alley**. A ball hit here is a "gapper."

BASEBALL BASICS: ABBREVIATIONS

HITTING

2B: Second base/double

3B: Third base/triple

AB: At bat

AVG: Batting average

BB: Bases on balls (walks)

CS: Caught stealing

G: Games played

GIDP: Grounded into double plays

GO: Ground outs

GS: Grand slam

H: Hit

HBP: Hit by pitch

HR: Home runs

IBB: Intentional walks (bases on balls)

LOB: (Runners) left on base

NP: Number of pitches

OBP: On-base percentage

R: Runs

RBI: Runs batted in

SAC: Sacrifice bunts

SB: Stolen bases

SF: Sacrifice flies

SLG: Slugging percentage

SO: Strikeouts

TB: Total bases

TP: Triple play

FIELDING

A: Assists

CS: Caught stealing

DP: Double plays

E: Error

FPCT: Fielding percentage

G: Games

INN: Innings

OFA: Outfield assists

PB: Passed ball

PO: Putout

Heat: A good fastball.

High and tight: Referring to a pitch that's up in the strike zone and inside on a hitter. Also known as "up and in."

Hill: Pitcher's mound.

Homer: A home run. Other terms include blast, **dinger,** dong, four-bagger, four-base knock, **moon shot, round-tripper, tape-measure blast,** and **tater.**

SB: Stolen bases (allowed)

TP: Triple plays

PITCHING
AO: Fly outs

APP: Appearances

BB/9: Walks per nine innings

BF: Batters faced

BK: Balks

CG: Complete games

ER: Earned runs

ERA: Earned run average

GF: Games finished

GS: Games started

H/9: Hits per nine innings

HB: Hit batsmen

IBB: Intentional walks

I/GS: Innings per game started

IP: Innings pitched

IRA: Inherited runs allowed

K/9: Strikeouts per nine innings

K/BB: Strikeout/walk ratio

L: Losses

LOB: Left on base

NP: Number of pitches thrown

OBA: On-base against

PA: Plate appearances

P/GS: Pitches per start

P/IP: Pitches per inning pitched

PK: Pickoffs

RW: Relief wins

SHO: Shutouts

SLG: Slugging percentage allowed

SV: Saves

SVO: Save opportunities

UR: Unearned runs

W: Wins

WHIP: Walks + hits/inning pitched

WP: Wild pitches

WPCT: Winning percentage

Hot corner: Third base.

In the hole: The batter up after the on-deck hitter is called "in the hole."

Jam: When a hitter gets a pitch near his hands, he is "jammed." Also when a pitcher gets in trouble, he is in a "jam."

Leather: Refers to how well a player plays defensively or handles the glove. Example: "He flashed some leather on that play."

Meatball: An easy pitch to hit, usually right down the middle of the plate.

Moon shot: A very long, high home run, hit as if it's heading to the moon.

Pick: A good defensive play by an infielder on a ground ball. Also a shortened version of "pickoff."

Pickle: See **rundown.**

Punch-out: A strikeout.

Ribbie: Another way of saying RBI.

Rubber game (or **rubber match**): The deciding game of a series.

Rundown: When a base runner gets caught between bases by the fielders.

Series: Most series are three or four games. Two teams play each other for three or four games at a time.

Setup man: A relief pitcher that usually enters the game in the seventh or eighth inning.

Southpaw: A left-handed pitcher.

Sweet spot: The part of the bat's barrel (the thick part of the bat) where balls are hit the best.

Table setter: Batter whose job is to get on base for other hitters to drive him in. Usually a leadoff or number-two hitter.

Tape-measure blast: An extremely long home run.

Tater: A home run.

Touch 'em all: Hitting a home run (touching all the bases).

Twin killing: A double play.

Utility player: A player who fills in at many positions. Most likely a "bench" player, meaning he doesn't start the game and comes off the bench.

Wheelhouse: A hitter's power zone. A ball in the hitter's "wheelhouse" is in his favorite spot, where he likely hits it every time.

Wheels: A ballplayer's legs.

Whiff: Strikeout.

Wood: Making contact with the ball. Example: "He put some wood on it."

2

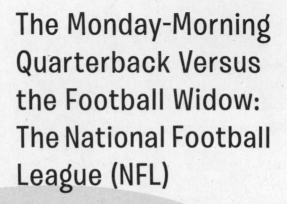

The Monday-Morning Quarterback Versus the Football Widow: The National Football League (NFL)

My family took my friend Andrea to her first professional football game. The Patriots were visiting the Dolphins, and the Miami air was thick and damp, filled with the smell of beer, bratwurst, and smoke from the pregame fireworks. It had rained earlier, so the narrow stairways were slick and muddy. Andrea sat down, quite uncomfortably, on the seat that was still sprinkled with raindrops and squirmed as the water soaked through her light khaki capris. Just before halftime, the Dolphins quarterback threw to the wrong team, and Andrea stood up and shouted at the top of her lungs, "Intersection!"

I'll never forget the horror on my father's face or the jeers from the other fans. Andrea was a good sport about confusing the word "interception" and decided to go get some food. Just as she took her first step up, she tripped over her three-inch stiletto heel and fell down about seven stairs, taking out a beer man and a hot dog vendor along the way.

THE GAME

Sunday.

In the fall, Sunday is more than a day of the week. It's an event. A day when men (and women) become couch potatoes, or grill masters, or party planners. The leaves are starting to change, there's a cold breeze in the air (well, for most of the country), and millions of fans are celebrating the return of football.

Football is a violent game. The padding the players wear on the field is necessary. Football is also (according to TV ratings) the most popular sport in America. This is nothing new. Violent sports have been around for centuries. While football's origins don't trace back to the days of the gladiators in ancient Rome, the premise is the same: watching people violently fight in order to win.

That's why the "shelf life" for an NFL player is only three and a half years. According to the NFL Players Association, such short careers are due to injuries or being cut from the team for younger, fresher talent. Although, of course, many players can have careers in the NFL for a decade or more, the average is still only three and a half years. Or in some cases, three and a half concussions. (In fact, some players sustain dozens of concussions over a career.)

Most of us know only the stars of the teams, but what you

The NFL is made up of thirty-two teams, split evenly into two conferences, the American Football Conference (AFC) and the National Football Conference (NFC). Unlike baseball, where the two "conferences" have different rules (like the DH rule), these two (the AFC and the NFC) have the same rules, and the game is  played the same way throughout. Each conference is split up into four divisions (North, South, East, and West) with four teams in each division.

AFC	NFC
NORTH	**NORTH**
Baltimore Ravens	Chicago Bears
Cincinnati Bengals	Detroit Lions
Cleveland Browns	Green Bay Packers
Pittsburgh Steelers	Minnesota Vikings
SOUTH	**SOUTH**
Houston Texans	Atlanta Falcons
Indianapolis Colts	Carolina Panthers
Jacksonville Jaguars	New Orleans Saints
Tennessee Titans	Tampa Bay Buccaneers
EAST	**EAST**
Buffalo Bills	Dallas Cowboys
Miami Dolphins	New York Giants
New England Patriots	Philadelphia Eagles
New York Jets	Washington Redskins
WEST	**WEST**
Denver Broncos	Arizona Cardinals
Kansas City Chiefs	San Francisco 49ers
Oakland Raiders	Seattle Seahawks
San Diego Chargers	St. Louis Rams

may not realize is that each team is allowed fifty-three players! Only eleven players are on the field at a time (twenty-two if you count both teams), but take a look at the crowded sidelines to see the immense size of the whole team. Every team has backups, and backups to the backups. These guys are the "second-string" and "third-string" players. Due to football's violent nature, the backups will usually get some playing time throughout the season.

Football is popular for many reasons but a major factor is that teams play only one game a week. So there is an excitement factor, foreplay if you will, of waiting all week for Sunday to come.

THE SEASON

Practice Makes Perfect: Training Camp

Training camp is similar to baseball's spring training. Camp starts in late July and runs until the exhibition season. This is when the team is all together for the first time (rookies and new players attend seminars and evaluations prior to training camp), and gives players and coaches a chance to get acclimated to one another for the upcoming season.

Training camp is held in the hot summer months. It consists of scrimmages and practices, meetings, weight-training sessions, and time for players to learn the playbook and various offensive and defensive schemes. Scrimmages and practices are sometimes held twice a day (two-a-days).

In most cases, training camp is held at a college or university near the team's home stadium. Camp runs right up until the preseason (exhibition season) starts in mid-August.

Preseason

Each NFL team plays four exhibition games before the start of the regular season. The preseason games do not count and are just practice. In most cases, the main starters and stars play only a quarter or two, and then the backups and reserves take over for the rest of the game. This could be the only real playing time for some rookies and backups.

Regular Season

The NFL regular season is played out over seventeen weeks. Each team plays sixteen games and has one "bye" week. A bye week is when a team is off and does not play. Most games are still played on Sunday. But now we have games on Saturdays (just after college football ends), Thursday nights (added in the 1980s), and of course Monday nights (added in the 1970s). The popularity of football and networks clashing for broadcasting rights were the reason for the additions. Games are broadcast on all different networks, including cable.

Teams play each team in their division twice, one home and one away game. (Each AFC East team, for example, plays other teams in the AFC East twice.) The rest of their games are against teams outside their division. And the schedule changes every year. The only teams that play one another every single year are the teams in the same division.

The regular season begins the Thursday evening after Labor Day, and then all teams (except bye-week teams and the teams that played on Thursday) play that Sunday.

Although the schedule usually changes, one constant remains the same. The Dallas Cowboys and the Detroit Lions always host a game on Thanksgiving. It's a tradition that began in 1970.

Playoffs

Twelve teams make it to the playoffs: the four division winners in each conference and two wild cards. The top two teams get a first-round bye and automatically advance to the second round.

Playoffs in the NFL are a one-game shot. Win and continue; lose and go home. Unlike in baseball, basketball, and hockey, there is no series. It's a one-and-done scenario. Lose and you are out and the season is over.

The top teams get "home-field advantage" throughout the playoffs. For example, if the Indianapolis Colts are the top-ranked team, they get to play all playoff games at their home field. If that is the case, you can expect to hear the phrase "the road to the Super Bowl goes through Indianapolis" repeatedly.

NFL PLAYOFFS BRACKET

The wild cards are the two best teams in the entire conference who are not in first place in their divisions. These games are first, held on "Wild Card Weekend."

Next comes the "Divisional Playoff" to see who makes it to the conference championship games.

The winners of the "Conference Championships" (the AFC and NFC champions) play in the Super Bowl.

The Super Bowl

Even non–football fans know what the Super Bowl is. The media and marketing circus is the most popular television program in the world. According to *Fast Company* magazine, more women have watched the Super Bowl than the Oscars.

The Super Bowl is always held in a warm climate or a stadium with a roof or a dome. It is always held on a Sunday, hence the term "Super Bowl Sunday." This is when the two top teams

---

SUPER BOWL FUN FACTS

- The Pittsburgh Steelers have the most Super Bowl wins with six, in seven appearances.
- The Dallas Cowboys have the most appearances with eight (five wins).
- There are only four active teams (as of the start of the 2010 season) that have never been in a Super Bowl. These teams are the Jacksonville Jaguars, the Houston Texans, the Detroit Lions, and the Cleveland Browns.

(the AFC and NFC champions) battle it out to see who the best in the league really is.

The winner of the Super Bowl receives the Vince Lombardi Trophy along with bragging rights until the next season begins. Not only that, the players and coaches get major pay bonuses and a championship ring worth tens of thousands of dollars to mark the occasion.

THE EXPERIENCE

Stadiums are large, almost twice the size of most baseball venues and in some cases three times the size of basketball and hockey arenas. Most are outdoors. (College football stadiums are even larger! See Chapter 5.)

Because the stadiums are so large, careful planning of their locations is crucial, both for the stadium's footprint and for the thousands of cars the fans will park there. Most stadiums are placed in a more-remote, less-developed area of the city in which the team plays. Parking can be difficult (imagine 65,000 people all trying to park and get to the game at the same time).

Once parked and ready to enter, you will most likely be walking by tons of people tailgating in the parking lots. When you make your shoe selection, anticipate your walk through the parking lot. It will probably be grass, dirt, and pebbles.

The smell of the gas and charcoal grills is intoxicating as you walk into the stadium. The parking lot is filled with revelers drinking beer, throwing footballs, and having a great time. Most people will get to the stadium very early just for this experience and make an entire day out of it.

When the teams take the field, there is usually a loud ovation, with most home teams doing some sort of entrance ceremony. Sometimes the announcer will introduce individual starters over the loudspeaker as they run up thorough the "tunnel" onto the field.

QUICK TIP:
BEST TIME TO LEAVE THE SEATS

The obvious time to leave the seats is at halftime; the problem is, that's when everyone is out of their seats. That means long lines at restrooms and concessions. Because a football game is divided into four quarters, with only two minutes between each one (just enough for a time-out or TV commercial), I have found it is best to leave my seat just after the second quarter has started. Yes, you can miss almost half the second quarter, but the lines will be short and you'll most likely be comfortable until at least the fourth quarter, when you should go if you want to leave your seat again. The beginning of the fourth quarter will also have shorter lines.

After the national anthem, the **kickoff** marks the beginning of the game. A coin toss decides who receives (gets the ball first) and who plays defense. The team that plays defense first gets the ball first in the second half. Because of this, the team that wins the coin toss can defer and elect to play defense first.

The game is made up of four fifteen-minute **quarters**. The teams switch sides of the field every quarter (not the sidelines, just the direction they are going in to score touchdowns). The first two quarters make up the first half, and the second two quarters make up the second half. In between the second and third quarters is a twelve-minute halftime.

During **halftime**, there will be on-the-field contests, cheerleader dances, and possibly some sort of ceremony honoring a local hero or event. The players are in the locker room re-grouping for the second half.

The **two-minute warning** is called when two minutes remain on the clock before each half ends (the end of the second and fourth quarters). The clock is stopped and it serves as a time-out for both teams.

Each team gets three **time-outs** per half. They do not roll over, so time-outs cannot be saved for the second half. A time-out can be called by any player on the field or by the head coach. Time-outs stop the clock and allow the teams to go over the play and discuss options. Sometimes before a field goal, the defending team will call a time-out to "freeze" (trip up or get into the head of) the kicker.

A **challenge** is an opportunity for coaches to try to reverse a call made on the field by the referee. Each coach gets two challenges. A coach can ask for the challenge by throwing a red flag onto the field. The head referee then reviews the play by video and either upholds or reverses the call. The team calling the challenge must have enough time-outs to support it. That is because if the call is not reversed, the team is penalized by losing a time-out.

QUICK TIP: CHEERING AND BOOING

In football, it is customary to boo or make as much noise as possible when your defense is on the field. Some people boo; others yell. I once had a guy behind me (every game, mind you) that would make the most annoying, mind-numbing yodeling/yelling/booing noise. This is all to try to confuse the offense. The noise can throw off the opposing offense when the players can't hear the quarterback's signals and the QB can't hear the calls from the sidelines.

It's also customary to do the opposite for your own offense. When your offense is on the field, it's best to be quiet or cheer quietly. Sometimes the quarterback or members of the offensive line will wave their hands in a downward motion to say "shh." This is so they can hear calls clearly and concentrate.

If the game is tied after four quarters, the game goes into sudden-death overtime. It's a fifteen-minute extra quarter where the first team to score wins. The winner of the coin flip will almost always take the ball. If the game is tied after the fifteen minutes, it ends in a tie—unless, of course, it is a play-off game or the Super Bowl; then more overtime quarters are played until a winner is decided. (At the time of printing, NFL owners have voted to change the overtime rule for playoff games to reflect more closely NCAA rules; each team's offense

BONUS POINTS: THE NAME GAME

Impress *and correct* friends and boyfriends (and TV broadcasters!) with proper pronunciation of some of the hardest-to-say names in the NFL.

T. J. HOUSHMANDZADEH JR.
(Seattle Seahawks, 2009)
(Hoosh-man-ZAH-deh)

NNAMDI ASOMUGHA
(Oakland Raiders, 2009)*
(NAM-dee Ah-So-MOO-wah)

BRENDON AYANBADEJO
(Baltimore Ravens, 2009)**
(Eye-on-buh-DAY-joe)

PISA TINOISAMOA
(St. Louis Rams, 2009)
(Tee-noh-EE-sah-moe-AH)

OSHIOMOGHO ATOGWE
(St. Louis Rams, 2009)
(Oh-SHIM-ago Uh-TOG-way)

*In 2009, Asomugha was the highest-paid player (per year) in the NFL ($15 million a year for three years).
**Ayanbadejo is not Spanish and the j is not silent.

will get a chance to score. This may also apply to regular-season games in the future. See Chapter 5 on college football and/or visit www.nfl.com for more information.)

INSIDE THE HUDDLE

The Offense

The offense is the team with the ball. The eleven players on the field have a simple set of instructions: Move the ball toward the opponent's end zone by ten yards or more within four plays. Each of the plays is called a down. The offensive players move the ball using a series of plays and strategies created by the coaches.

Although there can be many different formations, the one constant rule is that there must be seven players on the line of scrimmage (LOS—the imaginary line where the ball is placed).

The kickoff marks the beginning of the game. The receiving team's **kick returner** will in most cases catch the ball and

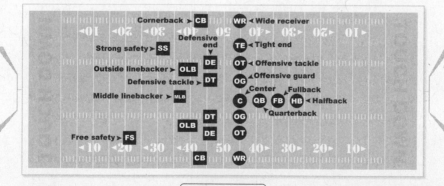

try to run with it as far as possible. Wherever he is when he is tackled (down) or runs out of bounds is the first LOS.

But the kick returner has another option too. He can signal for a **fair catch** by waving his hand in the air. If he does that, he is allowed to catch the ball and that's it. Nobody is allowed to tackle him. Once the catch is made, the play is dead. And that's where the LOS will be.

If the ball is kicked into the end zone, the returner can still try to run it out, but in a lot of cases he will just **take a knee** in the end zone. If the ball is downed by taking a knee in the end zone, the play begins (the LOS will be) on the twenty-yard line.

The Players

- The quarterback (QB) passes or hands off the ball.
- The center snaps the ball to the QB and blocks the defense.
- There are five offensive linemen: a center, two guards, and two tackles. They are responsible for blocking defenders, protecting the QB, and creating running lanes for the rushers and receivers.
- Two wide receivers are there to catch the ball when it is passed.
- Two running backs are there to run the ball; one, usually a big back, is called the **fullback**. He blocks more than he runs.
- One tight end blocks and also catches passes, and is sometimes seen as a "secret weapon."

Generally the quarterback is the star, the player who gets all the limelight. But he's also the player who takes the fall in a loss. Teams live and die by their quarterback. He needs to be a leader on and off the field, and he must be respected by his teammates in order to be successful.

Wide receivers have until recently been the prima donnas. Think big diamond earrings, flashy cars, loud mouths, and a "show me the money" attitude. This is because they are the "playmakers" and score a lot of touchdowns. Lately, the league has seen a turnaround of sorts, with less flash and a more team-oriented attitude. This is great for the game.

Downs

All progress in a football game is measured in yards. If the offensive team success-fully moves the ball ten or more yards within four plays, it earns a first down, and another set of four downs. If the offense fails to gain ten yards,

FIRST DOWN

it loses possession of the ball. The defense tries to prevent the offense not only from scoring, but from gaining the ten yards needed for a first down. If the offense reaches fourth down and isn't close enough for a field goal, it will usually **punt** the ball (kick it away).

The Run and the Pass

A play begins with the snap. At the line of scrimmage the quarterback loudly calls out a play in code (just like in the movies,

BEST FOOTBALL MOVIES

There are so many great football movies that it's really difficult to narrow them down to just a few. I chose movies based on the story and how well the movies show the game of football, in a manner that's easy to follow and helpful for learning.

Rudy (1993). This is a college football movie, but it is leaps and bounds greater than any other college football movie ever made, so it deserves a spot on this list. If any guy tells you that he didn't cry at the end of *Rudy*, he is lying. Based on the true story of Daniel "Rudy" Ruettiger, a small (five-foot-six) man with huge dreams, this emotionally charged flick follows Rudy's love for Notre Dame football and the adversity he endures while trying to make it there. *Rudy* is a must-see for all football fans.

Brian's Song (1971). *Brian's Song* was a made-for-TV movie that aired on ABC. The program went on to win three Emmy Awards, was nominated for a Golden Globe, and was so successful that it was later released in movie theaters. The poignant film is based on the real-life story of former Chicago Bears players Brian Piccolo (played by James Caan), a white football player terminally ill with cancer, and his friend Gale Sayers (Billy Dee Williams), a black teammate who helps his friend through this tough period. The story is emotionally and racially fueled and based on Hall of Famer Sayers's autobiography, *I Am Third*.

Heaven Can Wait (1978). Nominated for eleven Academy Awards (one win), *Heaven Can Wait* is a charming movie starring the gorgeous Warren Beatty as the quarterback of the L.A. Rams (now the St. Louis Rams) looking to take his team to the Super Bowl. He dies in an accident but wasn't "supposed to," so the angels send him back in the body of a recently murdered millionaire. He then buys the team. There are lots of interesting plot twists, but this movie has been remade so many times, chances are you've already seen some version of it. A few versions have taken out the football element altogether. If you see only one, make it this one.

Friday Night Lights (2004). Based on the 1990 nonfiction book by H. G. ("Buzz") Bissinger, *Friday Night Lights* is the story of the 1988 Permian High School Panthers football team in Odessa, Texas. The movie gives viewers a realistic look at small-town Texas football, where the entire town lives and breathes the high-school team. The only real way kids make it out of Odessa is by getting a scholarship, and the competition is fierce. The movie chronicles the team's run at the state championship. Billy Bob Thornton plays head coach Gary Gaines, but the real surprise is Tim McGraw's performance as an overbearing father to the team's running back. The television show with the same name and premise debuted on NBC two years after the film.

Remember the Titans (2000). Based on a true story, *Remember the Titans* takes place in 1971 Virginia and is a story about a recently desegregated high-school football team. The team has a black head coach (played by Denzel Washington), a white assistant coach, and a mixed team whose black and white members fight on and off the field. The story is emotional and a tad predictable but it's a feel-good football story sure to please everyone—football fans and nonfans alike.

Any Given Sunday (1999). This movie gives a look at front-office politics and a behind-the-scenes look at running a football team. Although many movies do this, this one is directed by none other than Oliver Stone. The talented cast (Al Pacino, Cameron

(Continued)

113

Diaz, Jamie Foxx, and Dennis Quaid) all give memorable performances. The kicker (pun intended) is that Cameron Diaz plays the demanding team president/owner who shows the boys who is boss. And boy, does she wear the pants.

Honorable mentions: *The Longest Yard* (1974), *Varsity Blues* (1999), *The Program* (1993), *Knute Rockne All-American* (1940), *The Waterboy* (1998), *North Dallas Forty* (1979), *Jerry Maguire* (1996), *The Replacements* (2000), and *Necessary Roughness* (1991).

it's a gibberish of sorts, like, "Blue 32, blue 32, hut, hut, hike!" but the players understand it), and the player in front of him, the center, snaps the ball under his legs to the quarterback. From there, the quarterback can throw the ball, hand it off, or run with it.

The Run

There are two main ways for the offense to advance the ball. The first is called a run. This occurs when the quarterback hands the ball off to a running back, who tries to get as many yards as possible by eluding defensive players. The quarterback is also allowed to run with the ball.

The Pass

The alternative to running the ball is to throw it. Usually, the quarterback does the passing, though there are times when another player may pass the ball to confuse the defense. Actu-

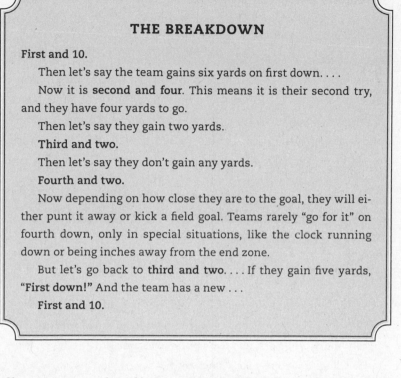

THE BREAKDOWN

First and 10.

Then let's say the team gains six yards on first down. . . .

Now it is **second and four**. This means it is their second try, and they have four yards to go.

Then let's say they gain two yards.

Third and two.

Then let's say they don't gain any yards.

Fourth and two.

Now depending on how close they are to the goal, they will either punt it away or kick a field goal. Teams rarely "go for it" on fourth down, only in special situations, like the clock running down or being inches away from the end zone.

But let's go back to **third and two**. . . . If they gain five yards, "First down!" And the team has a new . . .

First and 10.

ally, anyone on the offensive team is allowed to pass the ball as long as the pass is thrown from behind the line of scrimmage. A pass is complete if the ball is caught by another offensive player, usually the **wide receiver** or **tight end**. If the ball hits the ground before someone catches it, it is called an **incomplete pass**.

Turnovers

While trying to advance the football to the end zone, the offense may accidentally turn the ball over to the defense in one of two ways.

Fumble: When the player with the ball drops it, that's a fumble. Any player on the field can recover the ball by diving on it, or he can pick it up and run with it. The team that recovers a fumble gets the ball.

Interception: When a defender catches a pass meant for an offensive player, that's an interception. Both fumble recoveries and interceptions can be run back into the end zone for touchdowns. An interception is also called a **pick off**. When an interception results in a touchdown it is often called a **pick six**.

QUICK TIP:
TAILGATING—PRO FOOTBALL EDITION

Tailgating can be an art form. No matter who you are, tailgating is fun if you are prepared. To some, tailgating means bringing a cooler packed with beer, maybe some munchies, and hanging out in the parking lot, possibly throwing a football. To others, tailgating is a major event prepared days in advance, with tents, grills, music, full bars, and even personal Porta Potties. If you are attending someone else's tailgate, be sure to arrive early and bring cash to offer, at least $20, especially if you are eating their food and drinking their beer. Also bring at least a six-pack of your own beer per two people, if possible, and some water. You should contribute something. And please, wear comfortable shoes. For more info on tailgating see Chapter 5, about college football, which boasts the most hard-core tailgating in the country.

Defense

The players trying to prevent the offense from scoring are the defense. There are many strategies and schemes to prevent the offense from scoring. Defenders can play zone (cover an area) or man-to-man (cover a person), but the goal is either to take the ball away through a turnover or to prevent a first down and get the ball back on downs.

Defensive Players

- Three or four defensive linemen line up directly across from the offensive line (O-line). The linemen are responsible for stopping the run and getting to the quarterback. Best-case scenario: They **sack** (tackle) the QB.
- **Linebackers** (usually three) are among the most athletic guys on the field. They line up a few yards behind the line of scrimmage. They stop runs, rush the QB, and block or intercept passes.
- The "secondary" players (four of them), also known as defensive backs, are two **cornerbacks**, who cover the wide receivers (cornerbacks will get the most interceptions), and two **safeties**, jacks-of-all-trades who help defend wherever they are needed on the field.

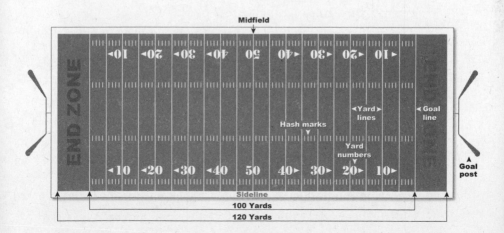

Special Teams

Special teams handle all of the "special" plays. These can be some of the most exciting plays in the game. These players take care of:

- Kickoffs
- Punts
- Extra points
- Field goals

Sometimes a member of the offense will also play special teams, especially a speedy punt returner or a lineman for blocking.

BASICS TO KNOW

- If a kick goes out of the other team's end zone it's called a **touchback**, and the ball is automatically placed at the twenty-yard line.
- The **center** position player snaps the ball to the quarterback.
- **Zone coverage** is when the defensive players cover a specific area of the field. **Man-to-man coverage** is when they stay with one specific offensive receiver.
- The **red zone** is the final twenty yards before the end zone. Doing well in this part of the field is a critical part of the game.
- Running the ball is an excellent "clock eater," meaning

it takes a lot of time off the clock, and so it is used in situations when a team wants to kill time.

- The clock stops only at the end of incomplete passing plays, when a player goes out of bounds, or when a penalty is called. The clock starts again when the ball is respotted by an official.
- The QB can stand **under center**, meaning he takes the snap directly from under the center (usually between his legs), or **in the shotgun**, where the QB stands about five yards back from the center.

POINTS

The whole point of the game is to score points. There are only five ways to score points in professional football.

Touchdown = Six Points

A touchdown is the biggest and best way to score. It is worth six points. To score a touchdown, a team must carry the ball across the goal line into the end zone, catch the ball in the end zone, or recover a fumble in the end zone.

TOUCHDOWN

Extra Point = One Point

Immediately following a touchdown, the ball is placed at the opponent's two-yard line. Usually the offense will kick an extra point, also called the point after touchdown (PAT) or the conversion. The kicker kicks the ball through the goalposts and earns one point.

Two-Point Conversion = Two Points

After a touchdown the team can choose to score two points by running or throwing the ball into the end zone the same way they would a touchdown. They choose between this and kicking the extra point. It's one or the other; they can't do both. Since going for two points is more difficult than kicking an extra point, the offense will usually kick the extra point.

Field Goal = Three Points

If the offense can't score a touchdown but is fairly close to the end zone, it will try to kick a field goal. It can be attempted from anywhere on the field on any down, but generally the decision is based on how far the kicker can "punch it." The field goal placement is set up seven yards back from the line of scrimmage. Then, add the end zone (another ten yards in length). So if the ball is on the twenty-yard line, it's a thirty-seven-yard field goal. For a field goal to be "good," the kicker has to kick the ball through the goalpost uprights and over the crossbar. The defense can try to block the kick, but it rarely succeeds.

Safety = Two Points

The defense scores two points by tackling the ball carrier behind his own goal line (in his own end zone).

OVERHEARD: PENALTIES

When a penalty occurs, the referee will throw a yellow "flag" on the field by the location of the foul. The "flag on the play" lets everyone know a penalty has occurred. Here are the most common penalties and their punishments.

HOLDING

Holding: Can be called on the offense or the defense. Offensive holding is when a member of the offense grabs a defensive player's jersey or arms or wraps his arms around the defender. Offensive holding is a ten-yard penalty. Defensive holding is when a member of the defense does the same, but it is only a five-yard penalty.

Pass interference: Can be called on the defense or the offense, but defensive pass interference is more common. When a player deliberately makes contact with an opponent more than five yards beyond the line of scrimmage and keeps the opponent from catching the ball, interference is called. This penalty is placed from the spot of the foul, so it can mean major yardage gains, depending on the intended length of the pass. I've personally seen fifty- and even sixty-yard gains from one penalty!

Personal foul: A flagrant, illegal act that could be harmful to another player. Examples of personal fouls are unnecessary roughness, hits to the head, roughing the passer, and roughing the kicker. When a player tries to tackle another player after the whistle is blown, that's also a personal foul. This penalty most often is fifteen yards.

Encroachment: When a member of the defense is in the neutral zone (the one-yard area between the offensive and defensive lines) when the ball is snapped. This is a five-yard penalty.

Offsides: A defensive foul is called when, before the ball is snapped, a defensive player crosses the line of scrimmage and touches an offensive player. The offense is penalized when an offensive player jumps or moves at all before the ball is snapped. Offsides is a five-yard penalty.

False start: When the offense is offsides and moves before the ball is snapped.

Face mask: There are two different kinds of face mask penalties. The smaller, five-yard penalty is when a player unintentionally touches an opponent's face mask and lets go quickly. The bigger, personal foul face mask penalty is when a player grabs, yanks, and/or pulls an opponent's face mask. This is a fifteen-yard penalty.

Delay of game: When the twenty-five-second clock reaches zero and the offensive team has not snapped the ball. A five-yard penalty is assessed.

Unsportsmanlike conduct: Deliberate bad conduct, like yelling at the referee or fighting. Two of these fouls called on one player result in the player's being ejected.

Not all penalties result in a first down; if a five-yard penalty doesn't add enough yardage to make it a first down, the down stays the same.

Sometimes you will hear that a team has "declined" a penalty. This is when the team benefiting from the penalty turns down the award given. This occurs only when the resulting play is more beneficial than the award. For example, the team is awarded five yards for the opponent's penalty, but its play resulted in a fifteen-yard completion and a first down. In this case, the benefiting team would decline the penalty and take the completed play instead.

HISTORY

Football is a soccer and rugby hybrid that eventually developed into what we know as American football. Just so there is no confusion, yes, in most places in the world, the word "football" is used for what we know as "soccer."

The first rules for American football were drawn up by a Yale player and coach named Walter Camp in the late 1870s, although his game was a kicking game only. It wasn't until 1906 that the forward pass (when the quarterback throws the ball downfield) was created and the modern game began. Football was strictly a college game in the beginning. For more on the history of the game see the college football chapter.

The first professional football league was created in 1920; it was known as the American Professional Football Association. It changed its name to the National Football League a couple years later.

The NFL proved to be successful and grew more popular after World War II. For this reason, another league was formed, called the American Football League (AFL). While originally seen as inferior, the AFL began to sign top talent by the mid-1960s. The two leagues merged in 1970 to create the NFL that we know today. While the united league kept the NFL name, the AFL brought many new ideas and inventions to the game, like the use of a stadium game clock, names on jerseys, the two-point conversion, and much more.

Most of the teams in the AFC today are the old AFL teams, while the NFC comprises mostly the old NFL teams.

What They Wear

Because of the violent and physical nature of the game, padding and helmets are a must for all players. During the game you hear the clinking of the armor as the players tackle and clash into one another.

All players wear a helmet with a face mask, shoulder pads, and hip pads. Many quarterbacks, running backs, and wide receivers wear a flak jacket—a padded vest—but some choose not to because they can't feel the ball when it's up against their body.

The NFL has very specific rules on jerseys, pants, and socks worn on the field. For example:

- A player's jersey must be tucked in at the waist.
- Towels can only be eight inches long and six inches wide, and must be tucked into the front of the pants.
- The uniform pants must meet the socks below the knee.

Shoes vary depending on what type of field the game is played on. On a wet grass field longer cleats (spikes at the bottom of the shoe) are used. On grass that's dry, shorter cleats are used. On artificial turf sometimes a player will wear no cleats at all and just a shoe with a rubber bottom, similar to a basketball shoe.

The jerseys are of high-quality nylon and made to be tough to handle all the on-the-field conditions, from rough weather to rough physical contact. In the NFL the numbers on the players' jerseys are assigned based on position, not preference.

1–9   Quarterbacks and kickers

10–19   Quarterbacks, receivers, tight ends, and kickers

20–49   Running backs and defensive backs

50–59   Centers and linebackers

60–79   Defensive linemen and offensive linemen

80–89   Receivers and tight ends

90–99   Defensive linemen and linebackers

DRAMA: NFL RIVALS

Who doesn't love some drama? There are so many football rivals that many games each season have some underlying meaning. Most of these games are divisional rivalries, because the teams play each other twice in one season. They play one home game and one away game against each other every year. Other rivals can be teams from the same state or teams that have played each other in the past and have a long-standing tradition of hatred. Here's a look at some of the most heated rivalries in professional football history.

Pittsburgh Steelers Versus Cleveland Browns

Also known as the "Rust Belt Rivalry" or the "Turnpike Rivalry" due to the short distance (about 130 miles) between the two cities, these two teams have played each other more than a hundred times and have ten titles between them. The rivalry dates back to 1950. Youngstown, Ohio, is midway between these cities and has dual television rights to broadcast both games. The ratings suggest an almost perfect fifty-fifty split.

Philadelphia Eagles Versus New York Giants

These two teams have been in the same division since 1933 and have played more than 150 times. Although this rivalry has always been popular, it really came to a head in 1978 at Giants Stadium in New York, in a game dubbed "the Miracle at the Meadowlands" by Eagles fans. The Giants had the lead and the ball with just twenty seconds left on the clock. Most expected the quarterback to just take a knee (literally, place one knee on the field and take the down to run out the clock), but instead the Giants fumbled the handoff and gave the Eagles new life. The Eagles recovered the fumble and ran it back for the touchdown and the win.

Chicago Bears Versus Green Bay Packers

This is the NFL's oldest rivalry, dating back to 1921. These two teams have played each other more than 175 times and combined for twenty-one championships, including four Super Bowls. There is no love lost between these two teams. In 1986 a member of the Packers body-slammed then–Bears QB Jim McMahon and took him out for the season with a separated shoulder. This was the season after the Bears won the Super Bowl.

Dallas Cowboys Versus Washington Redskins

Divisional rivals since 1961, these two teams have played each other more than ninety-five times. Although the Cowboys hold the edge with more wins over the Redskins, the Redskins are 2-0 against Dallas in the postseason. The rivalry became bitter immediately. In 1961, Dallas fans tried to smuggle huge crates of chickens into the Redskins' home stadium. The following year, Dallas fans successfully brought in two acrobats dressed in chicken costumes who sneaked on the field and threw eggs.

QUICK TIP: FOOTBALL = ALL WEATHER

Most of us females are not all-weather girls. I surely am not. I don't see a point in going out in rainy weather if I don't have to. My blow-dried and flat-ironed hair will be a frizz ball, and my perfectly made-up "natural-look" face will be a grease ball. Unlike baseball, another outdoor sport, football doesn't stop play for the weather unless there is severe lightning or a threat to life. It's hard to look hot when you are outside and it is 30 degrees and snowing. Some of football's greatest games in history are nicknamed the Ice Bowl, the Snow Bowl, the Freezer Bowl, etc. (you get the idea). Do not sacrifice health for fashion. Everyone will be dressed appropriately for the weather, and you should be too.

HISTORIC NFL GAMES AND MOMENTS

"The Frozen Tundra of Lambeau Field"

The 1967 NFL championship game is commonly known as "the Ice Bowl" and is considered one of the most famous pro football games of all time. The Dallas Cowboys played visitor to the Green Bay Packers at Lambeau Field. The game was played on December 31 and still holds the record for the coldest temperature for an NFL game (−13 degrees Fahrenheit). The referees' whistles stuck to their lips. The marching bands' instruments froze. The field was frozen solid. Some say it was as smooth as ice and ice skates would have been better than cleats. The game was a classic back-and-forth battle that ended with Green Bay's Hall of Fame coach, Vince Lombardi (the winner of the Super Bowl receives the **Vince Lombardi Trophy**), calling a risky quarterback sneak (when the QB takes the ball and pushes forward with his O-line to gain short yardage) to win and not tie the game. A tie would have sent the game into overtime, which was the last thing anybody wanted. "Let's run it and get the hell out of here," Lombardi famously said before the final play.

The game is even more famous now because of the well-known voice of NFL Films' longtime narrator, John Facenda. It is said that he coined the phrase "the Frozen Tundra of Lambeau Field" while making the NFL Films highlight reel for the game. However, there has been speculation that he never said it and that famous sportscaster Chris Berman actually invented the phrase while mimicking Facenda's distinctive voice. The label still exists today, and the phrase is something all football fans know well.

"The Immaculate Reception"

One of the most famous plays in NFL history occurred during the 1972 AFC divisional playoff between the Oakland Raiders and the Pittsburgh Steelers. The controversial play is commonly known as the "Immaculate Reception." The Raiders were up 7–6 with only twenty-two seconds left in the game. The Steelers had the ball on their own forty-yard line, facing desperate fourth and ten. Hall of Fame quarterback (and current TV broadcaster) Terry Bradshaw threw a pass, which was almost incomplete; amazingly, running back Franco Harris scooped up the ball just before it hit the ground. He then ran downfield to the end zone for the touchdown and the 12–7 win.

The play isn't without controversy. Some dispute its legality, claiming the ball hit the ground before Harris grabbed it, which should have caused officials to rule the play dead. The film has been studied, and most agree that the right call was made. In the end the play will always be a part of football lore.

"The Catch"

The San Francisco 49ers' dynasty began in 1982 in the NFC championship game against the Dallas Cowboys. With only fifty-one seconds left, from the Cowboys' six-yard line, Niners QB Joe Montana threw a very high pass to the back of the end zone, and receiver Dwight Clark made a leaping grab with his fingertips for the winning touchdown. The catch sent San Francisco to its first Super Bowl. The famous photograph of Clark's amazing catch graced the cover of *Sports Illustrated* the next week.

"The Tuck Rule"

The New England Patriots and the Oakland Raiders played a blockbuster AFC divisional playoff game in whiteout conditions during the 2001–2 season. The Pats were trailing by three late in the fourth quarter and QB Tom Brady appeared to fumble the ball, which would have given the Raiders a victory. But after an instant replay, the referee reversed the call, saying that the play was an incomplete forward pass (as Brady was intentionally moving his arm forward), and gave the ball back to New England. The "tuck rule," as it is now known, helped the Patriots to eventually win the game in overtime with a clutch field goal in the snow by kicker Adam Vinatieri. The Patriots went on to win the Super Bowl (their first ever) that year and then three Super Bowl championships in five years.

The entire game was played in a heavy snowstorm, so the game is also known as the "Snow Bowl." It was the last game played in the old and rundown Foxboro Stadium (the Patriots' home field) before it was torn down and replaced with the new, luxe Gillette Stadium.

"The Greatest Game Ever Played"

The 1958 NFL championship game between the Baltimore (now the Indianapolis) Colts and the New York Giants was played at the original Yankee Stadium in New York City and was the first game in NFL history to go into sudden-death overtime (first team to score wins).

The game was a gut-wrenching back-and-forth drama that ended in a tie. Although the NFL had incorporated overtime into its rules for playoff games in 1941, this was the first time it needed to be used. Baltimore ended up with the win. The epic battle was broadcast nationally on NBC, with more than 45 million people tuning in. The game itself was fantastic, but this is also the game that launched the NFL into mainstream popularity.

"The Perfect Season"

As of the end of the 2009 season, the 1972 Miami Dolphins are the only undefeated team in the history of the NFL. (The 2008 Patriots won all of their regular-season and playoff games but lost in the Super Bowl, and although they played more games than the 1972 Dolphins, this was not considered a perfect season.)

Led by Hall of Fame coach Don Shula, the Dolphins went a perfect 17-0, defeating the Washington Redskins 14–7 in Super Bowl VII. The feat has never been duplicated, and the '72 Dolphins have permanently cemented themselves in NFL history.

"The Super Bowl Shuffle"

The 1985 Chicago Bears recorded the "Super Bowl Shuffle" song and video just before their appearance in Super Bowl XX against the New England Patriots. The hilarious video (you must check it out on YouTube) features the Bears rapping and dancing in full-on '80s style. This was also when MTV and music videos were first becoming popular. The song was nominated for a Grammy and will forever be known by football fans. The Bears went on to win the Super Bowl to climax their spectacular one-loss season.

Pro Football Hall of Fame 🏆

The Pro Football Hall of Fame opened in September 1963 and is located in Canton, Ohio. Canton was chosen for a variety of reasons. The first is that the original American Professional Football Association, later renamed the NFL, was founded in Canton in 1920. The Canton Bulldogs, one of the first professional football teams, were an early league powerhouse. Last, the city of Canton created a huge marketing campaign and fund-raising event in the early 1960s. City officials and residents successfully lobbied the NFL to make their city the site of the hall.

The 83,000-square-foot hall honors those who have made major impacts in the game. It also preserves the history and mementos of the sport. For fans worldwide, the Pro Football Hall of Fame is the best football museum that exists and a football lover's dream.

Only the greatest players and coaches are voted into the Hall of Fame. Both players and coaches must be retired at least five years in order to be eligible. Contributors like owners and executives can be enshrined at any time.

Fans can get in on the nominations by writing to the Pro Football Hall of Fame. The main list is created by polling a forty-four-person selection committee called the Board of Selectors. (The board usually includes the beat writers from the major newspapers in the cities where NFL teams are located.) A list of fifteen finalists is eventually created.

The day before the Super Bowl the Board of Selectors votes on the final list. Only those with 80 percent of the vote are elected. However, the hall enshrines a minimum of four and a maximum of seven every year. So if four people don't reach 80 percent of the vote, the top four are inducted.

There is also a Seniors Committee, which reviews players and coaches who retired more than twenty-five years ago and may have been overlooked in the modern era.

The enshrinement takes place during "Hall of Fame Weekend," held every year to honor the new class of inductees. A bronze bust is created in the inductee's likeness. Unlike in other sports, the inductee enters the hall as an individual, with no specific team attached.

The weekend's festivities are elaborate, with more than fifteen events for fans and families. The enshrinement ceremony is nationally televised. For more information or to plan your trip (the hall offers specials in conjunction with the Rock and Roll Hall of Fame in Cleveland, just a short trip away), visit www.profootballhof.com.

THE BEST AND MOST TALKED-ABOUT PLAYERS IN HISTORY

Jim Thorpe was one of the first professional football players and stars. The Canton Bulldogs (one of the first pro football teams) hired Thorpe in 1915. He played on three championship teams from then until 1919 while at the same time also playing professional baseball. He also won two Olympic gold medals in 1912, in the decathlon and the pentathlon. Thorpe is consistently in the top five in any "best athletes of all time" lists.

Joe Namath ("Broadway Joe") played most of his twelve-year career with the New York Jets. The Hall of Fame quarterback was the first QB to throw for more than four thousand yards in one season; in the year he did it (1967), the season was only fourteen games. Namath is the first professional football "media star" whose flamboyant lifestyle was a hit with fans. He famously wore a full-length fur coat on the sidelines and starred in a not-to-be-missed pantyhose commercial, in which *he* is the one wearing the pantyhose (YouTube!).

Terry Bradshaw is a Hall of Fame quarterback who spent fourteen seasons in the NFL, all with the Pittsburgh Steelers. He led the Steelers to four Super Bowl titles in the mid- to late 1970s. He is well known now as an NFL television personality. His broadcast career started after his retirement in 1983, and he currently covers games in the studio for Fox. He is the only NFL player to have a star on the Hollywood Walk of Fame. Besides multiple commercial and television cameo appearances, he starred with Matthew McConaughey, Kathy Bates, and Sarah Jessica Parker in the 2006 movie *Failure to Launch*.

Walter Payton ("Sweetness") is known as one of the greatest running backs in the history of professional football, if not *the* greatest. He played thirteen seasons, all with the Chicago Bears, and was a nine-time Pro Bowl selection. He was well known not only for his physical ability and football talent but for his professionalism on and off the field. He never celebrated touchdowns. He also played practical jokes on teammates and media. He is in both the Pro Football Hall of Fame and the College Football Hall of Fame. The NFL honors him by handing out the Walter Payton Man of the Year award for achievements in community service.

Joe Montana ("Cool Joe," "Comeback Joe") played sixteen seasons in the NFL, fourteen with the San Francisco 49ers. He is the most celebrated quarterback of the 1980s. Montana led the Niners to four Super Bowl wins. The Hall of Fame QB's famous ninety-two-yard drive at the end of the NFC championship game in 1982, culminating in "the Catch," is legendary. Montana was elected to eight Pro Bowls and in some circles is seen as one of the greatest quarterbacks of all time.

Jim Brown was a Cleveland Browns running back for nine seasons (1957–65). The Hall of Fame running back was elected to the Pro Bowl nine times (every year he played) and won the NFL MVP three times. In 2002 the *Sporting News* named him the greatest football player of all time. He excelled in several sports in college and is also a member of the College Football Hall of Fame and the Lacrosse Hall of Fame. After retirement he went on to star in many movies and television shows, including *The Dirty Dozen.*

Roger Staubach ("Captain Comeback," "Roger the Dodger") is a Hall of Fame quarterback who spent his entire eleven-year career with the Dallas Cowboys. He led the Cowboys to two Super Bowl wins, including the team's first ever in January 1982, where he was named MVP. A family man and Vietnam vet, Staubach is credited with coining the phrase a "Hail Mary pass." In a 1975 playoff game versus the Vikings, with the Cowboys trailing late in the game, Staubach threw up a last-second fifty-yard pass to his wide receiver, who caught the ball and ran it in for a touchdown. Staubach was quoted after the game as saying that he prayed a "Hail Mary" before throwing the pass. Now the term is used commonly in the game.

Jerry Rice is regarded as the greatest wide receiver of all time and either still holds or broke every wide-receiver record ever created. He played twenty seasons (fifteen with the San Francisco 49ers) and was elected to thirteen Pro Bowls. He retired in 2005 and will surely be inducted into the Pro Football Hall of Fame on the first ballot when he is eligible. He is already a member of the College Football Hall of Fame. Most recently, fans know him as the runner-up on the second season of *Dancing with the Stars* and for guest appearances on television and sports talk shows.

Vince Lombardi is known as one of the best football coaches of all time. Although he never played in the NFL, he started coaching high school football while still playing college ball himself. He coached fifteen seasons (including as head coach and assistant coach) before his career was cut short by terminal cancer. Lombardi's overall record was an outstanding 105-35-6. He is famous for saying, "Winning isn't everything; it's the only thing." Players and coaches respected him greatly on and off the field. Just after his passing, the Super Bowl trophy presented to the winner was renamed the Vince Lombardi Trophy.

NFL DRAFT BASICS

Just like the Super Bowl, the NFL draft has become a marketing and media spectacle. Usually held the third weekend in April, the nationally televised seven-round main event is when the hopes and dreams of the best players in college football are fulfilled if they are chosen to play in the NFL. The draft takes place over two days, with rounds one and two on the first day and rounds three through seven on day two.

All NFL teams have draft selections. The selection order is determined in a "worst to first" format, where the Super Bowl champion has the last pick in the first round and the worst team picks first, as long as there aren't any expansion teams entering the NFL that year. (An **expansion team** is a brand-new team entering the league for the first time.)

There is always plenty of behind-the-scenes wheeling and dealing on and before draft day, so there is always a chance of your team trading away its pick for other picks, players, and/or incentives. Some teams can enter the draft with twelve picks and others with just four.

Almost all NFL players played college football. There is no minor league in football. All graduating seniors are eligible to be drafted, as are some sophomores and juniors who have "declared themselves" eligible to enter the draft.

Usually underclassmen will declare themselves if the chances are good that they'll be drafted early in the first round. Only the cream of the crop goes in the top ten. The higher a player is selected, the more money he will receive. Usually players in the top ten are also showered with marketing and sponsorship deals.

A player's worth is first determined by his college football career. But the NFL combine is a three-day event when the nation's top college players head to Indiana to perform mental and physical tests in front of NFL coaches and scouts. Cutting-edge fitness technology is used to determine the results, from how fast an athlete can run to how well his joints move. The combine can showcase a talented player from a smaller college and help an athlete who may have had a subpar college career but increased his stock with a great combine performance.

It's important to know that the draft isn't an exact science. Two words: Tom Brady. Two more words: Ryan Leaf. The first, Brady, is one of the greatest draft success stories of all time. He was drafted in the sixth round of the 2000 draft, 199th overall. Brady has gone on to win three Super Bowls and two Super Bowl MVP Awards (as of the 2009 season). Leaf, on the other hand, had a very successful college career and was selected in the first round as the number-two pick in the 1998 draft behind future Hall of Famer Peyton Manning. Leaf is widely regarded as "the biggest draft bust of all time." After being drafted he spent four terrible years in the NFL, filled with injuries, poor relations with teammates and the media, and inadequate performance on the field. Leaf is now in pop culture history. Every year just before the draft, media outlets and fans try to guess who the "next Ryan Leaf" will be. Believe me, a player does *not* want that honor.

THE OTHER LEAGUES

There are two other professional football leagues in North America: the Canadian Football League (CFL) and the Arena Football League.

The CFL has eight teams and is split into the East Division and the West Division. The season runs through summer and fall, not fall and winter like the NFL. Unlike MLB (pro baseball), the NBA (pro basketball), and the NHL (pro hockey), the NFL doesn't have Canadian teams in the league. The CFL is entirely Canadian. It officially became a league in 1958. While there are some rule differences—the CFL teams play on a larger field and get only three downs, while NFL teams get four—both the NFL and the CFL look for the same type of players. In some cases, a player seen as too small for the NFL might be perfect for the CFL and its quicker game.

There are a few players who have had success in both leagues, most notably quarterback Warren Moon, who is a member of both the Canadian Football Hall of Fame and the Pro Football Hall of Fame.

The Arena Football League, on the other hand, is quite

different from the NFL. The title alone should give it away. The games are played in an indoor arena on a smaller field. That translates into a higher-scoring, faster-paced game. The league was founded in 1987. The 2009 season was canceled to "work on the economic model," but there are plans to restart the league in 2010.

FOOTBALL FASHION AND FANDOM

Don't Let This Happen to You

A few years back I was attending the Patriots-Dolphins game in Miami with my brother, the same game we have attended for two decades together. I was wearing my cutest fitted football jersey, denim cutoff shorts (it was 90 degrees), and flip-flops. But not ordinary flip-flops: huge, platform, chunky flip-flops that raised me at least three inches off the ground. The kind that we short girls know well. They are hard to get used to walking in and look terribly ugly on and off your feet, but for short women they can be a casual lifesaver at a barbecue, at the beach, or, in my case, at a football game in Miami.

My father worked in shoes (no wonder I'm obsessed), and he had given me an ugly pair of multicolor hiking boots (think Timberland style but worse) he'd picked up at the office. The problem was that there is no hiking in South Florida. Since I knew I'd never wear them, I casually threw them in my trunk and forgot about them.

While walking to the stadium from the grass-and-dirt parking lot, passing all the tailgaters and football fans, I tripped over a rock in my chunky platform flip-flops and twisted my foot so badly that the toe thong popped off. They were now

OH NO SHE DIDN'T!
FOOTBALL FASHION FAUX PAS

"Unless you're performing at halftime, leave your skirts at home."
—Diana Vilibert, Web editor at marieclaire.com

"Don't be head-to-toe logo. If you must, wear one item with the team's logo and/or colors."
—Danielle Goldman, New York City fashion stylist

"If you wear sandals, you will be stepped on by a three hundred-pound fan and lose a toenail."
—Alyssa Roenigk, senior writer at ESPN *The Magazine*

"There is nothing worse than sitting in a stadium chair in a full-length coat or jacket."
—Hope Misterek, Seattle fashion stylist

"Do not wear stilettos to a football game. Just a huge no-no."
—Christine Garcia, Dallas-area photographer

ruined, and there was no way to walk in them. I had just a platform and no top to put my foot through.

I had to get the hiking boots out of my car and wear them with no socks the entire, super-embarrassing, game. Picture it: I was now wearing short cutoff denim shorts, a jersey (for the other team), and hiking boots. I may have cried a bit in the bathroom.

Moral of the story: Wear flats to a football game.

Football is all-weather. That's right; they will play through a tropical storm or a blizzard. Football games are rarely canceled or paused for weather, so keep that in mind when attending a football game. In this case, it is not right to sacrifice comfort for fashion.

If it's the dead of winter and freezing outside, what you wear to the game is really not important. The outerwear is the only thing most people will see. Bundle up and invest in a cute hat, scarf, and gloves, and maybe even a flask! "Football games are probably the most important games to dress appropriately for, especially if the stadium is outdoors," says *ESPN The Magazine* senior writer Alyssa Roenigk. "I cannot stress enough the importance of layering and tennis shoes. Football games last a very long time and often straddle two very different times of day and climates."

Just five years ago, women were really left out of the picture when it came to football-game fashion. Jerseys were made just for the boys. I'd try to squeeze my breasts into a kid's size to have a more fitted look, and I'd end up looking like a sausage. Or worse, one season I bought the smallest boy's jersey I could find and then cut it up to look like a baby tee. So it was a jersey half shirt. I was definitely a *Glamour* magazine don't.

Now we are lucky to have a huge selection of game gear specifically made for women. Through the NFL's Web site or in sporting goods stores across the country, finding the perfect-fitting jersey or T-shirt is easy. And you don't have to buy it in pink! (Unless you want to, of course!) Replica jerseys cut for a woman's figure are now available in regulation colors.

You don't have to wear a jersey or shirt with your team's name and logo on it, although most people will. Wearing team colors with no logo is always appropriate. In warm-weather places like Miami, L.A., and Arizona some women barely wear anything. Skimpy tank tops rule in cities where saline flows more freely on bodies than in the sea. Shorts and flip-flops are common in Miami but purely out of necessity. These women are smart and serious when it comes to skin care. They wear and bring SPF. When it's 90 degrees with close to 100 percent humidity, everyone will be sweating.

"Bring a sweater or a rain jacket (to protect against sudden rain, as well as drunken folks spilling food and drinks on you)," Roenigk recommends. "Tennis shoes are important to protect your toes (I've seen more fights break out in the stands of football games than at boxing gyms)."

Some layered tees in your team's colors, jeans, and flats are a can't-lose combination. Dress weather-appropriately, and remember, football is a blue-collar game. It's about having fun and braving the elements. Unless you are in a luxury box, comfort is key.

"Looking like you're trying too hard is far more unattractive than anything you can wear, so resist the temptation to dress sexy or hot. Stick with 'cute,'" says Diana Vilibert, Web editor at *Marie Claire*. "This is especially true if you're on a date, no matter how tempting it is to dress up a little. He won't notice how good you look—just how high-maintenance you are."

Please, absolutely no stilettos to a football game. If you must wear some sort of heel, make it a wedge built into fall or winter boots, and tuck skinny jeans in for a still casual but girlie look. In the South, where boots are too hot, a comfortable wedge sandal is acceptable, but I still don't recommend it.

"Sorry, there's just no way to casually scarf down hot dogs or teeter over to your nosebleed seats in a pair of heels, and you will call attention to yourself. Not 'Wow, she's hot' attention, but 'Wow, she looks like a moron' attention," Vilibert says. "If you're with a guy, trust me, he is not going to notice the way your favorite pair of heels makes your legs look a centimeter thinner. He *will* notice that you're wincing as you walk up each of the three hundred steps to your seat."

No matter what you wear, chances are you will look good. Football fans are some of the craziest fans of any sport. There will be people in full face paint, homemade attire, large hats, vests, wigs—everything and anything you can imagine. There will be middle-aged three-hundred-pound men with no shirts on and their chest hair painted in team colors. In December. In Buffalo.

As for accessories, less is definitely more at a football game. That is, of course, unless you want to be one of the people with the vest covered in every button your football team has ever produced. No? Didn't think so.

"Keep accessories understated and leave the serious bling at home," Vilibert says. "Now is not the time to dress up a casual jeans and T-shirt outfit with bold statement jewelry."

QUICK TIP: DO YOUR MAKEUP IN THE CAR

The sheer size of the stadiums alone should be the first tip that it is important to leave early; there will be two to three times as many fans at a football game as at any other pro sports event. Do your makeup in the car. Really. If you are running late, this isn't a 20,000-person arena for an NBA game. Or a 38,000-person baseball ballpark. It is more likely a 65,000-person stadium. I can't count the number of times I have sat in major traffic en route to a football game and had plenty of time to finish getting ready. In my opinion, an NFL game is the number-one sport for being stuck in traffic. If you are running late, it is best to finish getting ready in the car. Your friends will thank you.

Makeup

I love makeup and will not leave the house without something on, maybe just lip gloss or blush, even when just going to the gym. Makeup can be confusing at outdoor sporting events, so just stick with what you know. "Just because you're at a sporting event doesn't mean you need to look like you're there to join the team on the field, so go ahead and do up your usual makeup look," Vilibert says.

It's important to remember where you are going and what time of day it is. For hot daytime games in the South, try a tinted moisturizer instead of foundation.

"If it's an outside game, and during the day, keep the makeup to a minimum," says Roenigk. "You are going to sweat, and there's nothing cute about a gal with mascara running down her cheeks."

For day games in colder climates, your usual look is fine, but always check your makeup outside before heading out. "Make sure that if you're at an outside sporting event, your makeup is daylight friendly (step in your backyard with a mirror before you leave the house). What looks good in dim bar lighting usually translates to looking like an off-the-clock hooker in bright sunlight," says Vilibert.

For night games you can add more makeup in darker colors; just don't go overboard as if you were going to a club. If you are going out after, just make sure you bring some makeup with you to add on later.

"Heavier eye makeup, even a smoky eye, is a lot easier to pull off as part of a 'look' than lipstick or lip gloss is, so if you want a stronger (night-game) look, layer on the eyeliner but keep your lips nude," Vilibert says.

THE GIRLIE GIRL'S FOOTBALL GLOSSARY

All day: The quarterback has "all day" to throw the ball, meaning he has great pass protection from his O-line.

Backfield: Area behind the line of scrimmage, usually where the quarterback and running backs line up.

Blitz: When the linebackers and defensive backs all-out rush the quarterback in order to **sack** him.

Bomb: A long, high pass thrown far down the field. Also known as "going deep."

Bye: A bye week is when a team is off that week and does not play. This is also the case when a team advances in the playoffs without having to play.

Challenge: Coaches "challenge" a call from the referee that they think was incorrect. The instant replay is then reviewed.

Completion: A pass that is successfully caught.

Extra point: One point earned after a successful kick between the goalposts after a touchdown.

Fair catch: A catch of a punted ball after the receiver signals by raising his hand in the air that he will not run with the ball. He cannot be tackled after signaling for a fair catch.

Field goal: Three points earned when the ball is kicked through the goalposts or uprights.

Field position: The location of the ball on the field.

Flag: "A flag on the play" is commonly heard. It's small and yellow and is thrown on the field by an official to mark a penalty.

Formation: The way the offense and defense line up.

FOOTBALL BASICS: ABBREVIATIONS

AFC: American Football Conference

ATT: Attempts

AVG: Average

BLK: Punts or field goals blocked

C: Completion

DL: Defensive lineman

FG: Field goal

FGA: Field goals attempted

FGM: Field goals made

FUM: Fumble

INT: Interceptions

K: Kicker

LG: Long or longest

NFC: National Football Conference

OL: Offensive lineman

PCT: Percent

POSS: Time of possession

QB: Quarterback

QTR: Quarter

RB: Running back

RUSH: Rushing attempts

S: Safety

SACK: Sacks

SOLO: Solo tackles

TACK: Tackles

TB: Touchback

TD: Touchdown

TOT: Total

TP: Total plays

XP: Extra point

Y/A: Yards per attempt

YDS: Yards

Forward pass: A pass thrown to advance the ball in a forward (downfield) direction. The pass can be thrown only from behind the **line of scrimmage**.

Fumble: When the ball is dropped by a player when it is in play.

Incomplete: A pass that is not caught or intercepted.

Intentional grounding: When the quarterback intentionally throws an incomplete pass to avoid a loss of yardage.

Lateral pass: A pass thrown to the side or backward, but not forward. A legal lateral pass cannot be thrown forward, but it can be thrown from anywhere on the field, unlike a forward pass.

Line of scrimmage: An imaginary line where the play begins. It runs the width of the football field, sideline to sideline, from the tip of the football.

Pass rush: An attempt by the defense to tackle the quarterback before he can get rid of the ball.

Penalty: The punishment for breaking a rule.

Pocket: The area in the **backfield** created on a passing play where the O line forms a wall of protection so the QB can pass the ball.

Pump fake: When the quarterback fakes passing the ball in one direction to throw off the defense.

Punt: A kick when the punter holds and drops the ball and kicks it before it hits the ground on fourth down.

Rush: Running with the ball. Also used to mean **pass rush**.

Sack: To tackle the quarterback before he can get rid of the ball.

Safety: Two points are awarded if a team can force the opposition to down the ball in its own end zone. Also the name of a **secondary** position.

Secondary: The defensive players (cornerbacks and safeties) that cover the field farther from the line of scrimmage.

Shotgun: When the quarterback sets up five yards back from the center to take the **snap**. Usually used for a passing play, it allows the QB more time to set in the pocket to throw.

Snap: The action of the center handing the ball to the quarterback between his legs.

String: The order of starters at a position. First string starts and is backed up by the second string.

Take a knee: When the quarterback kneels to stop the play and keep the clock running. It usually happens at the very end of a game if the offensive team is winning.

Throwing it away: To avoid a sack a quarterback can throw the ball out of bounds and lose a down to stop play.

Touchback: When the ball is punted and it goes into the end zone. The receiving team gets the ball on the twenty-yard line.

Touchdown: When a team gets the ball into the other team's end zone. Six points are awarded.

Two-a-days: Usually during training camp, two-a-days are when teams practice twice in one day.

Two-point conversion: When, after a touchdown, the offense sets up again in formation on the two-yard line and tries to get the ball into the end zone.

Uprights: The two vertical posts of the goalpost.

3

The NBA Has a Dress Code; Why Shouldn't You? The National Basketball Association (NBA)

Basketball is a simple sport. In order to play you need only a basket and a ball. Anybody can play, and it's one of the only sports that you can play alone.

When I was a kid, my family had Boston Celtics season tickets at the old, not air-conditioned Boston Garden. (The old Garden was torn down years ago and replaced with a shinier, newer "Garden.") The term "garden" comes from the gathering places in the old days: A "garden" would serve as a venue for plays, shows, and sporting events. Originally the Boston Garden and its famous sister, Madison Square Garden in New

York City, were built specifically for boxing matches by a boxing promoter. The arenas were purposely built in an intimate manner because boxing promoters wanted the fans to be able to see the sweat on the boxer's brow from anywhere in the arena.

My family saw some great games at the old Garden, like the one during the 1986 NBA playoffs when a young future star named Michael Jordan scored 63 points (still a playoff record as of 2009). Hall of Famer Larry "Larry Legend" Bird called him "God, disguised as Michael Jordan."

But it's the other, simple part of basketball that still gets me to this day. My father put up a hoop on a utility pole outside the house I grew up in. We lived at the top of a hill, and all the neighborhood kids would come and use the hoop for pickup games. When I recently went back to visit that old neighborhood, one thing stuck out: After the decades of change, the old weathered hoop was still there, hanging high on the utility pole, serving as a spot to play for a new generation.

Basketball is a mix of luxury and the streets. It's urban glamour. It's the dressiest and most fashionable sport of all of the majors. Seats are set up on the court (courtside) for wealthier fans; these seats can cost anywhere from $2,000 to $4,000 apiece. These fans are usually celebrities and other moneyed individuals. The seats are practically on top of the players. (And in the case of a rough game, sometimes the players are on top of the seats.) Some courtside celebrities like Jack Nicholson (at Lakers games) and Spike Lee (at Knicks games) go to almost every game and are famous for their on-court antics. But being Jack Nicholson doesn't get you special treatment.

The National Basketball Association (NBA) is the highest-level professional basketball league in the United States and Canada. The league is set up into the Eastern Conference and the Western Conference. Those conferences are split into divisions.

EASTERN CONFERENCE

ATLANTIC DIVISION
Boston Celtics
New Jersey Nets
New York Knicks
Philadelphia 76ers
Toronto Raptors

CENTRAL DIVISION
Chicago Bulls
Cleveland Cavaliers
Detroit Pistons
Indiana Pacers
Milwaukee Bucks

SOUTHEAST DIVISION
Atlanta Hawks
Charlotte Bobcats
Miami Heat
Orlando Magic
Washington Wizards

WESTERN CONFERENCE

SOUTHWEST DIVISION
Dallas Mavericks
Houston Rockets
Memphis Grizzlies
New Orleans Hornets
San Antonio Spurs

NORTHWEST DIVISION
Denver Nuggets
Minnesota Timberwolves
Portland Trail Blazers
Oklahoma City Thunder
Utah Jazz

PACIFIC DIVISION
Golden State Warriors
Los Angeles Clippers
Los Angeles Lakers
Phoenix Suns
Sacramento Kings

Even he has been told to sit down and stop interfering with the game.

Basketball might have cornered the luxury market, but the regular fan can still get in on the action. Most upper-level seats are inexpensive, with some teams charging only $10 for special sections.

Some people call basketball a ballet because of the way the game flows and moves up and down the court. The players go back and forth in a graceful, hypnotizing way. In some cases while performing a **dunk** (when a player stuffs the ball in the basket by jumping to the height of the basket) a player has to leap, extend, and almost pirouette in order to complete the action successfully. The athleticism showcased by basketball players is beautiful and elegant.

It's also impossible not to notice that basketball players are generally very tall. A six-foot man in everyday life may be seen as tall or at least above-average height, but on the basketball court a player that is six feet tall is small.

THE GAME

The objective in basketball is simple: Put the ball in the basket and have more points than your opponent at the end of the game. Five players on each team play the game at one time; they are called the starting five. The remaining members of the team sit on the bench (literally a bench on the sidelines) and wait to be substituted into the game. In most cases, one of the first guys off the bench is called the **sixth man**—he has starter potential and usually gets more playing time than the rest of the bench. The NBA actually gives out an award called the Sixth Man of the Year Award, where an MVP bench player is named. During the game you will hear announcers talk about **bench points**. Those are the points scored by the nonstarters.

For regular games, the PA announcer will announce the starting five and the head coach in a fun fashion, with lots of fanfare before the national anthem. The **tip-off** marks the beginning of the game. The tip-off is when the referee tosses the ball up in the air and the two centers (usually the tallest men on the court) will jump and try to "tip" the ball to their teammates in order to gain possession. This can also happen during the game, but then it is called a **jump ball**. This happens when two players are both fighting for possession of the ball. The referee will call a jump ball, and a tip-off will be set up between the two contending players.

QUICK TIP: BEST TIME TO LEAVE THE SEATS

Since basketball is played in quarters, obviously the time between quarters is when most people will leave their seats so that they don't miss much of the action. The bathroom and concession lines will be shortest at the beginning to middle of the second quarter and halfway through the third quarter. The early part of the second quarter will be less crowded because most people will wait until halftime to leave their seats or they will have gone between the first and second quarters. Most fans won't want to miss the end-of-the-half action.

The middle of the third quarter and the beginning of the fourth will also be less crowded, because halftime just ended and most people left their seats then. Not only that, the fourth quarter is the most exciting, and fans won't want to miss much of it.

It's always best to look at a map of the arena online before the game to get familiar with your section's amenities.

By the Numbers

The game is split into four twelve-minute quarters, separated by a fifteen-minute halftime between the second and third quarters. Teams switch baskets at halftime but do not switch benches. There are 130 seconds between quarters. The game, like most major sporting events, usually takes around three hours, although technically they are playing for only forty-eight minutes. This difference is due to all of the time-outs (see page 155).

The Shot Clock

The offense has only twenty-four seconds to shoot the ball at the basket. Time is kept on the **shot clock** or the **twenty-four-second clock**. The ball must hit the rim in order for the clock to be reset. If the shooting team does not make a basket, both teams will try to **rebound** the ball (get the ball after the shot). If the offense gets the ball back (offensive rebound) and the ball hits the rim, they get a fresh twenty-four sec-

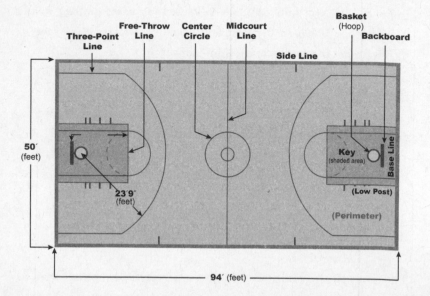

onds. If the defense gets the rebound, their clock starts at the other end of the court. As long as the ball is shot or is out of a player's hands before the clock hits zero, the ball is still in play. This is usually called a buzzer beater.

A Game of Seconds

Just as they say baseball is a game of inches, basketball is a game of seconds. Everything is timed. When you watch a game on television and see a referee who looks like he's counting and moving his hand when a player is dribbling downcourt, that's because he is counting. A player must **dribble** the ball while moving with it. Dribbling is the act of bouncing the ball back and forth between a player's hand and the court.

After a team makes a basket, the opposing team gets the ball out of bounds under the basket where the points were just scored. The problem is that their basket is on the other end of the court. The team that now has the ball must **inbound** (put in play) the ball within five seconds. Then they must take the ball downcourt toward their basket, passing the midcourt line within eight seconds. Failure to do either of these things results in a loss of possession.

Once the ball goes past midcourt, the player with the ball cannot cross back over the line. A player without the ball can cross back over the midcourt line, but if the ball crosses the line it also leads to a loss of possession.

Time-outs, Stopping the Clock, and Substitutions

Player substitutions can occur only when play is stopped. The new player goes to the **scorer's table** (a table located at midcourt where the official scorer is). The scorer's table also houses the possession-arrow box. Its lit-up arrows always show which team has possession by pointing the way the ball is going.

Each team gets six full time-outs and one twenty-second time-out per half. Any player on the court can call a time-out. The clock will also stop when the referee blows his whistle to signal a violation; when the ball goes out of bounds; when the quarter or half ends; and when a basket is made inside the last two minutes of an NBA game.

Time-outs are one hundred seconds long or sixty seconds long. The time-out rules in the NBA are rather complex. There must be certain amounts of time-outs per quarter, and if one isn't taken the referees will issue a mandatory time-out to the home team. It is not necessary to understand these rules in order to watch a game. You can ask any basketball fan what the NBA time-out rules are and he or she will likely know no more than this. No more than three time-outs can be called in the fourth quarter, and no more than two in the final minutes. This is to keep the game moving, though the final two minutes in basketball can be the longest two minutes in all of sports.

Overtime

Overtime (OT) in basketball is an additional five-minute "quarter." They play the game just like the other quarters, with the same rules and structure, but with only five minutes on the clock. If the game is still tied at the end of the first overtime period, they will play another, and it is called 2OT; and the game can go to 3OT and so on. It's pronounced as double overtime or triple overtime. Teams get an additional three sixty-second time-outs each for the overtime period.

Fouls

A personal foul is defined by the NBA as physical contact that disrupts the normal flow of the game. Officials try to determine if the contact helps the team that caused it. Some contact is inevitable in the game, but calling a foul is up to the referee's discretion. Three refs work a game at a time. If a player gets six fouls in the game, he has **fouled out**, meaning he is kicked out of the game. Once a player has four or five fouls, he is said to be in **foul trouble**.

If an offensive player commits a foul, the team loses possession of the ball. If a defensive player commits the foul, it's important whom the player fouls.

If the defensive player fouls the player who had the ball while he was attempting a shot, that fouled player will shoot **free throws**. (Also known as a foul shot, a free throw is an undefended shot made from the free-throw line at the top of the key.) Two free throws are awarded if the shot was missed. One free throw is awarded if the shot was made. If the shooter was attempting a **three-pointer**, and it missed, the shooter gets three free throws. If the three-pointer went in, the shooter gets one free throw.

If the defensive player fouls a player who didn't have the ball, then the offense takes the ball out of bounds and gets a fresh shot clock. That is only if the team that committed the foul is not **over the limit**.

Just as the players have limits on how many personal fouls

SHE'S GOT GAME

they can commit, teams are also limited. Each team can commit only four fouls per quarter. Once the team commits more than that they are over the limit, and any further fouls committed after that will cause the other team to get two free throws, even if they weren't shooting the ball.

A foul committed with what is deemed to be excessive force is known as a **flagrant foul**. This penalty results in the other team being awarded free throws and possession.

The most common offensive foul is called **charging**. It's when the player with the ball pushes into the defender while the defender is not moving at all and is in a stationary defensive position.

A **technical foul** (sometimes called a "T") can be called on a player or a coach. It is called when unsportsmanlike conduct occurs either physically or verbally. If a player or coach gets two technical fouls called on him, he is ejected from the game. The other team is awarded one free throw after a T is called, and play resumes where it was before the violation.

Nonfoul Violations

The following violations result in a change of possession:

Twenty-four-second violation: NBA teams must attempt a shot within twenty-four seconds.

Three-seconds rule: An offensive or defensive player cannot remain in the foul lane—in the "painted" area—for more than three seconds at a time.

Double dribble: A violation in which a player dribbles the ball, stops, then begins to dribble again.

Traveling: A violation in which a player takes too many steps (more than the allowed two) without dribbling the basketball.

Eight-second violation: After a basket, the offensive team has eight seconds to get the ball over the midcourt line.

Palming or carrying: A violation in which a player moves his hand under the ball and scoops it while dribbling.

Goaltending: When a defensive player interferes illegally with a shot on the rim or on a downward path to the hoop; the shot is assumed in, and the offensive team receives the basket.

Points

- Free throws are worth one point.
- Any shot from inside or on the three-point line is worth two points.
- A shot from behind the three-point line is worth three points.
- Both two-point and three-point shots are called **field goals**.

A **second-chance** basket is when a team misses a shot but then gets its own rebound and then scores. Another term to know is **points off turnovers**, meaning points the team scored after it got the ball due to a turnover. This is also a football term.

Common types of shots are the **bank shot**, the **layup**, the **jump shot**, also known as a jumper, and the **fadeaway**.

- A bank shot is a shot that bounces off of the backboard and goes into the basket.
- A layup is when the player puts the ball in the basket by leaping from below, very close to the basket, and uses one hand to bounce the ball off the backboard. Most layups happen when a player is running to the basket.

BEST BASKETBALL MOVIES

There are a lot of fantastic basketball movies. Here are some of the best for both entertainment and learning about the game and the passion behind it.

Hoosiers **(1986).** Nominated for two Oscars and a Golden Globe, *Hoosiers* is about a small-town high-school basketball team in Indiana. A coach looking for redemption, played by Gene Hackman, and an ex-ballplayer turned town drunk (Dennis Hopper) lead the team to the state championship in an unlikely run, overcoming hurdles and obstacles along the way. The movie is set in 1952 and is loosely based on the Milan High School team in Indiana that won it all in 1954. *USA Today* called *Hoosiers* "the best sports movie of all time."

Love and Basketball **(2000).** This movie straddles a fine line between sports movie and chick flick. Whichever it is, it is the best combo ever made. It's a love story between a man and a woman, but also between them and the game of basketball. It starts in 1981 when the two characters are eleven years old and meet on the basketball court. The story takes them through high school and college, and then to after college, when they meet again, and play the most important game of one-on-one in their lives. Winner takes the other's heart.

White Men Can't Jump **(1992).** The hilarious and sometimes heart-tugging story of two men, black and white, who hustle their way through the basketball courts of L.A. by manipulating others' racial prejudice. They take in a lot of money but lose it as quickly as they win it. Woody Harrelson and Wesley Snipes play the lead characters, and Rosie Perez plays Harrelson's girlfriend. Perez adds flavor and comedy to the movie, and the street basketball is top-notch.

Hoop Dreams **(1994).** My favorite movie on this list is a documentary about two black teenage athletes who are bused ninety minutes each way to a predominantly white school in Chicago. The athletes dream of making it to the NBA and use that as motivation while dealing with the issues that arise with going to this school. Originally the documentary was supposed to be a thirty-minute piece for PBS, but the filmmakers had so much great footage that they turned it into a 170-minute film. The intimate film's themes—race, economic class, and American life in the inner cities—are riveting. The film won major awards at Sundance and was nominated for an Oscar. Many critics put *Hoop Dreams* on the "best" lists for 1994.

He Got Game **(1998).** Directed by Spike Lee, *He Got Game* stars Denzel Washington and NBA veteran Ray Allen (who was a young up-and-coming NBA talent when the movie came out). They play a father and son. Allen's character is a top high-school recruit, about to sign with the college of his choice because everyone wants him. Washington plays his imprisoned father, who is let out by the governor to try to persuade his son to take the scholarship to the governor's alma mater. The premise is not far off, as for years backhanded politics have played a role in sports, but this movie does not conform and in typical Spike Lee fashion, goes against the grain.

Honorable Mentions: *Blue Chips* (1994), *Above the Rim* (1994), *Rebound: The Legend of Earl "the Goat" Manigault* (1996), *The Air Up There* (1994), *Go Man Go* (1954).

- A jump shot is when a player jumps in the air and shoots from the air.
- A fadeaway is a jump shot, but one where the player is jumping away from the basket in order to create space between him and the defender.

Statistics are an important part of basketball, as in all sports, and terms like **assist** and a **triple double** are part of the lingo.

An assist is when a player passes the ball to another player and that player scores. So if player A passes to player B and then player B scores, player A gets an assist. It's an important part of the game, and a good player will have a lot of assists per game. It shows he is an unselfish player, or a "team player."

There are five major statistical categories: points, assists, rebounds, steals, and blocked shots. When a player reaches double digits in two of the five categories in one game, it is called a double double. That is a good game for a player but fairly common.

Getting double digits in three of the four categories is called a triple double, and although it isn't that rare, it is still a great performance by a player.

The quadruple double, however, is very rare. Only four players in NBA history have ever put up double-digit numbers in four of the categories in one game. However, the NBA didn't start counting some of these statistics until the 1973–74 season, so a few greats who played earlier than that might have recorded quadruple doubles.

OFFENSE

The five players on each team on the court play offense and defense. Players can be substituted in and out of the game as many times as the coach wants. In basic basketball, the five positions are one center, two forwards, and two guards.

The guards are called the **point guard** and the **shooting guard**. The point guard is the "quarterback" of the team. He leads the team on the court and generally is the best ball handler. He is usually the one who takes the ball from the inbound pass and brings it up the court. He reads defenses and calls plays on the court.

The shooting guard is usually the team's best shooter. He is someone who can consistently take all kinds of shots (jumpers, layups, three-pointers) from all over the court.

The two forwards are called the **power forward** and the **small forward**. The power forward usually plays down in the post, the area closest to the basket but outside of the free-throw lane, or the key. The power forward's bigger size lets him also take on a center position's role when necessary.

The small forward is quicker than the power forward. He acts as a forward that sets up at the perimeters (the area farthest from the basket, outside the free-throw lane but inside the three-point line) but is also quick enough to play a guard role as well.

The **center** is the big man on the court and usually plays at the bottom of the key, also known as the **low post**. He is usually the tallest guy on the court and uses his big physique to score baskets from "low in the paint"—just under the basket.

OVERHEARD: SLANG AND TRASH TALKING

These are common terms that might be shouted when watching a game.

Denied! Usually yelled after a blocked shot.

Brick! An ugly shot that hits or clanks off the rim or backboard.

Airball! When a shot hits nothing but air. The shot misses the rim and backboard completely. When an opposing player shoots one, the crowd will shout it slowly: "Aaaaaaaaair-baaaaaaaall."

Swish! Nothing but net. When the ball gracefully sails through the basket and hits only net. Makes a swish noise on its own.

And one! When a player scores a basket and is fouled, he will get to take one free throw, worth an additional one point.

The Pick-and-Roll

Coaches draw up all kinds of plays in order to make baskets, and their playbooks are filled with new schemes every game. But one of the most common and oldest plays in basketball is the **pick-and-roll**. The terms associated with it, like "setting a screen" and "cutting to the basket," are commonly heard during a game.

When a player makes a **cut**, he is making a quick movement down, around, or across the court in order to gain a beneficial position.

An offensive player can try to stop a defender from guarding a teammate. He will step in front of the defensive player who is guarding the ball handler. That is called **setting a screen**

Zone Defense   Man-to-Man Defense

or **pick**. Now the defender has two players to worry about. If he chooses to guard the ball handler, then the player who set the screen can **roll** (turn around and run) to the basket and wait for a pass. If the defender chooses to block the player who set the screen, he leaves the ball handler open to take a shot. The complete play is called the **pick-and-roll**.

DEFENSE

Basketball players are in great shape and must have excellent conditioning. There is not a break to set up for the next play when the teams switch from offense to defense, as in other sports. There are fast breaks (when after a turnover or a quick rebound the offense takes the ball to its basket and shoots as quickly as possible so the defense doesn't have time to set up), which can make the offense and defense change every few seconds. So players must be ready to play either offense or defense at any moment.

The two most common defensive schemes are the **zone defense** and the **man-to-man**.

A zone defense is when the players on defense guard whichever offensive player enters their zone. The zones can be set up in many ways, like a 1-2-2 or a 3-2.

Man-to-man defense is just what it sounds like. The defenders cover the man they are assigned. Usually coaches will match up players that are similar in height and weight in order to defend properly. Obviously a coach isn't going to put a small guy on a big guy. It wouldn't make any sense. On the flip side, however, a coach will try to make mismatches if possible if it is to their advantage. Usually the other coach will discover it right away and adjust immediately.

An important part of defending is to **box out** (when a defender positions himself between the ball handler and the basket, in order to get a rebound and block his shot). Coaches will also be looking for players to **hustle** to get back on defense to prevent the fast break.

QUICK TIP: CHEERING AND BOOING

Obviously, when your team scores a basket, you cheer. But there are some other times when you shouldn't cheer for your team. When a player on your team is shooting free throws it is best to keep quiet. The arena will be unusually silent in order to let the player concentrate on the shot.

However, when someone on the opposing team is shooting free throws, it is appropriate to make as much noise as you can. Boo and shout in order to distract him from making the shot. Fans sitting directly behind the baskets will usually have thundersticks (a noise-making prop given out by the team when you enter the game) to wave around and try to distract the player visually as well.

The NBA season is eighty-two games long and usually starts in early November and ends in late April. The playoffs start after that, and the championship series is usually in mid-June.

Eight teams in each conference qualify for the playoffs. They are then seeded one through eight based on their records. The top teams in each division are seeded one through four, and the rest are seeded after that based on record.

The first round is called the **conference quarterfinals**, in which the first-seeded team plays the eighth-seeded team, the second plays the seventh, and so on. The second round is called the **conference semifinals**. Next, the **conference finals** determine the **conference champions**, who play each other in the **NBA finals**.

All rounds are best-of-seven series (four wins takes the series). Home-court advantage for each round is determined by regular-season record, regardless of seed. The best teams get home-court advantage.

NBA PLAYOFFS

HISTORY OF THE GAME

The game of basketball was invented in 1891 in Springfield, Massachusetts, home of the Basketball Hall of Fame. Springfield is located in western Massachusetts, about a two-hour drive from Boston. The game was invented by Dr. James Naismith in order for his students at the YMCA to keep physically fit during the long, cold New England winter. Naismith was trying to create a game that could be played in an indoor gymnasium. He took a peach basket and nailed it to the wall, and basketball was created.

Naismith put nine players on each team and handed them a soccer ball. Every time the ball went in the basket the team that put it there would get one point. The first game on record was played at the YMCA's gymnasium on January 20, 1892. It ended with a 1–0 score.

With so many players on the court the game was clumsy and crowded, especially because the original court was half the size of today's. In 1897 the nine-player teams were cut down to the five-player teams that we know today. The peach baskets had a bottom, so the ball had to be retrieved manually every time someone scored. A hole was cut in the bottom of the baskets soon after, and a long dowel was used to poke the ball through the top.

The peach baskets were used until 1906, when a metal hoop and backboard were introduced. This allowed for rebounding to enter the game. The baskets were made so that the ball could pass right through the hoop, just like in today's game.

In 2006, Naismith's granddaughter found his handwritten diaries, which give a fascinating glimpse into how the game was created. Naismith suggests in his diaries that the game is loosely based on a children's game called Duck on a Rock, but at first he didn't think it would be successful, because many others had tried similar things before that hadn't worked out. He called his new game "basket ball."

Basketball proved to be a very popular sport immediately. It was one of the first sports to allow women to play. In 1892, just a few months after the original game was played, a physical education teacher from nearby Smith College (a women's college) went to Naismith to learn more about the game and develop it for her students. In 1893 women were successfully playing basketball at Smith.

The game of basketball spread very quickly. The YMCA dispatched the game to its locations in the United States and

---

THE NAME GAME: NBA EDITION

Impress and correct your friends and boyfriend (and TV broadcasters!) by mastering some of the hardest-to-pronounce names in the NBA.

PREDRAG "PEJA" STOJAKOVIC
(New Orleans Hornets, 2010)
PRAY-drog Stoy-AK-o-vich

IME UDOKA
(Sacramento Kings, 2010)
E-may You-DOH-kah

PAU GASOL
(Los Angeles Lakers, 2010)
Pow Ga-SOUL

VLADIMIR RADMANOVIC
(Golden State Warriors, 2010)
VLAD-a-meer Rod-MAH-nah-vich

WALLY SZCZERBIAK
(Cleveland Cavaliers, 2010)
SIR-bee-ack

ZYDRUNAS ILGAUSKAS
(Cleveland Cavaliers, 2010)
ZEE-droon-is Ill-GOW-skus

THABO SEFOLOSHA
(Oklahoma City Thunder, 2010)
TAH-bow Sef-o-LOH-Sha

YAKHOUBA DIAWARA
(Miami Heat, 2010)
Yah-KOO-bah DEE-a-WAH-rah

Canada. And by 1895, just three years after the game was invented, it was already being played in U.S. high schools.

For about fifty years before the NBA was created, basketball was a popular sport throughout the country in colleges, recreational leagues, and high schools. Basketball became popular for many reasons, but a key factor was how inexpensive the game was to equip. Teams needed only a ball and a hoop in order to play. No special uniforms or equipment were necessary. That is also a reason why basketball is so popular in inner cities. Anyone can attach some sort of basket to a pole and grab some sort of ball. Basketball is a game that a person can play by himself and not only get a great workout, but improve his skills at the same time.

For more information on the history and roots of the game, see college basketball in Chapter 5.

The NBA

The National Basketball Association (NBA) as we know it today formed in 1949, after the Basketball Association of America (BAA—the major league at the time) merged with a smaller league called the National Basketball League (NBL). For the next decade the league's number of teams fluctuated from as many as seventeen to as few as eight. The only two original teams that have never changed locations are the Boston Celtics and the New York Knicks.

The NBA faced competition from the start-up American Basketball Association (ABA), which formed in 1967. Because of the NBA's success, investors thought a new league that added some fanfare could rival the NBA. In the early 1970s the ABA became popular due to the creation of the three-point shot and the slam-dunk contest. The two leagues merged in 1976, and while the NBA kept its name, it did adopt the ABA's three-point shot and added the slam-dunk contest at the All-Star Game.

Harlem Globetrotters

The Harlem Globetrotters team was created in Chicago in 1926 as an all-black basketball team. They adopted the "Harlem" part of their name in 1930 even though they had never played in Harlem, because Harlem was seen as the epicenter of black culture, so the name would market the team efficiently. The Globetrotters were one of the first professional teams and played in and won many professional tournaments of the early 1940s.

The Globetrotters were so good that they started adding comedy and showmanship to their game. But when the NBA formally integrated and the first black player was drafted by the Boston Celtics in 1950, the team lost a lot of its talent, and the Globetrotters started focusing mainly on the comedy and special tricks of their game. Although from then on the Globetrotters played mainly exhibition games and toured the country showing off their special skills, some NBA greats once played as Globetrotters, like Earvin "Magic" Johnson and Wilt Chamberlain.

The famous whistled tune that is always played when showcasing the Globetrotters is "Sweet Georgia Brown" by Brother Bones. The Globetrotters are well known for their red, white, and blue uniforms, ballhandling tricks, and amazing skills displayed on the court.

NBA D-League

The NBA Development League (D-League) is the NBA's "minor league" system. Before it was created in 2001, most NBA talent came from colleges. The number of teams in the D-League has grown over the years from eight when it started to twenty in 2009.

The NBA teams have affiliates and can send two roster players to the D-League; the rest of the team is made up from D-League draftees, undrafted free agents, local tryouts, and high-school graduates who are at least eighteen. Since the NBA allows players only nineteen years old or older, the D-League offers a way for players who choose not to attend college to continue playing after high school.

The D-League has its own championship and all-star games and gives smaller cities without an NBA team a chance to watch some quality live basketball in their hometown.

The NBA Draft

The nationally televised NBA draft uses a lottery system for the teams that don't make the playoffs. The teams that make the playoffs are ranked in the order they finished the season, with the NBA champions taking the last pick.

The nonplayoff teams are a part of the "draft lottery." Fourteen Ping-Pong balls are numbered and placed in a lottery-type machine, where they are shuffled around. The nonplayoff teams are ranked and numbered, with the worst team in the league on top. Each team is assigned Ping-Pong balls and combinations, with the worst team receiving the most combinations and, therefore, the best chance of getting the first pick.

The athletes that are picked in the top ten get the most money and endorsement deals. In some cases, a team that selects a top-ten pick will try to build an entire franchise around that particular player.

Most NBA players come straight from college, where they have honed their skills for at least three or four years. Most have been heavily scouted. Players that do not attend college can be drafted out of high school, but the rules have changed over the years. As of 2009, a player must be at least one year out of high school and at least nineteen years old. There are many stars and future Hall of Fame players who went to the NBA straight from high school before this rule was created, like Kobe Bryant and Kevin Garnett.

International players have similar rules. They must be at least nineteen and declare themselves eligible by submitting written documentation at least sixty days before the draft. They are also eligible if they play professionally in another country.

WNBA

The WNBA is a professional women's basketball league run by the NBA. It was founded in 1996 and play began in 1997. As of 2009 there were thirteen teams, and most shared an arena with their NBA counterparts. The season runs during the NBA off-season, from June to September, with playoffs running through October.

USA BASKETBALL AND THE DREAM TEAMS

USA Basketball is the nonprofit governing body of the national team that competes in the Olympics and foreign tournaments (the International Basketball Federation, FIBA, hosts tournaments and the World Championships around the world). Prior to 1989, only amateur (usually college) players could represent the country in these events, but when the rules changed to allow professionals, the Dream Team was created and sent to Barcelona to compete in the 1992 Summer Olympics.

That team, the original Dream Team, was a sight to behold. The most prolific stars of that time, mostly all-stars and current Hall of Famers, all playing on the same team for the country, was a ratings gold mine. Michael Jordan, Larry Bird, Magic Johnson, Charles Barkley, Patrick Ewing, and on and on . . . a true basketball fan's "dream."

The original Dream Team went on to win the gold medal that year. With the addition of professional players to the team, the USA continued to dominate the Olympics in 1996 and 2000, also taking home gold medals. While the team changed with the new stars of the day, the outcome was the same.

In the 2004 Summer Olympics in Greece, with a new group of NBA superstars at the helm, it seemed another gold medal was inevitable. But the USA team lost three games and only took home a bronze medal. Team USA had lost only two games total in Olympic play since 1932. The team—and entire country—was disappointed and shocked.

In 2008, at the Summer Olympics in Beijing, China, USA Basketball and the media called themselves the "Redeem Team" to show the world that they were back and better than ever. And they proved it, returning home with another gold medal. The losses in 2004 really changed Team USA forever, and now the team isn't just thrown together; they really practice and work together as a team in the off-seasons.

DECADES AND DYNASTIES: WHAT TO KNOW

The Boston Celtics have the most NBA championships with seventeen. From 1957, when they won their first, to 1969, the Celtics owned the court, winning eleven championships in thirteen years, including eight in a row, a record that no other professional team has ever accomplished.

For the league, the 1970s was all about expansion. The league went from nine teams to twenty-two teams, and by the end of the 1970s nearly every major city had a team. The NBA also incorporated four ABA teams during this period.

The 1980s became a very popular decade for the NBA. In 1979 two rookies made their debuts, Earvin "Magic" Johnson and Larry Bird. Johnson went to play for the Los Angeles Lakers, and Larry Bird went to the Boston Celtics. Johnson led the Lakers to five championships in the 1980s, and Bird led the Celtics to three. The Lakers and Celtics had a notorious rivalry during this time, one of the most heated in all of sports. The rivalry still exists today though the teams have met in the finals only once since the 1980s (the Celtics beat the Lakers in the NBA Championship in 2008).

Michael Jordan entered the league in 1984, during the height of the Lakers-Celtics rivalry. The NBA was already on an upswing, thanks to Johnson and Byrd, but it was Jordan who took the league to a whole new level. The shooting guard was amazing to watch on the court, and many players and fans took notice. Jordan single-handedly changed the game forever with his athleticism and graceful play. He led the Bulls to six NBA championships in eight years in the 1990s. The Bulls dynasty brought the NBA unprecedented popularity.

The NBA saw an influx of foreign-born talent in the last

THE BASKETBALL HALL OF FAME

The Basketball Hall of Fame is located in Springfield, Massachusetts, where the game of basketball was born. It originally opened in 1968 but was in the planning stages for many years before that. The growth and popularity of the game in the 1980s and 1990s forced three relocations, and in 2002 a brand-new hall opened with more than forty thousand square feet of space on the banks of the picturesque Connecticut River.

In order to be considered for the Basketball Hall of Fame, a player or coach must be fully retired for five years. Basketball history, skills challenges, live clinics, and the enshrined players' exhibits fill the hall's space. The hall's mission is to "honor and celebrate basketball's greatest moments and people."

decade. As of 2009, more than seventy-five international players from thirty-two countries graced the court, including forty-five European players. The NBA also has offices in China to expand the game into Asia.

WHO TO KNOW IN HISTORY

Michael Jordan is known as the greatest basketball player of all time. That can be said with little argument. He burst into the league and immediately began entertaining fans with his prolific slam dunks and the "air" he would grab while dunking. He is one of the most marketed athletes of all time. He introduced Nike's Air Jordans in 1985, a sneaker still popular more than twenty years later. He won six NBA championships, all with the Chicago Bulls, where he spent most of his career. He was a fourteen-time All-Star. Rumor has it that he dropped out of the slam-dunk contests at the All-Star Game after a few wins to make the contest fair. He famously retired from the game in the mid-1990s to play professional baseball; he never advanced past the minor leagues, and returned to the NBA one season later.

Earvin "Magic" Johnson spent his entire career with the Los Angeles Lakers and helped lead the team to five NBA championships. He was a twelve-time All-Star and is currently a television announcer for the NBA. Johnson is well known for living with HIV since 1991 and for being the first famous professional athlete to announce he had contracted the disease. HIV education was still fairly new after the epidemic emerged in the 1980s, and after a physical for the upcoming 1991–92 season, Johnson learned he had tested positive. He famously played in the 1993 All-Star Game even though he had technically retired and some players were against his playing. He won the All-Star MVP that year. Johnson has dedicated his life to philanthropy and HIV/AIDS education. As of 2009, he was living a happy and healthy life with HIV.

Larry Bird played twelve NBA seasons, all with the Boston Celtics. He was an All-Star in each of his twelve seasons. He led the Celtics to three NBA championships and was one of the best shooters of all time. He won Rookie of the Year his first year in the league and also won the three-point shoot-out at the All-Star game three times. He is currently the president of basketball operations for the Indiana Pacers, located in his home state of Indiana. He is also responsible for an NBA rule named after him, the Bird Collegiate Rule, which changed draft eligibility rules. The Celtics drafted Bird after his junior year of college; he then stayed in college for his senior year. The Celtics had a year to sign him, essentially locking in Bird before he was ready to enter the NBA, keeping him from other teams. The NBA changed that rule so that such an arrangement wouldn't happen again.

Jerry West played his entire fourteen-year career with the Los Angeles Lakers and was elected to the All-Star game all fourteen seasons. After retiring in 1974, he went on to coach the Lakers for three seasons starting in 1976. After coaching, he was a Lakers scout and eventually the team's general manager; he is credited with designing the teams that won four championships in the 1980s. West's average of 27.0 points per game is the fourth highest in NBA history. West was the only player to win an NBA Finals MVP Award (1969) but be on the losing team. The famous NBA logo is modeled after West's silhouette.

Bill Russell's amazing NBA career began in 1956. He was a defensive specialist and is well known as the best shot blocker of all time. During his thirteen seasons with the Celtics they won an amazing eleven championships, including eight in a row. He was a twelve-time All-Star and five-time NBA Finals MVP. That award is now called the Bill Russell MVP Award. Russell was the first African American coach in the NBA, but what is even more spectacular is that he was a player-coach, meaning he actually played on the team as the Celtics' starting center while also serving as head coach. The Celtics won two championships with Russell as coach. His personality is also notorious. He and Wilt Chamberlain (see below) had a famous rivalry—a term Russell disliked—and friendship throughout the 1960s. When Chamberlain famously signed a $100,000 contract in 1965 (the most for any NBA player at that time), Russell went to management and demanded $100,001, which he received immediately.

Kareem Abdul-Jabbar played in the NBA for twenty years, from 1969 to 1989. He is most famous for his hook shot (when a player takes a shot with his body perpendicular to the basket and makes an arc with his arm, like a side shot, and the follow-through ends up over the head). Because he is seven-foot-two, it was called the "sky hook" shot—no one could defend it. He won the Rookie of the Year Award in 1970. Abdul-Jabbar changed his name from Lew Alcindor after he converted to Islam in 1971. He holds the record for most MVP Awards (six) and went to the All-Star Game nineteen times in his twenty years in the NBA. He also won the NBA championship six times with the Los Angeles Lakers.

Wilt Chamberlain was a thirteen-time All-Star and two-time NBA champion who played center on five different teams during his career, including the Harlem Globetrotters. He and fellow Hall of Famer Bill Russell were major rivals and friends. Their rivalry is said to be one of the best in all sports. Russell spent some Thanksgivings with Chamberlain. Chamberlain is most remembered for scoring a hundred points in one game in 1962. No other player has ever accomplished that feat or even come close. The seven-foot-one Chamberlain is also notorious for his personal life. He partied like a rock star, bought lavish homes, condos, and cars, and was known to "collect" women. In his autobiography, he famously claims to have slept with more than twenty thousand women.

Julius Irving ("Dr. J") was an ABA star before the leagues merged, and pioneered the slam dunk as we know it today. He is considered one of the best slam dunkers of all time. He also was the first to slam-dunk from the foul line. He made slam-dunking a part of the basic basketball skill set. He joined the NBA in 1976 with the Philadelphia 76ers and was an eleven-time All-Star and the fifth-highest scorer of all time. Irving's fast and fan-friendly play made him popular, and he was one of the first basketball players with endorsement deals, commercials, and his own shoe to market.

John Stockton spent his entire career (1984–2003) with the Utah Jazz. He is considered one of the best point guards of all time and holds the records for the most assists (passing to the player that scores) and steals (stealing the ball, forcing a turnover) by large margins. He won two Olympic gold medals in 1992 and 1996. He never won an NBA championship, though, and is considered one of the best players to have never won it all. He was elected to the Hall of Fame on the first ballot and is immortalized in a bronze statue in his honor outside the arena in Utah. He holds the record for most seasons and consecutive games played with one team.

WHO TO KNOW NOW: FUTURE LEGENDS

As of 2009, these athletes are on NBA rosters and are poised to become the legends of the future. These stars have likely already punched their tickets to the Hall of Fame.

Kobe Bryant was the youngest player to ever start an NBA game. He was drafted in 1996 and has played all of his games with the Los Angeles Lakers. He already has four NBA championships, eleven All-Star selections, a slam-dunk contest win, an NBA MVP Award, and an NBA Finals MVP Award.

Shaquille O'Neall was the first player selected in the 1992 draft. He already has four NBA championships and has played for four different teams so far. His skills on the court are rivaled only by his larger-than-life personality. Shaq has rapped, acted, and even become a police officer in Miami. He's a fifteen-time All-Star, won the Rookie of the Year Award in 1993, and garnered the NBA MVP Award in 2000. He also won the NBA Finals MVP Award three times.

Dwyane Wade was drafted fifth overall in 2003. He won the

NBA Finals with the Miami Heat in 2006 and the NBA Finals MVP Award. He is already a five-time All-Star, has won a scoring title, and was *Sports Illustrated*'s 2006 Sportsman of the Year.

LeBron James was picked number one in the 2003 draft by the Cleveland Cavaliers. He won the 2009 NBA MVP Award and is a five-time All-Star. He made the Cavaliers a competitive playoff team. He signed a $90 million shoe contract with Nike before playing in his first professional game.

COURTSIDE CHIC

Basketball is a stylish sport. Even the players have a specific dress code when engaging in team or league activities (see "The NBA's Dress Code," page 187). Players at the game but sitting on the bench, not playing due to injury, even have a dress code. Many NBA coaches wear suits to coach the games.

A basketball game is the easiest sport to dress for because it is the dressiest of all the major sports. A nice, climate-controlled 72-degree arena is sports paradise, and it means there will never be any surprises in the weather department. Most arenas are also newer than baseball and football venues, so the bathroom facilities and concessions will probably be clean, and in some cases luxurious. It is really hard to go wrong at a basketball game.

Of course, there will be people in basketball jerseys. Some people will be in tees and jeans and flats, the usual staples for a game. But at a basketball game it is perfectly acceptable to wear heels. While I still don't recommend stilettos, since most of us will be walking and climbing narrow stairs, a slightly chunkier heel or platform is fine.

BANNED IN THE NBA

Players may not wear the following while on team or league business:

- Sleeveless shirts
- Shorts
- T-shirts, jerseys, or sports apparel (unless appropriate for the event [e.g., a basketball clinic], and then it must be team-identified, and approved by the team)
- Headgear of any kind while a player is sitting on the bench or in the stands at a game, during media interviews, or during a team or league event or appearance (unless appropriate for the event or appearance, team-identified, and approved by the team)
- Chains, pendants, or medallions worn over the player's clothes
- Sunglasses while indoors
- Headphones (other than on the team bus or plane, or in the team locker room)

Most people come straight from work or at least look like they do. There will be lots of people wearing suits; expect a well-dressed, well-heeled crowd effortlessly mixing in with the more casual fans. Because of the intimacy and luxury, basketball has become as chic as the celebrities sitting courtside. Tailored pants, heels, and a fitted sweater are classic. Jeans and boots paired with a camisole and blazer are another option.

Heather Walker, public relations manager for the Boston Celtics, works every game and wears a suit. She's been attending basketball games regularly for more than six years and has worked in sports for more than a decade. As a fan, she wouldn't wear her suit if she didn't have to, but she would still keep it chic and classic. "As a fan I would wear a nice collared shirt and jeans. I'd dress up but be hip and casual," Walker says. "I'd put on some funky boots and earrings. You want to dress to impress, especially if you are sitting courtside, but not overdo it."

The problem with basketball jerseys is that they are tank tops. I do not think any man over the age of eighteen should wear a basketball jersey. But if they insist, try to get them to wear a T-shirt underneath it. For women, it's the same rule; although tank tops can be cute, it may be a bit chilly in the arena, so a shirt underneath is recommended.

"I am not a big fan of NBA jerseys being worn to the games without an undershirt on. Love the jerseys but I personally would wear the jersey with a shirt with sleeves underneath," Walker says.

The NBA4her line launched in 2003. The NBA took notice and began to offer fan gear for fashion-conscious women. Now you can get fitted, curve-hugging tees, tanks, and even jeans with your team's logo on the back pockets! Team shops offer everything from halter tops to crystal-studded team logos on a shrunken T-shirt. The styles go from cute to classic, so there is something for everyone. For the diehards they even offer watches, necklaces, and team-logoed flip-flops.

Because basketball games allow for a more fashionable environment, the question of showing off "the girls" comes up all of the time. For some women, cleavage is a part of everyday life (to each her own), but for the rest of us, the girls come out at special times. Diana Vilibert from marieclaire.com has it right. "If you have your heart set on showing off the girls a little, the key is to ditch the supertight tank top in favor of a casual V-neck T-shirt."

You are still at a game, and although basketball is dressier than other sports, it's still not going-out-to-the-club dressy— although on weekends, a lot of people might be going to the club after the game. Or at least they look that way. As with any sport, tight short skirts and tank tops are never recommended, nor are thin stiletto heels. But high-heeled boots, pumps, or booties are all perfect.

The bottom line is that at a basketball game, no matter where you live, the crowd will be in everything from suits to sweat suits. So unless you don a prom dress or a club outfit, there's not much of a chance of being overdressed. You can, however, be underdressed. This is not a flip-flop and cutoff-shorts event. If casual clothing and flats are preferred, of course jeans, a tee, and flats or city sneakers are fine, but leave the flips-flops at home.

During the playoffs or big games, it is common now for the team to give out free T-shirts when fans enter the area to make the stands look uniform. Some teams have done the "whiteout," where they give out white T-shirts and request everyone wear them, or a "blackout," giving out black T-shirts. It is to create an intimidating environment for the visiting team (and it looks pretty cool on television!). Yes, the T-shirts will be big and one size and definitely not fashionable, but please put one on and be a part of the crowd. You don't want to stick out as the girl that is too cool to participate.

Don't Let This Happen to You: Be Camera Ready

One afternoon during my sophomore year of high school I at- tended track practice after school, took a quick shower in the locker room, and ran out the door to meet my father, who was waiting in the parking lot to drive me down to Miami for an NBA game. I was wearing a huge surfing-logo T-shirt and baggy jeans. It was comfy, and what was in my gym bag. I had no makeup on, and my hair was in a wet ponytail. I was fifteen years old and still a tomboy. Although I was starting to experiment with makeup, it was not a priority. But this is the game that would change that forever.

The Miami Heat were playing the Chicago Bulls. It was late in Michael Jordan's legendary career, and the Heat had never beaten the Bulls (the Heat joined the NBA in 1988). The game was nationally televised and a big deal to the home team.

We had really good seats for that game, about eight rows up, directly behind a basket. The game was amazing, and the Heat pulled out their first-ever victory over the Bulls. I had a great time with my dad and didn't think much about the way I looked.

The next morning I got a lot of attention in the hallways at school. At least three different senior boys said they saw me on television. These were guys that had never talked to me before. Then two teachers mentioned it. Then a few of my own classmates said something. Apparently the TV cameraman spent a lot of time on my father and me. It was embarrassing having my classmates explain to me in detail how I chewed my popcorn and what I looked like giving high fives to my seat neighbors.

Moral of the story: I never attended another game without makeup on. I will always be camera ready. And I will chew with my mouth closed.

Who Wears Short Shorts?
What the Pros Wear

The basketball uniform has changed throughout the years. Look up a picture from the 1980s or earlier of NBA players and you may just blush. They look like they could be auditioning for a Nair commercial. Since then, the shorts have gotten longer (thank goodness) and much baggier. And just like in fashion, when it comes to basketball, it's all about the shoes.

Basketball sneakers made their big breakthrough in the 1950s with the original Chuck Taylor Converse All-Stars. They were just plain canvas high-tops with a rubber sole.

High-top sneakers are generally still popular in basketball because they give great ankle support—if you've ever done "suicides" in a workout you know what I'm talking about. All of the shuffling and foot movement involved in basketball can produce many twisted ankles.

In the 1960s low-tops came into fashion because they made some athletes feel quicker and lighter on their feet. Now a popular style is a three-quarter-cut sneaker. It's halfway between the high- and low-tops and gives ankle support but doesn't go up as high as a traditional shoe.

The first sneaker endorsement was by Walt Frazier of the New York Knicks in the early 1970s. Frazier was one of the game's first showmen. He was given the nickname "Clyde" because of his fashionable manner of dressing. Inspired by *Bonnie and Clyde,* he dressed in a gangster-type suit and took on a larger-than-life persona. Puma paid Frazier $5,000 to wear a suede low-top sneaker named "the Clyde." Frazier went on to win two NBA championships and is in the Hall of Fame.

The most famous sneaker of all time, the Air Jordan, was

coupled with one of the largest marketing and advertising campaigns in history. Nike has released a new Air Jordan shoe every year since 1984, sometimes even re-releasing classics that sell out almost instantaneously in the USA and abroad.

Basketball sneakers are not cheap. They average more than $100, with the latest Air Jordans priced at $230. The news has featured stories of children robbing each other for their sneakers. That's why NBA player Stephon Marbury created the Starbury leather basketball shoe priced at only $15.

As for clothing, jerseys must be tucked into shorts at all times. Shorts may not be more than one inch longer than the knee. Usually the home team will wear the lighter jersey and the away team a darker jersey. That's why, as in most sports, different-color uniforms are worn for home and road games.

The NBA's Dress Code (for Players)

In 2005 the NBA was suffering from a tarnished image. After a nasty on-court fight during a game that escalated into the stands, and a few key players having legal woes off the court, the NBA's image was seen as thuggish, street, and too hip-hop. Advertisers were pulling out and sponsors were leaving the arenas. In an effort to clean up its act, Commissioner David Stern set forth a dress code. At first it was seen as a joke, mocked by players and the press, but now most players oblige without much comment. And the dollars have increased too, with sponsorship levels at an all-time high.

THE NBA DRESS CODE (NBA.COM)

BUSINESS CASUAL

Players are required to wear business casual attire whenever they are engaged in any team or league business, including All-Star festivities.

To the NBA, "business casual" attire means:

- A long- or short-sleeved dress shirt (collared or turtleneck), and/or a sweater.
- Dress slacks, khaki pants, or dress jeans.
- Appropriate shoes and socks, including dress shoes, dress boots, or other presentable shoes, but not including sneakers, sandals, flip-flops, or work boots.

EXCEPTIONS TO BUSINESS CASUAL

Players who are in attendance at games but not in uniform are required to wear the following additional items when seated on the bench or in the stands during the game:

- Sport coat
- Dress shoes or boots, and socks

Players leaving the arena may wear either business casual attire or neat warm-up suits issued by their teams.

Teams can make exceptions to the business casual policy for special events or player appearances where other attire is appropriate, like participation in a basketball clinic.

THE GIRLIE GIRL'S BASKETBALL GLOSSARY

Air ball: A shot that completely misses the **basket** and **backboard,** hitting only air.

Alley-oop: When a player lobs the ball toward the **basket** in the air and a teammate jumps up, catches it, and dunks the ball.

Assist: When a player **passes** the ball to a teammate who then scores.

Backboard: The flexiglass or wood frame that supports the **basket.**

Backcourt: A team's backcourt is its defensive back of the court.

Bank shot: A shot attempt that uses the **backboard**.

Baseline: The line on the end of the court that separates in-bounds from out-of-bounds.

Basket: The iron rim and netting (also called the goal).

Blocked shot: When a defensive player bats away an opponent's **shot** attempt.

Box out: Using the body to block or shield an opponent from getting a **rebound** and increase your own chances.

Board: Slang for **rebound**.

Breakaway: When the **defense** steals the ball and races to the **basket** to score. Usually results in a **slam dunk** or an **alley-oop** trick shot.

Brick: An ugly **shot** that clanks off the rim.

Bucket: Slang for **basket**.

Center: The position that is usually filled by the team's tallest member. Plays close to the basket, gets the most rebounds, and blocks shots.

Charge: Illegal personal contact when an offensive player pushes or moves into a defender. The defender must be stationary or the call is a block.

Crossover dribble: When a player in a stationary position dribbles the ball from one side of his body to the other, then switches back to the original hand to throw off the defender.

Cut: To move quickly from one spot on the court to another in order to elude a defender.

Dead ball: Any time the referee whistles for play to stop.

Defense: The team without the ball; it tries to prevent the other team from scoring.

Double dribble: A violation in which a player dribbles with both hands simultaneously or stops his dribble and then starts again.

Downtown: A shot attempted from far away from the **basket**.

Dribble: To bounce the ball to the floor repeatedly.

Dunk: To stuff the ball through the **basket**.

Fast break: When the **defense** rebounds the ball and races to get to their **basket** ahead of their opponent.

Field goal: A **shot** that goes in, other than a **free throw**.

Flagrant foul: A **personal foul** that involves violent contact.

Forward: A position on the court. There are usually two forwards per team on the court.

Foul out: To be disqualified and kicked out of the game for having committed six fouls.

Foul trouble: When a player is close to fouling out—usually when he has four or five fouls.

Free throw: A **shot** in which one point is awarded. The shot is not defended and is made from the free-throw line at the top of the key.

Goaltending: A violation that involves touching the ball after it has already hit the **backboard** or is heading into the **basket**. The shooting team is awarded the basket.

BASKETBALL BASICS: ABBREVIATIONS

3PT: 3-point field goal

3PA: 3-pointers attempted

AST: Assist

BLK: Block

BS: Blocked shots

C: Center

CONF: Conference

DIV: Division

DNP: Did not play

FF: Flagrant foul

FG: Field goal

FGP: Field goal percentage

FT: Free throw

FT–FTA: Free throws made–Total free throws attempted

G: Games

GB: Games back

L: Lost

L10: Last 10 played

MIN: Minutes

MPG: Minutes per game

NBA: National Basketball Association

NBDL: National Basketball Development League

OFF: Offensive rebounds

OT: Overtime

PCT: Percent

PF: Personal foul and power forward

PTS: Points

REB: Total rebounds

RPG: Rebounds per game

S: Steals

SF: Small forward

SG: Shooting guard

STL: Steals

TO: Turnover

W: Win or won

Guard: A player position. Usually two guards per team are on the court.

Hack: Slang for foul.

Hoop: Slang for **basket**.

Inbounds pass: Putting the ball in play from out-of-bounds.

Intentional foul: A foul committed purely to foul the person and not to go after the ball.

Jump ball: Putting the ball in play by the official tossing it in the air and two players jumping and trying to tap the ball to a teammate.

Jump shot: A **shot** when the player jumps in the air, then shoots.

Lane: The painted rectangular area in front of the **basket**.

Layup: A **shot** where the player **dribbles** to the **basket** and bounces the ball lightly off the **backboard** and into the **hoop**.

No-look pass: A **pass** when the player purposely does not make eye contact with the intended receiver, to throw off the **defense**.

Offense: The team in possession of the ball.

Officials: The referees.

Overtime: The five-minute session that occurs if the regulation game is tied at the end.

Paint: Slang for **lane**.

Pass: When one player throws or bounces the ball to another player.

Personal foul: A violation where illegal contact occurs.

Pick: A **screen** for the player with the ball.

Pivot foot: A player who is holding and not dribbling the ball must keep one foot anchored to the ground. That is the pivot foot.

Point guard: The primary ballhandling position.

Post: The area outside the **lane** near the **basket**.

Rebound: Retrieval of a missed **shot**.

Screen: When an offensive player legally stands or blocks the opponent from reaching the **basket**.

Shot: When the ball is thrown at the **basket** in order to score.

Shot clock: Also known as the twenty-four-second clock; tells the amount of time left before the **offense** must shoot and at least hit the rim with the ball.

Sideline: The lengthwise boundary of the court. Also where the team benches are.

Slam dunk: A fantastic **dunk**.

Technical foul: A foul by any member of the team, including coaches and attendants, for unsportsmanlike conduct of any kind.

Three-pointer: A **shot** from behind the three-point arc—worth three points.

Time-out: Stoppage of play by a team, usually to discuss strategy.

Tip-off: Starts the game. When the ball is thrown in the air and the **centers** try to tap it to their teammates.

Travel: When a player moves illegally by taking more than two steps, or if the pivot foot is moved, or if a player holding the ball jumps in the air and lands without shooting or passing the ball.

Turnover: When the **offense** loses the ball to the **defense** without taking a **shot**.

Violation: An action that causes the team to lose possession of the ball.

Walk: A synonym for **travel**.

4

Hockey and Heels: The National Hockey League (NHL)

*Hockey has some of the most pas-*sionate fans in professional sports. They are hard-core fans, and because hockey doesn't have the nationwide popularity that some of the other professional sports have, the fans really know their stuff. There are areas of the United States where hockey is one of the most popular sports, like Detroit and Minnesota.

My first job after college was an internship with a National Hockey League (NHL) team. The first thing I noticed as a female was that the typical hockey stereotype wasn't true. When I thought "hockey player," I thought big, hairy toothless wonders skating around the rink and punching each other out. That wasn't the case at all. There were the veterans who looked a little beat up after years of their bodies taking abuse from the violent game. But most of the guys were young and foreign and excited to be playing in the NHL.

Hockey is the most popular sport in Canada. The country's passionate fans follow their teams closely, and teams like the Toronto Maple Leafs have huge followings all around the country (and even in the United States). Their Canadian fans actually leave the country to travel to away games in U.S. cities.

The NHL is made up of thirty teams in the U.S. and Canada.

EASTERN CONFERENCE	WESTERN CONFERENCE
ATLANTIC DIVISION	**CENTRAL DIVISION**
New Jersey Devils	Chicago Blackhawks
New York Islanders	Columbus Blue Jackets
New York Rangers	Detroit Red Wings
Philadelphia Flyers	Nashville Predators
Pittsburgh Penguins	St. Louis Blues
NORTHEAST DIVISION	**NORTHWEST DIVISION**
Boston Bruins	Calgary Flames
Buffalo Sabres	Colorado Avalanche
Montreal Canadiens	Edmonton Oilers
Ottawa Senators	Minnesota Wild
Toronto Maple Leafs	Vancouver Canucks
SOUTHEAST DIVISION	**PACIFIC DIVISION**
Atlanta Thrashers	Anaheim Ducks
Carolina Hurricanes	Dallas Stars
Florida Panthers	Los Angeles Kings
Tampa Bay Lightning	Phoenix Coyotes
Washington Capitals	San Jose Sharks

Hockey Night in Canada (*HNIC*), televised nationally every Saturday night, is one of Canada's highest-rated broadcasts. It started in 1931 as a radio broadcast and premiered on television in 1952. The broadcast is a hockey doubleheader featuring at least two of the six Canadian teams. The first game usually involves the Toronto Maple Leafs, and the second game involves one of western Canada's teams. When I worked for the NHL team it was a huge thing to be a part of *HNIC*. The few times we got to be a part of it (when we played a Canadian team on a Saturday night) there was always extra electricity in the air.

THE GAME

Hockey is played at indoor arenas, except when the league is running a promotional event and holding a special game at an outdoor venue. Most NHL teams share their home ice with the NBA franchise in their city. The ice is covered with hardwood for the basketball games throughout their overlapped seasons. When I worked for that hockey team the arena we played in was not shared by an NBA team. So the ice was covered only when a concert or circus came to town. Watching the ice being prepared was amazing. The process took great skill, and many hours to get the ice just right.

When changing the ice to a basketball court, most arenas have a permanent layer of ice that is covered with insulation, usually fiberglass, and then the wooden basketball court is put down in pieces. Seats are added (since the ice hockey playing surface is much larger than the basketball playing surface), and then the clear wall that separates flying pucks from fans is removed. The process can take between five and eight hours and the manpower of fifteen to thirty people. For teams that share an arena with an NBA team, this process may have to be done a few times a week.

Making the ice is an intricate and scientific process that requires extreme attention to detail. Just one millimeter of extra water or temperature one-half of a degree off and the ice can be ruined. In professional NHL rinks, the ice temperature is usually between 24 and 26 degrees Fahrenheit. Hockey players prefer a colder, harder ice than figure skaters do because it's "fast ice" that makes for easier passing and skating. It also prevents injuries and damage to their blades.

Hockey is played in winter, so in most parts of the country it is cold outside. Growing up in South Florida, it was always odd to be outside in 90-degree weather and then go inside to a 30-degree temperature drop, but it sure felt good. In warm climates, a hockey game can be the only time a person sees ice all winter.

NHL players have complained about ice conditions for years. This is especially true in warm climates because the heat and humidity outside can soften the ice. Arena and ice workers take extreme measures to make sure the ice stays cold and hard even though the heat from outside comes in every time a door opens. On the other hand, in Canada in the middle of winter sometimes the arenas have to be heated (even close to the ice) because the temperature outside is too cold, and that also affects the ice negatively.

The ice is surrounded by **boards**, which are covered in advertising. These advertisers get a lot of airtime during televised games because the camera consistently follows the puck around the ice. The boards can be used to a team's advantage by deflecting the puck and for **body checking**, which is legal

BEST HOCKEY MOVIES

Here's a look at some of the best hockey movies of all time. Unlike other sports, there aren't very many hockey movies. And there are even fewer *good* hockey movies. The best are the ones that bring extra comedy and/or drama to the film while still showcasing classic hockey in a way that a new fan can learn the game.

Slap Shot (1977). This movie is on some sportswriters' all-time best-movie lists for any sport. The hilarious comedy stars Paul Newman as the player-coach of a minor league hockey team that is scheduled to fold at the end of the season due to a string of losses and because the town's resources are drying up. Newman's character lies to motivate the team and tells them that the team has been sold and is moving to Florida at the end of the season. In addition, three new faces grace the team, the gritty, fight-loving Hanson brothers. The movie is a comedy and showcases the violent minor league hockey of the 1970s. Although it is fiction, it is inspired by a true story.

Miracle (2004). There have been a few films and television movies about the "Miracle on Ice," but this excellent one won an ESPY (ESPN award) for best sports movie of 2004. It tells the historic and true story of the 1980 USA Olympic hockey team, which beat the heavily favored Soviet team during the height of Cold War tension. Kurt Russell stars as legendary coach Herb Brooks, who led the team to the unlikely victory. The Soviet team was made up of the country's professionals, and the U.S. team was made up of a bunch of college kids. Although everyone knows the ending, it is still a must-see hockey movie.

Youngblood (1986). Okay, so this is your typical 1980s cheesefest, but the bad outfits and bad music and just the overall badness make it almost good. Did I mention a young and gorgeous Rob Lowe costarring with an equally young and gorgeous Patrick Swayze (in a mullet)? The plot revolves around Lowe's character and his desire to reach the NHL, and focuses on his rough journey to get there. The silver lining is the hockey. It's good hockey, rough and testosterone-fueled with just the right amount of drama.

The Mighty Ducks (1992). Don't let the name fool you. This is actually a decent movie and the hockey is really good! And it's all played by kids. A lawyer played by Emilio Estevez is court-ordered (drunk-driving charge) to coach a peewee hockey team. But Estevez's character has demons to contend with. He played hockey when he was a kid and lost the championship game for his team. This is something that still haunts him as an adult. He takes his band of misfits all the way to the championship, where he faces his old coach. It's a fun, feel-good movie that inspired two sequels and the name of the NHL team the Mighty Ducks of Anaheim, now the Anaheim Ducks.

Mystery, Alaska (1999). This is a fictional movie about a small Alaska town called Mystery that has an amateur hockey team. The town rallies around this team of talented players. A former town resident (played by Hank Azaria) writes an article for *Sports Illustrated* about how great the players are. The team accepts an offer/challenge to play the New York Rangers, and things spiral from there. The publicity this small town gets changes the residents forever, and the game changes the lives of some of the players as well. The team's player-coach, played by Russell Crowe, shines as the driving force behind the film.

Honorable Mention: *The Rocket* (2005).

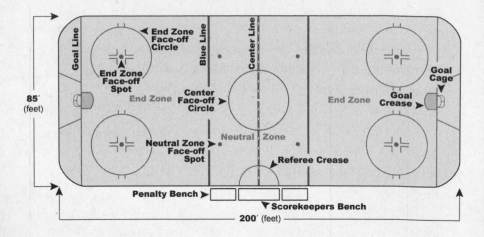

physical contact. When a player **checks** he uses his hip and shoulder to hit the opposing player against the boards in the hopes of getting the **puck** away from him.

Six team members, including the goalie, are on the ice at a time. Each NHL team is allowed to carry eighteen position players and two goalies on its roster. The object of the game is to get the puck into the opponent's goal. The puck is made of vulcanized rubber, and it is frozen before the game so that it glides across the ice and does not bounce.

The puck is moved by sticks with curved blades at the end. The puck can touch any part of a player's body, including the hands, although holding the puck or kicking it purposely is not allowed. Just like baseball players have their own special bats, hockey players have their own sticks made to their specific tastes. Some prefer a lighter stick, others a heavier stick. The curvature of the blade is also done to a player's preference.

A hockey game is divided into three periods, each twenty minutes long. The time between periods is usually fifteen to twenty minutes, depending on commercials and the time needed for the ice to refreeze. That time is needed so that the players can rest and the **Zamboni** can do its job. A Zamboni is an ice resurfacer invented by Frank Zamboni, and the name Zamboni is actually trademarked. Although it is a brand, it has become a generic colloquialism for any ice resurfacer.

Between periods, the ice resurfacer cleans the ice by shaving the top layer and sweeping away the shavings. It also releases a thin layer of water to smooth the ice and bring it to a nice finish to start a new period of play.

Hockey games are fun and flashy. Just like in basketball, the arena's intimate setting allows for fun and fanfare before, during, and after the game. The team's personnel will make use of lights and pyrotechnics before a game to get the crowd riled up. When a goal is scored, the noise is deafening—not from the cheering but from the loud horn that blows for a few seconds to signal that the home team has made a goal. Be prepared, it is loud, almost obnoxiously loud. It is necessary, though, because sometimes the puck is so hard to see, you won't know a goal has been scored until you hear the horn.

QUICK TIP: BEST TIME TO LEAVE THE SEATS

Hockey's three periods can get confusing, since there is no set "halftime." There is plenty of time in between periods (usually seventeen minutes) to leave the seats. Generally, concessions and bathrooms will be less crowded at the midpoint during the periods. I usually leave my seat with about five minutes left in the first or second period. This way, I don't miss too much action but avoid the lines and crowds when the period is over.

When a Canadian team is playing a U.S. team, there will be two national anthems, "The Star-Spangled Banner" and

Canada's national anthem, "O Canada." The song became Canada's national anthem in 1980. Hard-core hockey fans have it memorized in both French and English.

The game begins with a **face-off**, where the two teams line up facing each other and the puck is dropped by a referee in between the sticks of the two centers (see "The Skaters," below). The centers will try to tap the puck to a team member to gain possession. Face-offs also restart the game after play has been stopped for any reason.

Overtime (OT) in hockey is a sudden-death overtime period of only five minutes. The clock is reset, but the teams do not have to play the whole five-minute additional period, because as in all sudden-death overtimes, the first team to score wins. Only four skaters and one goalie participate in OT in order to speed up the game. If the game remains tied after the five-minute OT period, then a **shoot-out** occurs. This was created in 2005 because of the large number of ties in professional hockey. In order to make the game more "fan friendly," the shoot-out was added to bring an exciting new element to the game.

The shoot-out begins with three players on each team taking one free shot each at the goal. It's just the shooter and the opposing goalie. One team goes at a time. The home team decides who goes first. The team with the most goals at the end wins. If the score is still tied at the end of the shoot-out then it moves to a sudden-death format like the OT period. There are no longer ties in NHL hockey. Also, the goals scored in a shoot-out do not count toward the total goals scored in the game. The winning team is awarded one extra goal for its work in the shoot-out.

If a team is losing late in the game (with only a minute or so left) it may **pull the goalie**. This allows the team to have an extra skater, an attacker, to try to score to tie up the game. This can backfire and the opposing team can gain control of the puck and score an **empty-netter** by shooting into the now unguarded net.

The **three stars** of the game are awarded at the end of a hockey game. This has been a tradition for many decades. The NHL awards the three stars after every game played. The first star will go to the best player in that game, usually a high goal scorer or a goalie that made outstanding defensive efforts. The next two stars are awarded to the other top players in that game.

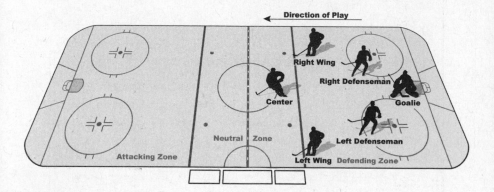

THE SKATERS

There are six players on the ice for each team most of the time.

- Goalie: Defends the goal.
- Center: A forward. Kind of like the quarterback or the point guard of the team. He handles the puck the most,

and tries to bring it to the opposing goal by passing to his two wings.

- Left wing and right wing: Also forwards. They pass with the center to try to score goals.
- Two defensemen: Defend their goal at the blue line and try to break up passes and shots from the opposing team. On offense, the defensemen try to get the puck to their forwards.

The center and two wingers (the forwards) usually form a **line** that is always together. Teams change lines every sixty seconds or so to keep skaters fresh. The coach will have a sig-

---

THE NAME GAME: NHL EDITION

Hockey is easily the sport with the most difficult names to pronounce. With an influx of Eastern European players over the last two decades, television broadcasters, announcers, and even official NHL guides can't get it right. There are so many hard-to-pronounce names that the NHL publishes an official "pronunciation guide" every season. Impress and correct everyone with these hard to pronounce names.

ALEX OVECHKIN
(*Washington Capitals, 2009*)
(Ah-VEHCH-kin)

EVGENI MALKIN
(*Pittsburgh Penguins, 2009*)
(Yev-GAY-knee MALL-kin)

VINCENT LECAVALIER
(*Tampa Bay Lightning, 2009*)
(Vin-sint Luh-KAV-uhl-yay)

DANIEL BRIERE
(*Philadelphia Flyers, 2009*)
(Bree-AIR)

PAVEL DATSYUK
(*Detroit Red Wings, 2009*)
(PAH-vel Daat-ZOOK)

LUKAS KRAJICEK
(*Tampa Bay Lightning, 2009*)
(CRY-check)

---

nal or the team will already have created a way to know when to exit and enter the ice. That's why you'll see players constantly jumping over the boards to enter or leave the game. The lines usually stay together because they have proven that they work well together. The defensemen are usually the same way, with two players working with each other all the time. Different lines specialize in different things. When you see players leave the ice and others enter it's called a **line change**. Substitutions are allowed at any time during the game.

Defensemen traditionally score fewer goals because their main focus is keeping the puck out of their net. Right and left wingers are usually the quickest skaters and have excellent stick-handling skills. The center will usually score the most goals.

In NHL hockey there are five officials (three on the ice) for each game.

- The **referee** is the head official and supervises the game.
- Two **linesmen** are used to call offsides and icing violations, and handle all face-offs not occurring at center ice.
- **Goal judges** sit behind each goal, off the ice, and when they see the puck cross the red line into the goal they turn on the red light to indicate a goal has been made.

BASIC RULES TO KNOW

Offsides

When a member of the attacking team enters the attacking zone before the puck does. Some sort of offsides rule is used in many sports, including soccer.

Icing

When a player shoots the puck across at least two red lines. A member of the other team (but not the goalie) must touch the puck with his stick for icing to be called. The puck then goes to a face-off back in the defending zone of the team that caused the icing. Unintentional icing usually happens when a team is defending their goal and a player accidentally slaps the puck too hard and it travels all the way to the other end of the ice.

Icing may not called for a few reasons; one is when a team is **shorthanded** (see "Penalties," below). Another reason icing wouldn't be called is if the linesman believes the pass was an attempted receivable one.

Penalties

While offsides and icing are infractions, they are not penalties. Penalties in the NHL are mostly for illegal contact and result in the team that committed the penalty having to play shorthanded for an assessed amount of time. The player that committed the penalty is sent to the **penalty box**, literally a separate little glassed-in booth where he sits and waits out his penalty. It is like watching a child in "time-out" in elementary school. He is separated from the pack and must just sit back and watch while his team is shorthanded.

Common Hockey Penalties

Boarding: Pushing an opponent violently into the boards while the player is facing the boards.

Charging: Taking more than three strides or jumping before hitting an opponent.

Checking from behind: Hitting an opponent from behind is a penalty. It carries an automatic minor penalty and misconduct, or a major penalty and game misconduct if it results in injury.

Clipping: Delivering a check below the knees of an opponent. If injury results, a major penalty and a game misconduct will result.

Cross-checking: Hitting an opponent with the stick when it is held with two hands and no part of the stick is on the ice.

Fighting or fisticuffs: Engaging in a physical altercation with an opposing player, usually involving the throwing of punches with gloves removed.

High-sticking: Touching an opponent with the stick above shoulder level.

Hooking: Using a stick as a hook to slow an opponent; no contact is required under new standards.

Interference: Impeding an opponent who does not have the puck, or impeding any player from the bench.

Roughing: Pushing and shoving or throwing punches that are not severe enough to be considered fighting.

Slashing: Swinging a stick at an opponent.

Spearing: Stabbing an opponent with the stick blade. It carries an automatic major penalty and game misconduct.

Tripping: Using a stick or one's body to trip an opponent; no contact is required under new standards.

When a team has an advantage with more skaters than the other, they are said to be on a **power play**. A power play occurs when someone on the other team commits a penalty. Only two people on a team can serve a penalty at once, so sometimes the advantage can be five on three. If more than two penalties are called on one team, the third will be delayed until one is over so that the advantage is never more than five on three.

Minor penalties usually last for two minutes, while major penalties last for five. Most minor penalties, like **high-sticking**, can be deemed major if they are seen as malicious. If a skater has a **breakaway** (when a player has the puck and is racing to the opponent's goal with the defenders behind him) and he is tripped, he is awarded a **penalty shot**. A penalty shot is when a skater is given a free shot. The puck is placed at center ice and the player is allowed to skate a little to gain momentum and then shoot with no defenders except the opposition's goalie.

Fighting is actually illegal in the NHL rule book. But there's an unofficial code among players, coaches, and officials that lets the fights happen even though they are usually penalized with a major penalty (five minutes). Fighting in hockey is a sore subject. Some people hate it and think it should be barred from the game. Others enjoy the fighting and see it as the main draw. It is not allowed in college hockey and players are ejected there for fighting. In the NHL, the referees will attempt to break up fights but only after some time has passed so they can assess who is to blame. They also hold back so they do not get injured themselves. Most fights are not premeditated and happen because something occurred on the ice, but others are planned in advance between players that have a grudge or something to prove to another player.

POINTS AND STANDINGS

Hockey is unlike the other major North American sports when it comes to how the teams are ranked in the standings. It is not purely a win-or-loss format. The winning team is awarded two points. If the game goes into overtime, both teams get a point and the winning team gains another point in order to get their two. The losing team in overtime keeps its one point. The teams with the highest points at the end of the season are seeded for the playoffs. During the season, the rankings are based on point totals and games played.

The playoffs in the NHL consist of four rounds. Each round is a best-of-seven series, meaning the first team to win four games wins that round. The first round is called the conference

NHL PLAYOFFS

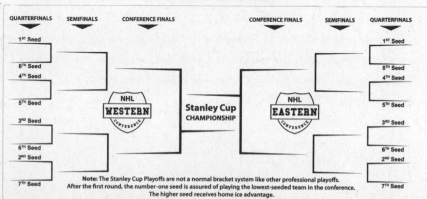

Note: The Stanley Cup Playoffs are not a normal bracket system like other professional playoffs. After the first round, the number-one seed is assured of playing the lowest-seeded team in the conference. The higher seed receives home ice advantage.

quarterfinals; the second round is the conference semifinals. The third round is the conference finals, where the top two remaining teams in the conference play to see who will represent the conference in the Stanley Cup Finals.

The **plus/minus** statistic is an unofficial way to rate a player or to compare players on a line to see who is better for the team. It is used to measure how successful a team is when a player is on the ice. When a goal is scored, each player on the ice for the team that scored is awarded a point (+1). This happens whether he had anything to do with the goal itself or not. Each player on the team that gave up the goal receives minus one point (–1). This happens when teams are even strength or if the scoring team is shorthanded. Teams are not awarded points if they are on a power play, and players that are shorthanded are not given minus points if they give up a goal while shorthanded.

So a plus/minus ratio of +4 is much better than a ratio of –4. The stat is a goal differential tool that helps determine who is effective on the ice even if they do not score very much.

QUICK TIP

The record for the highest plus/minus in one season is held by Hall of Famer Bobby Orr at +124. The best plus/minus over a career is held by Hall of Famer Larry Robinson, who spent most of his tenure with the Montreal Canadiens, at +730. The worst plus/minus ratio is held by a former player from the 1970s, Bill Mikkelson, at –82.

HISTORY AND DRAMA

Nobody knows exactly how long the game of hockey has been around. Some versions of hockey, like field hockey, are among the world's oldest sports—ancient in fact: The earliest reports of hockey, known then as the game with a "ball and a stick," date back to ancient Rome and China some four thousand years ago.

Ice hockey started in Canada in the early to mid-1800s, and it seems to have developed from people adapting to the icy conditions of the land. British soldiers in Canada and Arctic explorers recorded playing shinny (an informal game of hockey, like a pickup game with few rules).

The game of hockey similar to what we know today was created in 1875 at McGill University, where the first indoor organized game was played at the college's ice rink. A law student named James Creighton played the game with other students, and two years later he drew up seven original rules and formed the McGill University Hockey Club. The game became popular quickly, and soon other teams formed in and around Montreal. It even jumped over the pond to England, where Oxford University started its own club in 1885.

By 1893 there were more than a hundred teams in Montreal alone and even more throughout Canada. The game traveled south to the U.S. that year, and the first game in the States was Yale University versus Johns Hopkins University. Three years later an amateur league formed in New York City, and in 1906 the U.S.'s first pro team was formed in Michigan.

Lord Stanley's Cup

Hockey tournaments and carnivals were held all over Canada, and in 1892 the governor-general of Canada, Lord Stanley of Preston, recognized that there was no formal award for the best team in Canada. He purchased a silver bowl to be the trophy for the champion.

After the bowl served as the championship trophy in a few early hockey leagues, the NHL took it over to give to its champion in 1926. The original bowl is in a vault in the Hockey Hall of Fame. The cup used today is much bigger than the original. It's made of silver and nickel, and the top of the cup is a copy of the original bowl donated by Lord Stanley.

The Stanley Cup, as it is known today, is unlike any other trophy in professional sports. First, there is only one Stanley Cup—well, one that a team wins. There are actually three: the original in the Hall of Fame's vault, a replica that is used as a stand-in at the hall when the awarded trophy isn't there, and of course the awarded trophy.

Unlike other sports, where a new trophy is made every year, the Stanley Cup is passed from championship team to championship team each season. Every team member, including coaches, owners, and team presidents, has his name engraved on the cup. New rings are added to the bottom when necessary for space.

The Stanley Cup is rich with traditions. Immediately after the Stanley Cup is presented to the winner, it is usually passed to the captain, who hoists it above his head and skates a lap around the rink. He then passes it to a teammate, and this continues until every team member has carried it above his head and skated around the rink.

It is also tradition to drink champagne out of the cup. This started back in 1896 with the then-champion Winnipeg Victorias.

In 1995 a new tradition started where each member of the team takes the cup "home" for a day. He spends a day with the trophy (and of course is accompanied by a representative of the Hockey Hall of Fame). Some bizarre but true stories have come out of the home visits. A few players have used the Cup to baptize their children. Others have used it as a dog bowl and let their dogs eat out of it. One NHL star (that we know of) used it as a ring bearer when proposing marriage to his girlfriend.

THE NHL

The Beginnings

The NHL was formed in 1917 just when its predecessor (the National Hockey Association, or NHA) was unraveling due to internal fights and tension among owners. The NHA had become the first real professional league after amateur hockey became so popular. The newly formed NHL and its teams were all in Canada, and it wasn't until 1924 that the U.S. gained a team, the Boston Bruins. By 1926 the league was expanding and had teams in Canada, the Great Lakes region, and the northeast United States. As the league expanded so did the game itself. The rules changed often for the first few years to improve and evolve the game from a backyard sport to a sport that can be enjoyed by fans.

Early in the 1920s the NHL had competition from the Pacific Coast Hockey Association and the Western Canada Hockey League. They competed for talented players, and the winners of the leagues would compete for the Stanley Cup. At this time, hockey players were some of the highest-paid athletes of the day, rivaled only by major league ballplayers.

The league expanded in the 1920s to ten teams but then lost teams to bankruptcy during the Great Depression in the 1930s. Some teams still thrived during this time, like the Toronto Maple Leafs, whose new owner built a brand-new arena. The owner, Conn Smythe, wanted the new place, Maple Leaf Gardens, to be a place where people wore evening clothes and could have a party or dinner. He also wanted it to be a place where men would be proud to bring their wives or girlfriends.

The Original Six

The Great Depression and World War II caused the NHL to go from ten teams to only six. The six remaining teams, now called "the Original Six," were the only NHL teams for twenty-five years. They are:

- Montreal Canadiens
- Toronto Maple Leafs
- Detroit Red Wings
- Boston Bruins
- Chicago Blackhawks
- New York Rangers

From 1942 to 1967 these six teams fought each other for the Stanley Cup and bragging rights, as well as for players. With only six teams, this was an era of dynasties. The Maple Leafs won four Stanley Cups in the late 1940s. The Red Wings won four in the early 1950s, and the Canadiens won five in a row in the late 1950s.

Competition and Expansion

In 1967 the NHL finally expanded after twenty-five years by adding six teams to the league. The "Original Six" became the East Division, and the six new teams became the West Division. By 1974 the NHL added another six teams in order to compete with the newly formed World Hockey Association (WHA). In 1979 the WHA folded and the NHL absorbed its teams.

The 1970s is when the NHL first became involved in international play. But it wasn't until the late 1980s and the fall of the iron curtain that the league become what we know it as today. The fall of the Berlin wall in 1989 allowed Russian and Eastern European players to come to the U.S. and play. Before that there had been some Soviet and Eastern European players in the league, but there was a lot of red tape and even instances where team owners sneaked players out of their countries in order to bring them to North America to play.

For example, in 1979 there were only six European players selected at the NHL entry draft. In 1989 there were thirty-two. And in 2000 there were 123 Europeans selected. During the 2008 season, Europeans made up more than 25 percent of the NHL's rosters.

The NHL Draft

Like the NBA, the NHL also holds a "lottery" to determine the order of the draft. The nonplayoff teams all have a shot at the top pick and are ordered in a worst-to-first format. The winner of the Stanley Cup gets the last pick. The worst team in the league has the best chance of getting the first pick, although it does not always get that pick.

Professional hockey players come from three places: juniors, college, and European leagues.

The "juniors" is a really broad term, encompassing all of junior hockey, which is usually for sixteen- to twenty-year-olds. The term "junior" really means amateur hockey, and there are countless amateur leagues all around Canada and the United States. The levels are broken down by tier and age. Some players choose to stay in the junior leagues while others play college hockey, but both levels are highly recruited and scouted. Most players will go from juniors to the minor league NHL system, the American Hockey League (AHL).

QUICK TIP: BRING A SCARF OR A WRAP

The closer you sit to the ice, the colder it will be.

The AHL

The AHL isn't exactly the minor leagues of the NHL. Technically it is its own professional league, but it really serves as the developmental system and minor league system to the NHL. Most of the NHL teams have an exclusive affiliation with one of the AHL teams and will send younger or less-experienced players down to their AHL club when they need some help. They can bring the players back up to the NHL at any time. When I worked as an intern for an NHL team, there were a few times when I had to drive a player to the airport who had been sent down.

The AHL helps the NHL by producing top talent and giving younger players the chance for ample playing time. This provides training for the NHL. The AHL has its own All-Star Game and playoff tournament, called the Calder Cup.

THE MIRACLE ON ICE

Every hockey fan knows the now-famous phrase "Do you believe in miracles?," yelled by legendary sports broadcaster Al Michaels in the closing seconds of the game between the U.S. and the USSR at the 1980 Lake Placid Olympic Games. Many people consider this game the greatest sports moment of all time.

The USSR team was the best all-around team coming into the Olympics. The Soviets were long criticized by many other countries, including Canada, for using "professionals" in the Olympics even though at this time the competition was supposed to be for amateurs. The Russians were so good that they even beat the NHL's New York Rangers and New York Islanders in exhibition matches. When they arrived at the 1980 Games, the Soviets had won every ice hockey gold medal except for one (1960) since 1956, and they were the heavily favored team in the Lake Placid Olympics.

The two teams were automatic rivals due to the decades of the Cold War, and they actually had already met in a practice game at Madison Square Garden in New York City just before the Olympics. The Soviets easily beat the Americans, 10–3.

The Olympics were a hard-fought battle for Team USA, and head coach Herb Brooks's team of college players had to come from behind in most of their games leading up to the medal rounds. The game against the Soviets was mentally and physically challenging, and the score was tied during the third and final period 3–3. Team captain Mike Eruzione scored a goal to put the Americans on top by one with just ten minutes left to play in the game. The next ten minutes became the most excruciating and nail-biting minutes in all of sports. Minutes felt like hours as the U.S. had to defend their goal and keep the usually high-scoring Soviets from tying it up. With all eyes on the clock, goalie Jim Craig had to defend his goal from an onslaught of quality shots from the Soviets.

Ten minutes became five and five became one and soon the patriotic crowd was in disbelief as they started the countdown led by Michaels in the booth with his now famous line, "Eleven seconds! You've got ten seconds! The countdown going on right now . . . Five seconds left in the game! Do you believe in miracles? Yes!"

The moment was voted the greatest sports moment of the twentieth century by *Sports Illustrated*. But this game was not the gold medal game, something most people forget when they talk about "the Miracle on Ice." In fact, the U.S. team had to go on and play Finland in order to win the gold medal, and they did, of course, in come-from-behind fashion like every other game of those amazing Olympics.

The U.S. team famously stood on the podium together at the gold medal ceremony.

WHO TO KNOW IN HISTORY

Wayne Gretzky is nicknamed "the Great One" and is considered one of the greatest hockey players of all time. He is one of a handful of players (including everyone on this list) so good that the waiting period to enter the Hockey Hall of Fame was waived so that he could be inducted immediately. Upon his retirement, after playing in the NHL for twenty years, Gretzky held more than forty regular-season records and fifteen playoff records. He is the only player in NHL history to total more than 200 points in one season. And he did it four times! He won four Stanley Cups, all in the 1980s. Gretzky's number, 99, was retired by all teams in the NHL, an honor that only one other athlete in all of professional sports has received, MLB's Jackie Robinson.

Bobby Orr is considered the best defenseman of all time. He led the Boston Bruins to two Stanley Cup wins in the 1970s. He played for twelve years, mostly with the Bruins, and is currently a players' agent in Boston. Orr's waiting period to enter the Hall of Fame was waived after his retirement, and he was the youngest member ever inducted, at age thirty-one. In 1970 he received *Sports Illustrated*'s Sportsman of the Year honor. Orr still holds many records, including the most points ever by a defenseman in one season with 139, and most assists by a defenseman in one season with 102. He also holds the record for highest plus/minus in one season with +124.

Gordie Howe ("Mr. Hockey") is considered one of the best hockey players of all time. Gordie Howe was in the Detroit Red Wings organization for twenty-five years and led the Red Wings to four Stanley Cups in the 1950s. Howe's Hall of Fame career (his waiting period was also waived) didn't end when most players' careers did. Howe played into his fifties and was the oldest player ever to play in an NHL game (at fifty-two years old for the Hartford Whalers). He scored fifteen goals that season and helped the Whalers make the playoffs. Howe still holds the records for most NHL regular-season games played, most NHL seasons played, and most goals, points, and assists from a right winger in the NHL.

Mario Lemieux ("Super Mario") played seventeen seasons for the Pittsburgh Penguins from 1984 to 2005. He retired twice due to illness but came back in between with excellent skill and strength. He purchased the Penguins team in 1999 to save the team from bankruptcy. Lemieux won two Stanley Cups with the Penguins, one while he was an owner. That is a first in any sport. After retiring the first time due to Hodgkin's lymphoma, he was immediately inducted into the Hall of Fame. But he returned to the league two seasons later and is one of three players to be a member of the hall while still playing. He retired for the second and final time in 2006 with a heart problem, but is co-owner and chairman of the Penguins.

Maurice Richard ("The Rocket") played for the Montreal Canadiens from 1942 to 1960. He won the Stanley Cup eight times and played in twelve straight All-Star Games. He was inducted into the Hall of Fame in 1961, and he also had his waiting period waived. At the time of his retirement he was the NHL's all-time leading scorer, and he led the league in scoring five times. He was one of the first true Canadian sports celebrities and even did a hair-color commercial in the 1980s. When he died in 1993, the funeral was broadcast to all of Canada, and more than 115,000 went to see him as he lay in state at the Molson Centre in Montreal.

Bobby Hull was nicknamed the "Golden Jet" because of his blond hair and incredibly fast shooting and skating. He played for twenty-three years in both the NHL and the WHA. He won the Stanley Cup with the Chicago Blackhawks in 1961. Hull is said to have had the fastest slap shot of his time and possibly in hockey history. He was one of the biggest NHL stars of the 1960s. His third-youngest son, Brett Hull, was a huge NHL star in his own right. Brett retired with the third-highest total goals in the NHL, and the father-son duo is the only one where both had more than fifty goals in a season. Bobby Hull was inducted into the Hall of Fame in 1980, and his number has been retired by both the Chicago Blackhawks and the Winnipeg Jets (now the Phoenix Coyotes).

Guy Lafleur won five Stanley Cups with the Montreal Canadiens during his seventeen years of professional hockey. He is the Canadiens' all-time points leader (combining goals and assists) leader. The Hall of Fame right winger is well known for his off-the-ice antics. After the Canadiens won the 1978 Stanley Cup, he notoriously "borrowed" the trophy for a weekend and placed it on his front lawn for all the neighbors to see. This predated the tradition of taking the cup home. He also released a disco album called *Lafleur* on which he recited hockey instructions and sang to disco music. Comedy aside, he was an excellent hockey player and is currently a restaurant owner in Quebec.

Mark Messier spent twenty-five years in the NHL, winning six Stanley Cups, five with the Edmonton Oilers and one with the New York Rangers. He is the only player in history to be the captain of two Stanley Cup–winning teams. He played in fifteen All-Star Games, and his number has been retired by both the Oilers and the Rangers. Messier was inducted into the Hall of Fame in 2007. He holds the record for most NHL regular-season and playoff games played at 1,992. He has been featured in many television commercials and has become very active in charity work after his retirement.

Ray Bourque played twenty-one seasons with the Boston Bruins and finished his career with the Colorado Avalanche, where he finally won the Stanley Cup in his last professional game. He holds the NHL records for most goals, points, and assists by a defenseman. His Hall of Fame career with the Bruins was bittersweet because although they went to the playoffs almost every season he played (and every season in the 1980s), they did not win the cup with Bourque. His number, 77, is re-tired by both the Bruins and the Avalanche. He stayed in Boston after his long tenure there and opened a restaurant in the historic North End neighborhood, just blocks from where he played for two decades. He also is a consultant with the Boston Bruins. Both of his sons play in the NHL system.

NHL TROPHIES: END-OF-THE-SEASON AWARDS

These trophies are awarded to exceptional players at the end of the hockey season. The trophies are named after either the individuals that donated them to the league or past players.

Hart Trophy: Best overall player in the league

Vezina Trophy: Best goaltender

Norris Trophy: Top defenseman

Calder Trophy: Best rookie in the league

Lady Byng Trophy: League's most gentlemanly player

Frank Selke Trophy: Top defensive forward

Jack Adams Award: League's best coach

Art Ross Trophy: Player who leads the league in scoring points

Maurice Richard Trophy: Leading goal scorer

FASHION AND FANDOM

First things first: The game is played on ice and ice is cold. It's too cold for a tank top or short sleeves. Most people will wear a sweater, sweatshirt, jacket, or long-sleeved jersey. It does not matter what the temperature is outside or how cute your new top looks; it is very important to bring something to cover up with or you will be cold. And braving it will make you look just plain stupid, at least at the beginning of the game. The arena will warm up a bit, even though the ice stays the same temperature; the more people in the arena, the warmer it will be. And you will get used to the temperature. What starts at around 58 degrees can easily feel like 70 by the end of the game.

Alyssa Roenigk from *ESPN The Magazine* has spent plenty of time in hockey arenas, both for work and for fun. There are a few tricks of the trade that she says every girl should remember before going to a hockey game. "There is one very important thing to remember about attending a hockey game. It is cold in those arenas. The playing surface is made of ice," Roenigk says. "Wear a thick bra. I don't think I need to elaborate."

Hockey has some of the most passionate fans in sports, hardcore fanatics. I can say with absolute certainty that hockey games have more people wearing team jerseys in the stands than any other North American sporting event. It could be that the jerseys are long-sleeved—since it's cold at a game, it's easy to know what to wear if you have a jersey. Or it could be that hockey fans are just the most passionate fans in sports. Regardless of the reason, you will see that most people will be wearing team jerseys. Personally, I'm not a huge fan of hockey jerseys. They are not the most flattering jerseys out there, because they are baggy and potato-sack-like. Nevertheless, there is still no problem with wearing one.

Now female fans can get their hands on smaller, somewhat form-fitting jerseys cut for a woman's figure. The NHL's official Web site offers gear like most other professional sports do now. Fans can purchase anything from crystal-covered team-logo T-shirts to headbands to over-the-top handbags made out of recycled team license plates. There are lots of cute fitted team T-shirts that can easily be layered for a comfortable and fan-friendly game look.

Because the game is often played in the same arena as the city's NBA affiliate, the same fashion rules apply for hockey and basketball. Although hockey is a more casual sport, the venue is just as nice, so it is okay to be a bit dressier for a game. The clean indoor arenas make for a pleasant viewing experience, especially considering the weather, so as long as you bring a sweater, anything you wear will be appropriate. I usually wear a fitted V-neck sweater layered over a tank top or T-shirt, depending on the weather outside. Jeans and heeled boots complete a look that can be worn in any arena. Of course flats are appropriate too, but due to the temperature inside the arena I do not recommend flip-flops or open-toed shoes of any kind.

Roenigk, who now lives in fashionable Los Angeles, moved there from even more fashionable New York City, so she has seen her fair share of horrors when working at or attending games. "In most instances, you want to steer away from looking like you're going to the club," Roenigk suggests. "However, for some this is acceptable attire at the Staples Center, as night games are often followed by a stop at a downtown L.A. club. Same goes for games in major cities like New York and Chicago."

THE GIRLIE GIRL'S HOCKEY GLOSSARY

Assist: A pass of the puck that leads directly to another player scoring a **goal**.

Blue line: One of the lines on either side of the **red line** that divide the **rink** into zones. These lines govern the offside rule and define the offensive, defensive, and neutral zones.

Boarding: A penalty called when a hockey player violently knocks an opposing player into the boards.

Center forward: The **forward** who plays in the middle of the **rink**. Primary job is to score **goals**.

Checking: Keeping an opposing hockey player from advancing to where he wants to by keeping him "in check," by using one's body to move, stop, or muscle the opponent out of position.

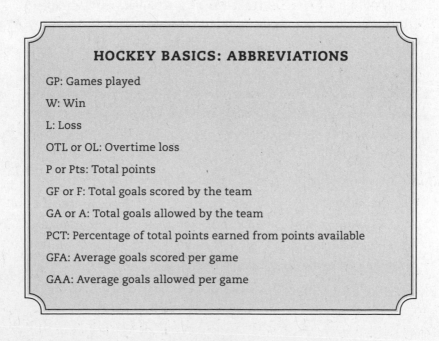

HOCKEY BASICS: ABBREVIATIONS

GP: Games played

W: Win

L: Loss

OTL or OL: Overtime loss

P or Pts: Total points

GF or F: Total goals scored by the team

GA or A: Total goals allowed by the team

PCT: Percentage of total points earned from points available

GFA: Average goals scored per game

GAA: Average goals allowed per game

Crease: Area right in front of the **goal** where the **goaltender** is not to be interfered with or a penalty will be called.

Defenseman: One of two players whose main job is defense and who play back near their own goal.

Face-off: The method of starting play. Two players stand inside the face-off circle, a referee drops the puck between them, and each tries to pass the puck to a teammate.

Forward: Player whose primary responsibility is offense and scoring goals. There are usually three forwards per hockey team on the ice.

Goal: When the puck enters the net or gets beyond the goal line inside the net. This is the only way to score in hockey. Each goal is worth one point.

Goaltender: The player who stands in front of the goal and whose job is to prevent the other team from scoring. The goalie, as he's called, wears extra pads and a mask, as high-speed shots are aimed at him throughout the game.

Hat trick: When a hockey player scores three goals in a single game.

Icing: A violation that occurs when a hockey player shoots the puck across both the **red line** and the opposing team's goal line without the puck going into the net. See "Icing," page 206, for more details.

Penalty box: Where a player sits to serve penalty time.

Penalty shot: Awarded when a hockey team loses an obvious scoring chance because of a foul committed by the opposing team. One hockey player gets to take a shot at the goal with only the **goaltender** playing defense.

Power play: When one team commits a penalty and one of

their hockey players has to go to the penalty box. The non-penalized team now has more players on the ice.

Red line: Splits the rink down the middle.

Rink: Where the game is played.

Save percentage: The percentage of shots on goal that a **goaltender** successfully stops. Judges goalie performance.

Slap shot: A shot where the player actually slaps the hockey stick onto the ice and uses the snap of the stick and the follow-through to propel the puck at great speed.

Slot: The area on the hockey rink in front of the **goaltender** and between the face-off circles.

Snap shot: A shot done with a quick snap of the wrists.

Zamboni: The machine that smoothes the surface of the ice.

5

College Football and College Basketball

COLLEGE FOOTBALL

I attended the University of Florida in Gainesville, where the Florida Gators play at Ben Hill Griffin Stadium (known as the Swamp or Florida Field). College football is very popular in the South. The South has the most fanatical fans and they take their football seriously. The first thing I noticed at my very first game was the sheer size of the stadium. I had been to NFL games and some college games before, but it wasn't until I entered the Swamp that I actually felt intimidated. The Swamp holds more than ninety thousand fans. And while that is almost a third larger than many NFL stadiums, it's not nearly the biggest. There are five college stadiums that hold more than a hundred thousand people. And these venues sell out for every game! Purchasing tickets to some college games can be harder than getting tickets to the Super Bowl. Not only do the current students want tickets, but so does everyone in the whole town or city, never mind the thousands and thousands of alumni who travel to games all over the country.

Game days in Gainesville are like those in many other big college towns where football rules the land. The sights, sounds, and smells are different from those you'll find at any other sporting event. The entire town walks the streets, all clad in school colors, like a festival filled with fans showcasing their school pride in a way unmatched by any professional sport. This scene is just one reason to attend a big college program's football game. The action starts early, and patrons must be prepared to make a whole day out of it.

Most college football games are played on Saturdays during the day. However, some big schools will play nationally televised night games as well. Many schools are "dry campuses," which means no alcohol will be served at the game. That is one reason the tailgating usually starts very early. So it's important to check your team's Web site to know the lay of the land.

In some big college towns, the RVs start wheeling in on Thursdays and Fridays before the games, and once that happens, it is officially the weekend. Town parking lots become campsites, and businesses thrive, while excitement fuels the electricity in the air in anticipation of game time. It's not only the businesses that thrive. Savvy students figure out ways to make an extra buck or two during the season as well. My senior year of college I lived in a house near the stadium, and we used to make our rent in less than two hours on early Saturday mornings by letting cars park at our house on the front lawn.

Walking into a college football stadium of any size will have a different feel from the NFL. For one thing, it's a younger crowd. Students of the home university usually get some sort of ticket discount. At my college we got season tickets for the price of a nice steak dinner. Then we could (illegally) sell our tickets to a big game for hundreds of dollars apiece! Most universities now require a student ID in order to use student tickets, preventing the moneymaking schemes of days past. One side of the stadium was mostly dedicated to students, and the other was mainly for alumni.

There are men on the cheerleading squads at college games, and the college cheerleaders rely more on acrobatics than the dancing all-women NFL squads. But the key ingredient at a college football game is the band. The clashing cymbals and drums are loud and pulsate through the crowd, leading the fans through their school cheers.

For many college football fans, it's never just a game; it's more like a way of life. There are entire cities that prepare their budgets and events around Saturdays in the fall. For some of these places, football season is the foundation of their entire economic plan for the year. There is more history and passion in college football than in professional football. The rivalries are deep; many date back more than a century. Identifying with a particular school is a badge of honor. Whether the loyalty is due to location, an alma mater, or a childhood memory, college football fans are committed to their teams.

College football is special because not only is it a look at the future of the NFL, it is rich with tradition, culture, and history. Many people prefer college football to the NFL and have valid reasons for doing so. One reason is that the players do not get paid. There's no showboating. No "show me the money"

STADIUM FUN FACTS

- The two largest college football stadiums (by seating capacity) are Penn State's Beaver Stadium and the University of Michigan's Michigan Stadium. Both hold more than 105,000 people.
- Five college football stadiums have 100,000 seats or more.
- Only four of the twenty-five largest stadiums in the U.S. are NFL stadiums.
- Sixteen college football stadiums average more than 80,000 people a game.
- Four college football stadiums average more than 100,000 fans a game.

attitude. No training-camp holdouts. No whining about contracts. It's just a group of young athletes playing football while living the rest of college life (studies, parties, and girls). For some players, a football scholarship is their only opportunity to go to college. For others, a love for the game keeps them playing. And for the elite few, it's a chance to make it to the NFL (and then get shown the money).

But it really is just an elite few who make it. According to the NFL Players Association, more than 100,000 high-school students play football. Only 9,000 of those athletes make it to play college ball. And then only 310 are invited to the NFL combine. Finally, only 215 will ever grace an NFL roster. That's only a 2.4 percent chance of making it to the pros from college.

College athletes pay their dues. They have to be students and athletes at the same time. They have to complete classes while completing passes. Some have to deal with celebrity and national television cameras but still eat dinner at the dining hall with their peers, or worse, try to avoid the paparazzi and media while running late to class. I can't imagine how difficult it would be to have to travel to different cities almost every weekend to play ball and then make sure to be back and prepared when the Philosophy 101 paper is due by Monday. Yes, the universities obviously offer some relief to the players during the season, but they still have to keep up grades in order to play.

COLLEGE FOOTBALL VERSUS THE NFL

The game of football is fundamentally the same at all levels. Because the NFL does not have a minor league system, college football basically serves as this system. But there are a few key differences between college and NFL rules. Here are the most important differences to know:

- Overtime: In college football, each team gets to be on offense. The first team starts at the opponent's twenty-five-yard line and gets one "possession," meaning it has the ball until it either scores or loses the ball on downs or by turnover. Then the other team gets its turn. The team with the most points then wins. If nobody scores, the process starts over again, with each team getting a new chance. If one team scores a touchdown and the other only a field goal, then the touchdown obviously wins. If both teams score the same points and the score is still tied, they start over.

- Only one foot needs to be inbounds and touching the ground when catching a pass in order for it to be complete. The NFL requires that both feet must be inbounds and touching the ground.
- In college football, the clock stops after a first down is made. In the NFL it does not.
- In college football, the hash marks are closer to the sidelines, so most plays start closer to the sidelines.
- Extra-point attempts are from the three-yard line in college football, while in the NFL they are from the two-yard line.
- In college ball, a player is considered down if any part of his body besides the hands and feet touches the ground, whether he is touched by the other team or not. In the NFL, if a player goes down but is not touched by a member of the other team, then he can get back up and keep going.
- There is no two-minute warning in college football.

DIVISIONS AND CONFERENCES

The National Collegiate Athletic Association (NCAA) is the governing authority for all college athletics. Schools belong to divisions based on the number of students, the size of the football program, attendance at games, and scholarships available for athletes.

The **Football Bowl Subdivision** (FBS, previously called Division I-A) is the highest level of intercollegiate athletics. The college football games seen on national television are mostly FBS games and involve the most well-known teams.

The biggest programs with the most students, scholarships, and best facilities are in the FBS. Examples of FBS teams are Miami (FL), the University of Southern California, Oregon, Nebraska, and Texas.

The **Football Championship Subdivision** (FCS, previously Division I-AA) is for schools that are almost big enough but just not yet ready for FBS play. Many of these schools are also well known, like the Ivy League schools, but their football programs aren't as large. Some of these schools move up into the bigger division after a few years of their football programs gaining national attention. The "midmajors," as they are called in the FCS, are determined based on attendance at games and scholarships provided.

There are also **Division II** and **Division III** football programs that have loyal followings, but these are at much smaller schools with smaller football programs, and they have their own tournaments and championships. The rules are the same, however, for whichever division a school plays in. There are more schools in Division III football than in any other division. But for this chapter's purposes we are focusing only on the big boys.

The FBS is made up of eleven conferences and Independents, mainly split up by regions. Below is a list of the eleven conferences and some notable teams that are a part of each conference (not all teams in the conference are listed); also listed are some well-known Independents.

Atlantic Coast Conference (ACC): Florida State, Boston College, Miami (FL), Clemson

Big East: South Florida, Rutgers, Syracuse, West Virginia

Big Ten: Michigan, Ohio State, Penn State, Wisconsin

Big 12: Nebraska, Oklahoma, Texas, Texas Tech

Conference USA: East Carolina, Marshall, Tulsa, Texas El Paso (UTEP)

Mid-American Conference (MAC): Ball State, Miami (OH), Temple

Mountain West Conference (MWC): Brigham Young, Air Force, Utah

Pacific 10 (Pac-10): California, UCLA, USC, Oregon, Arizona

Sun Belt: Florida Atlantic, Florida International, Middle Tennessee State, Troy

Southeastern Conference (SEC): Florida, Alabama, Georgia, Auburn, LSU

Western Athletic Conference (WAC): Boise State, Hawaii, Idaho

I-A Independents (not affiliated with any conference): Army, Navy, Notre Dame

Some conferences are bigger than others, and I don't mean just by size. The SEC, Pac-10, Big 12, Big East, Big Ten, and ACC are the best-known, big-name conferences. They not only get a lot of television time but almost always produce the national champion. That is because those six conferences are known as the **BCS Conferences** (see "The BCS" below). It's important to find out which conference your school is in and learn about the rivals you will most likely play during the season. Not all conferences have their own championship, but for those that do, it is an honor and a big deal to win the title. This is separate from the BCS bowl games and championships. Conference championships count as regular-season games in the eyes of the BCS.

THE BCS

The Bowl Championship Series (BCS), begun in 1998, is always controversial, dramatic, and full of surprises. It is the system that decides the bowl berths in FBS college football. The debate rages on year after year about whether or not the FBS should have a playoff or tournament system. Everyone from the mailman to the president of the U.S. has an opinion on it. But the BCS system has always prevailed, even when threatened with action by Congress.

The BCS determines who plays in the BCS National Championship Game, basically the Super Bowl of college football. The BCS system uses a mix of human polls and computers to determine the rankings, and the top two teams play in the big game. The BCS system also determines who is invited to play in other BCS bowl games, still prestigious but nowhere near the national championship game. The six champions of the BCS conferences all get invitations to a prestigious bowl game. The four BCS bowls are the **Orange Bowl** in Miami, Florida, the **Sugar Bowl** in New Orleans, Louisiana, the **Fiesta Bowl** in Glendale, Arizona, and the **Rose Bowl** in Pasadena, California. The National Championship Game takes place a week after the BCS bowls (which take place around New Year's Day), and the location of the event rotates among the four BCS bowl sites, so each site hosts the championship as well as its bowl once every four years.

The BCS is a complex statistical system but it is not an exact science and definitely has its flaws. The rankings are determined by formulas processed by computers, the **coaches poll,** and the **Harris poll**.

THE POLLS

The polls rank the **Top 25** programs in the country. The different polls are:

- Associated Press: sixty-five sportswriters cast their votes for the top teams
- Coaches: All FBS coaches cast their votes
- Harris: Votes are cast by a group made up of former players, coaches, and current and former media members chosen at random by the Harris Interactive organization
- BCS: Combines six different computer rankings, the coaches poll, and the Harris poll

The polls reflect what has happened during the previous day's games. The polls will change weekly depending on who wins and who loses. Most of the polls come out on Sunday afternoons. The BCS and Harris polls do not start until halfway through the season, since it isn't till then that enough results have accumulated to meaningfully rank teams. The AP does a preseason ranking that most people use as the main poll to begin the season. Many publications and television networks do their own polls—for example, Fox Sports.

THE OTHER BOWLS

Since the BCS came into the picture, some of the other bowls have suffered a bit. Years ago, just making it to any bowl game was a big deal; now only the BCS bowls get major attention.

The bowl games mark the end of the season for college football. In order to be "bowl eligible," meaning having the chance to be invited to a bowl game, a team must have won at least six games and not have finished with a losing record. Some conferences are associated with certain bowls; traditionally, the SEC champion always played in the Sugar Bowl, for example, and the Pac-10 and Big Ten champs always played in the Rose Bowl. Before the BCS, the conference champions would play in their respective bowl games, and then poll rankings would decide the national champion. Now there is the championship game to make it easier (at least it's supposed to make it easier) on the voters. The winner of the National Championship Game wins it all.

Many bowls are household names but not part of the BCS, like the Cotton Bowl and the Citrus Bowl. For some smaller schools, just getting an invitation to a bowl game is a tremendous feat. The most important bowls will be the last ones held. Usually the bowl season starts just before Christmastime, on the 20th or 21st of December, and runs through the first week of January. In 2009 there were thirty-four bowl games including the four BCS games and the national championship. New Year's Day has the most bowl games and is historically a day for college football. Just like Thanksgiving is associated with turkey and NFL football, New Year's Day is the best day in the world for college football fans. It's nonstop football all day and all night.

The first "bowl" game, in 1916, was called the Tournament of Roses Football Game. Once Rose Bowl stadium was completed in 1923, the name of the game was changed to just the Rose Bowl. The Rose Bowl holds the record for highest attendance for bowl games with more than 105,000 people a year. The Tournament of Roses is a festival of flowers, music, and

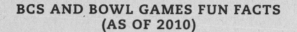

BCS AND BOWL GAMES FUN FACTS (AS OF 2010)

- The University of Nebraska holds the record for the most bowl game appearances in a row with thirty-five (1968–2003).
- Two active streaks of bowl appearances are Florida State with twenty-eight and Florida with nineteen.
- The University of Alabama holds the records for most bowl games played (fifty-seven) and won (thirty-two).
- The SEC has the most BCS bowl game wins.
- The most BCS bowl appearances go to Ohio State, USC, and Oklahoma.

equestrians that holds a major parade every New Year's Day. Originally, the football game was held as a way to fund the parade in Pasadena, California.

Other cities in warm climates saw this as a great money-maker and a way to drive tourism. By 1940 other cities got in on the action to promote winter tourism when air travel was not yet commonplace. The next bowls to pop up after the Rose Bowl were the Cotton Bowl in Dallas, the Sugar Bowl in New Orleans, and the Orange Bowl in Miami.

THE SEASON

Every game in the FBS is like a playoff game. Lose one and your school's national championship hopes are probably over. Although in recent years, one-loss teams have made it to the championship game (and won it all), the only way to almost guarantee your spot is to go undefeated. And even then you may not have a chance if your school is in a less prestigious conference. In a few instances, undefeated teams have not gone on to the championship game. The teams were good but played in conferences that didn't measure up according to the voters. There really isn't a set way to determine who should go. There is lobbying and debate every bowl season as to who "really" should be going to the championship. It's all just hype leading up to the final game.

Some games during the season are seen as "throwaways," where a school will play a grossly overmatched opponent. That's why sometimes you will see highlights on *SportsCenter* where the score was 65–0. It happens every season. A big-time school will usually play a couple of these "practice" games before getting into the conference matchups. These are the big rivalry games. Unlike the NFL, where rivals play each other twice a season, one game in each hometown, in college football, conference teams play each other only once a season, and the home-field advantage switches every year.

THE HEISMAN TROPHY

Ask any football fan to name the last five NFL MVP winners and there might be some head scratching. Ask a football fan who won the last five Heismans and the answers will flow as easily as a river. The Heisman Trophy is by far the most prestigious award football has to offer, including all the awards in professional football. Winning the Heisman is an honor that stays with a player for his entire life. A Heisman winner will always have that distinction.

The Heisman Trophy is awarded to the most outstanding

player in college football and is presented after the regular season, but before the bowl games begin. It is named after legendary and pioneering college football coach John Heisman. After Heisman's passing, just one year after the award was created (in 1935 it was called the Downtown Athletic Club Trophy, named after a private club formerly in downtown Manhattan), the award was renamed after Heisman. Heisman had a lot to do with the creation of the game of football that we know today and was a prominent figure in many rule creations, including the forward pass, the hike, and game flow (quarters instead of just halves).

The famous trophy is made of cast bronze and was modeled after a player named Ed Smith in 1934. Smith is not a well-known player or Hall of Famer, but he seems to have had a great season the year the award was created and so was considered the future of football. But Smith never won the Heisman. The trophy depicts a player running with the ball tucked under one arm, and the other arm stretched out for a straight-arm.

The trophy has its own history. Many players have sold theirs at auction for some extra money. They always sell for hundreds of thousands of dollars. In 1966 then–University of Florida quarterback Steve Spurrier donated his Heisman Trophy to the school so that the award could be shared with the students and faculty. The heartfelt action was so well received that the student government raised funds to purchase a new one for Spurrier. The gesture had lasting effects around college football because now there are two Heismans presented, one for the winning player and one for the winner's school.

The first African American to win the Heisman was the legendary running back Ernie Davis of Syracuse. Davis was one of the greatest college players of all time. But he never played in the NFL. He was diagnosed with leukemia shortly

after winning the Heisman in 1961 and died in 1963. Davis was the MVP of both the Cotton Bowl and the Liberty Bowl in the early 1960s.

All players in college football are eligible to be nominated for the Heisman, although all modern-age winners have come from the Football Bowl Subdivision (Division I-A) and most winners are from schools that are also contenders for the national championship. The voting is done by media representatives and split up into six regions in order to avoid regional bias. There are 145 media votes in each region. In addition, all previous Heisman winners have a vote. Each voter ranks his or her top three players one, two, and three. Nominees get three points for being ranked first, two points for being ranked second, and one point for being ranked third. All the points are tallied, and the athlete with the most points wins the Heisman.

HISTORY OF COLLEGE FOOTBALL

The first game on record called "football" was played in 1869 in New Jersey between Princeton and Rutgers. But the game was very different from today's. They used a round soccer ball, there was no forward pass, and the game was more of a soccer-rugby hybrid. The game was also more of a social event, with both teams dining together after the match. Its popularity grew at universities, and by 1875 Columbia, Harvard, Tufts, and Yale had added teams. By then, the ball was an egg-shaped rugby ball. The first newspaper to report a score of the game was *The Boston Globe*: In 1875 it reported the final score of a match between Tufts and Harvard. That game is also commemorated in the College Football Hall of Fame in South Bend, Indiana.

But it wasn't until 1880 that the "father of college football," Yale player Walter Camp, changed the rules to be more like what we know today. For an additional two years he continued to create innovations, introducing the concept of downs, specifying eleven players on each side, and devising verbal signals and strategy.

Although the sport had fans (records show that in 1878, two years before Camp's rule changes, Princeton and Yale played a match in front of four thousand in Hoboken, New Jersey, just across the Hudson River from Manhattan), it wasn't until 1903 that college football's popularity skyrocketed. That was the year that Harvard unveiled Harvard Stadium, a concrete, horseshoe-shaped football stadium. At the time, it was the largest project of its kind in the United States, and it was built as the first permanent football stadium. The architecture looks almost like the Colosseum in Rome. It is the oldest stadium in the country and is still used today in Allston, Massachusetts, home of Harvard's football team.

This new game called football became increasingly violent. Many injuries and even deaths occurred around the turn of the century. Padding wasn't sufficient, and the rugby-style rules didn't offer much protection for the players. There was a public outcry to change the rules to make it safer or to ban the game altogether. In 1905, President Theodore Roosevelt threatened to ban the game because of the number of on-field deaths. This is what led to the creation of the NCAA. It was necessary to have an organization that could control and regulate the game.

There were suggestions to widen the playing field in order to open up the game. But the expensive new Harvard Stadium had just been built, and widening the field would make the stadium useless. Instead, the NCAA added the forward pass to the rule book. They also banned "mass momentum" plays like the flying wedge, a play responsible for some deaths. The flying wedge was based on a military tactic: One team would be in a V-shape, and an opponent would throw himself at the legs of the wedge, almost like a bowling ball trying to knock down the pins. The person assuming the role of the bowling ball was sometimes seriously injured.

THE PROGRAMS

College football teams are sometimes called programs. That is because unlike professional football, where players come and go yearly due to trades and free agency, college teams are built to last. Most players stay for at least four years, sometimes five if redshirted. A player who is redshirted is "held out" his freshman year, when he takes classes and practices with the team but does not play in games. This is done for various reasons, mainly to let the player mature and learn a bit before heading into real playing time. It also gives the player five years of eligibility instead of the normal four years.

In the NFL today dynasties are rare due to salary caps (see "Sports Business Terms" in the Quick Guide) and even playing fields. College is all about recruiting. The candidates being recruited want to play for a team that has a winning program. They want a team that has a longtime coach with good standing at the school and within the community. And they want to play for a program that is among the best in the country over time. That's where the expression "rebuilding years" comes in. A school will need a lot of depth to stay strong over the course of a few years or even a few decades, but there will always be a time when most of the top talent leaves (either due to graduation or leaving for the NFL) and the team will have to make do with its younger players. Some top schools may have one or two rebuilding years but usually shoot back up to the top with their talented recruits.

RIVALS AND DRAMA

Because of college football's rich tradition and history, there are many rivalries. Here's a look at some of the best and most famous:

Harvard Versus Yale ("The Game"): This rivalry dates back to 1875. The two teams have played each other more than 125 times. But it is much more than just an old-time rivalry. These two schools are the most distinguished and oldest in the nation, which makes the game very intense. Ivy League schools rarely participate in postseason football games, and Ivy League players rarely go on to the NFL. (In 2008 there were ten Ivy Leaguers total in the NFL; the University of Miami alone, for example, had fifty-five.) For both schools, "the Game" is like their championship game. It doesn't matter what the season record is; all that matters is if you win. "The Game" is the last game of the season for both teams, in late November. The game is played at the Yale Bowl or Harvard Stadium and alternates yearly. It is also well known for having a large joint tailgate every year at each venue.

Army Versus Navy: The United States Military Academy (Army) versus the United States Naval Academy (Navy) just sounds like drama with no explanation needed. With the stands filled with men and women in uniform, plus a national television audience, this game is always a must-see for the season. It is the very last game of the season, usually played when other teams are playing their conference championships. As of 2009 the game is held the second Saturday in December, making it the last regular-season game of the year in any conference. Army and Navy have played each other since 1890. Players from these two schools rarely go to the NFL (the players will usually be too old to begin NFL play once they have finished their military commitments), but there have been some exceptions, like NFL Hall of Famer Roger Staubach. Because these players' careers end after college, winning this game becomes a rite of passage. The game is held at a neutral location (now in Philadelphia) in order to keep it fair.

Michigan Versus Ohio State: These two teams have played each other more than a hundred times. Their first meeting was in 1897. They compete almost annually for the Big Ten Conference title and a spot in the Rose Bowl. They have more than seventy-four conference titles and nineteen national championships between them. The big yearly game between these two storied squads has been held at the end of the season since 1935 due to the national interest and bowl implications. Both teams usually have national title hopes coming into the season, so this game sometimes determines more than just the conference champion.

Florida Versus Georgia ("The World's Largest Outdoor Cocktail Party"): These two SEC rivals have played each other since 1915. The game is played in Jacksonville, Florida, ostensibly neutral ground, even though Jacksonville is 73 miles from Gainesville, Florida, but 342 miles from Athens, Georgia. Still, the home team switches every year, and each team gets its own ticket allotments, to make things fair. The "Cocktail Party" is more like a weekend-long tailgate with one big party held at the Landings, a waterfront plaza with restaurants and bars. Following the 2005 season, the SEC asked all broadcasters to stop calling it the "Cocktail Party" because it associates both schools with alcohol, something neither school wants due to the rowdiness, injuries, and even deaths that have occurred during the weekend.

Texas Versus Oklahoma ("The Red River Rivalry"): This rivalry is more than a hundred years old. Both schools are usually at the top of their conference, and this annual match is a huge battle. Even though it isn't the Big 12 championship game, it very well could be—or should be. Originally the rivalry was called the "Red River Shoot-out," named after the river that separates parts of Texas and Oklahoma, but "Shoot-out" was dropped in 2006. This game is played at a neutral site halfway between both schools, at the Cotton Bowl in Dallas. Rumors say that this game may eventually be moved to the schools' own stadiums and will rotate annually. Both programs also usually have national title hopes, so this one game can make or break a school's entire season.

Lafayette Versus Lehigh ("The Rivalry"): Unless you are an avid college football fan, or live in eastern Pennsylvania, you may not have heard of either of these schools. They are much smaller than the other programs on this list, but they have such a storied history that this rivalry deserves a spot. Less than twenty miles separate the two schools. They have played each other since 1884 and have met more than 144 times, making it the most-played college football rivalry in the nation. Although Harvard and Yale began playing each other earlier, there were many years when they did not play but Lehigh and Lafayette did. Also, Harvard and Yale's early games were more like rugby, as the football rules didn't really change until 1883, one year before this rivalry started. But good luck getting a ticket—families, neighbors, and friends have been divided for more than a century over this game, which is on everyone's must-see-once-in-a-lifetime list.

Alabama Versus Auburn ("The Iron Bowl"): While other teams may get more attention paid to their rivalries, these two teams seem to really hate each other the most. The game is called the "Iron Bowl" because for most of its history it was played in Birmingham, Alabama, known for its iron and steel manufacturing. Now, however, the game is played at each school's home stadium, rotating yearly. The game is nationally televised, and there has been a lot of fighting, drama, and mudslinging between these two schools dating back to the very first game in February 1893, where Alabama said the game was the final matchup of the 1892 season and Auburn said it was the first of 1893. The fighting between coaches, players, and officials got so bad that play between these two schools was canceled in 1907 and did not resume again until 1947, when the Alabama House of Representatives passed a resolution urging the schools to resume the matchup.

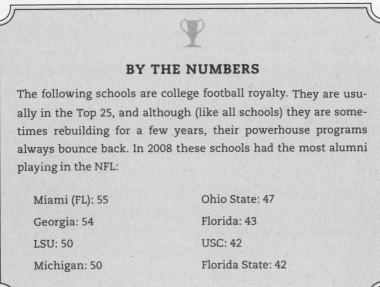

BY THE NUMBERS

The following schools are college football royalty. They are usually in the Top 25, and although (like all schools) they are sometimes rebuilding for a few years, their powerhouse programs always bounce back. In 2008 these schools had the most alumni playing in the NFL:

Miami (FL): 55	Ohio State: 47
Georgia: 54	Florida: 43
LSU: 50	USC: 42
Michigan: 50	Florida State: 42

Honorable Mentions: Florida versus Florida State, Florida State versus Miami (FL), Georgia versus Auburn, USC versus Notre Dame, USC versus UCLA, Kansas versus Missouri, Nebraska versus Oklahoma.

COLLEGE FOOTBALL LEGENDS

Joe Paterno ("JoePa") has been the head coach at Penn State since 1966 and holds the record for most games coached at the same school. He started at Penn State in 1950 as an assistant. Born in 1926, Paterno has won two national championships and countless Coach of the Year Awards. He also holds records for most bowl appearances (thirty-six) and victories (twenty-four). He has led Penn State to twenty-nine Top 10 end-of-season rankings (as of 2009). He is not just a Penn State institution; he is a college football institution, and his name is well known by all college football fans. Paterno was elected to the College Football Hall of Fame while still coaching.

Lou Holtz is the only college football coach to lead six different schools to bowl games and the only coach to lead four different teams to finish in the Top 20 at the end of a season. His college football expertise landed him a commentator role on ESPN, and he can be seen as an analyst talking about college football. Holtz has won many Coach of the Year honors and is enshrined in the College Football Hall of Fame.

Bobby Bowden was born in 1929 and since 1976 has been the head coach at Florida State University (FSU), where he has won two national championships and twelve ACC titles as of 2009. Bowden retired at the end of the 2009 season. He is second all-time in wins and bowl wins behind only Joe Paterno. He led FSU to fourteen straight finishes in the Top 5, an unheard-of feat that has not been duplicated and may never happen again. He was elected to the College Football Hall of Fame in 2006 while still coaching, something that only Paterno and two others have accomplished. Bowden is the patriarch of a distinguished college football family. His son Tommy Bowden was once the head coach at Clemson. Another son, Terry, was once the head coach at Auburn. Both had success on the field.

Ernie Davis ("The Elmira Express") was one of the greatest running backs in college football history. He was the first African American to win the Heisman Trophy and the first to be drafted number one in the NFL draft. But he never played an NFL game. Just after his historic number one selection in the NFL draft, he was diagnosed with leukemia, and he died shortly after that. His career at Syracuse was legendary; his team won the 1959 national championship, and he was chosen MVP of both the Cotton and Liberty bowls. His career is profiled in the 2008 movie *The Express* starring Dennis Quaid.

Paul "Bear" Bryant coached at Alabama for twenty-five years and won six national championships and thirteen conference championships. He was a ten-time SEC Coach of the Year winner and was inducted into the Hall of Fame in 1986. City streets, museums and even the stadium in Alabama are all named after Bryant. When he retired, he held the record for most wins as a head coach. Bryant was well known for his trademark houndstooth cap, which he always wore on the sidelines.

COLLEGE FOOTBALL TRADITIONS AND LORE

College football is all about tradition. The little things that each school does are what make it unique. Almost every school has some sort of tradition surrounding its football games. Unfortunately, it would take an entire book to examine them all. Here are some traditions that are famous throughout the country and college football.

Dotting the i in Script Ohio: Ohio State University's famous all brass and percussion 225-piece band (the largest of its kind) spells out "Ohio" in cursive on the field in remarkable precision, and then a fourth- or fifth-year sousaphone player gets to "dot the i." Once "Ohio" is spelled out, the sousaphone player selected for that game trots to his "dotting" position and takes a bow to each side of the stadium. This ritual dates back to 1937. Sometimes, an honorary "i dotter" is selected; Bob Hope and Jack Nicklaus have been among those chosen.

Howard's Rock at Clemson: Legendary Clemson coach Frank Howard received a two-and-a-half-pound rock as a gift from a friend who found it in Death Valley. Lore says that Coach Howard gave it to a Clemson booster, who put it on a pedestal at Clemson's Memorial Stadium. After that Clemson came back and won a big game they'd been losing by eighteen points, and the rock became a symbol of luck and legend. Now, and every game since 1967, the Clemson football players all rub the rock before running down a grass hill to enter their stadium, dubbed "Death Valley."

Pink Locker Room at Iowa: The visitors' locker room at the University of Iowa's Kinnick Stadium is pink. Really, really pink. But it isn't just on the walls. It's on the floor. The lockers. The showers. The toilets. Everything is pink. It was the brainchild of former Iowa coach Hayden Fry, who also had a degree in psychology. He ordered the pink walls because it was supposed to be calming. And calm is the last thing any football coach wants. He wants fire and passion. But some people say Fry did it strictly to mess with his opponents' heads. Either way, it worked and the pink locker room is still at Iowa.

The Sooner Schooner: Oklahoma University's (OU) Sooner mascot is a covered wagon called the Sooner Schooner. It is pulled by two white horses named Boomer and Sooner. The Schooner is pulled across the field after every OU score.

Traveler: The University of Southern California's recognizable mascot is Traveler, a pure white horse. Various Travelers have trotted up and down the sideline at every home game since 1961. When USC scores, Traveler and his rider (a student dressed up as a Trojan) gallops up and down the sidelines at the L.A. Coliseum, where USC plays its home games.

Running through the T: The University of Tennessee Volunteers marching band forms a T on the field during the pre-game festivities. Then they open up the T into a block letter. The football team then sprints from their tunnel through the T, with 100,000 fans at Neyland Stadium screaming them on. Tennessee's Neyland Stadium is also famous for its checkerboard end zones, a unique feature that has been copied but will always be a Volunteer tradition.

The 12th Man: Texas A&M University's trademarked 12th Man is actually the entire student body in the stands. The tradition of calling the fans the "12th Man" started in 1922, when the underdog Aggies were playing the top-ranked team in the nation, Centre College, and were losing badly. With the sidelines getting thin and reserves getting hurt, the head coach, Dana X. Bible, remembered that an eligible player named E. King Gill was up in the press box. Although Gill was actually playing only basketball and not football anymore, he was still on the roster. He was called up in the stands and came down, suited up, and stood by on the sidelines in case he was needed. The Aggies came back to win the game. Gill never played, but his gesture of taking the call and being ready to play was warmly received by all involved, and he became known as the 12th Man; the term is now used for the whole student body in spirit. The Aggies' fans are also famous for another tradition: After every touchdown the men in the stadium all kiss their girlfriend, wife, or fiancée.

"We are the Boys from Old Florida": The song "We Are the Boys from Old Florida" has its own lore because there are so many contradictory stories about who actually wrote the tune. It is still a mystery to this day. But Florida Gator fans have been singing it since the 1930s. At the end of the third quarter at football games at Ben Hill Griffin Stadium all of the fans lock arms, sway in unison, and sing the song. Just after the second-to-last line everyone takes a long pause and the ninety thousand singing fans all stop in unison before finishing the last line swaying.

Touchdown Jesus: Notre Dame Stadium, home of the University of Notre Dame Fighting Irish football team, is watched over by a neighbor, a mural on the side of a library building that overlooks the stadium. The top of the mural is a resurrected Jesus with his arms held up over his head like a referee signaling for a touchdown.

Chief Osceola: The Florida State University Seminoles' mascot is Chief Osceola (named after the famed Seminole Indian leader); he rides Renegade, an Appaloosa horse. To begin every home game, Chief Osceola rides Renegade down the field and hurls a burning spear at midfield. Only when the Seminoles play in-state rival Florida at home does Osceola jump off the horse before hurling the spear. Although in recent years there has been much controversy about sports teams and their names and mascots portraying Native Americans, the university has a good relationship with the Seminole Tribe of Florida and has received its blessing to continue using the name.

Nittany Lion Roar: The Penn State mascot, the Nittany Lion, roars when the team scores and leads the crowd in the famous "We are . . . Penn State" cheer during every game.

Boats on Lake Washington: Perhaps the most scenic stadium in the country is the University of Washington's Husky Stadium, where fans can arrive at the game by boat. The stadium overlooks Lake Washington, and with mountains in the background, the gleaming water, and the boats just off the east end zone, the picturesque scenery makes this a can't-miss stadium visit. The boats also take part in a great tailgate party.

TAILGATING: COLLEGE FOOTBALL EDITION

Tailgating is an art, and in college football the work is among the best in the world. This list of the best tailgates in the nation could be fifty deep. Some fantastic tailgates are left off this list due not to lack of creativity, but to lack of space. This list is based on every-game fun, not just a single-game event (sorry, Harvard versus Yale, though your joint tailgate is amazing) and not just the number of people that attend (sorry, Ohio State, though your 100,000 fans surround the stadium every game day). The quality of food, tradition, atmosphere, and that certain je ne sais quoi make these tailgates the best.

Ole Miss: The University of Mississippi's weekend-long party is held at a place called "the Grove," a ten-acre oasis of oak, magnolia, and elm trees. Getting tent space is like handling a real estate transaction. Frat boys and CEOs mix together in the shade under leafy canopies, eating off of silver trays, not paper plates. The Grove has strict rules (including setup times and a ban on cars) and unwritten rules that are followed by all. For example, the fashion: Flip-flops are acceptable at this party only after your feet hurt from your high heels. That's right. A new dress and pearls are a given every weekend for the females at Ole Miss football games and tailgates (see "Fashion," page 257).

Penn State: Pennsylvania State University turns State College into the third-largest city in the state on game days. With more than 100,000 people joining in on just the tailgate, things started to get a little crazy in "Happy Valley" (the town nickname). So crazy, in fact, that the town had to enact a law banning drinking outside the stadium during the game in order to keep the party in check.

Tennessee: The University of Tennessee's tailgate is something to see. Hundreds of thousands of people line the streets on one side of the stadium, and boats tie up on the nearby Tennessee River and hold their own tailgate. This event has the beauty of the water and boats, but also the passion of football in the South. Tennessee is also well known for its delicious, award-winning pregame barbecue.

Wisconsin: Since the state is known for its cheese, beer, and bratwurst, and there isn't a more perfect combination for throwing a great tailgate, of course the University of Wisconsin Badgers had to make the list. The fantastic tradition of the "Fifth Quarter" means that the Badger band stays after the game (along with an estimated thirty thousand to forty thousand fans) and plays songs and performs a choreographed show. The tailgating outside is waiting for them, with the region's specialties chilled or fired up on the grill.

LSU: Louisiana State University, located near Baton Rouge, is as Deep South as you can get. This is Cajun country, where Southern and French cuisines and styles mix. While LSU fans take their successful football program seriously, they also take their tailgating seriously. It is all about the food. This isn't your typical burger and hot dog grill-out. Jambalaya, crawfish, boiled shrimp, gumbo, rabbit dishes, Cajun sausage, and alligator stew fill up the plates and stomachs of students and alumni attending the weekend-long festivities. The party starts Wednesday night because the RVs and tailgaters arrive early to start the action. The tailgating is so serious that some people have their parties sponsored by local bars, restaurants, and companies.

COLLEGE FOOTBALL AND COLLEGE BASKETBALL

FASHION

There are no rules for college football attire because each individual school and each individual game is so tied in to traditions, history, and culture. From one week to the next the atmosphere can change depending on who the opponent is and where the game takes place. Every school has its own style and its own way of attending football games. For some, it's just like a normal football game. The difference between these games and NFL games is that college has more fanfare. As a student of that university, you feel passionate about the game. This is your school, your team, your campus. There are temporary tattoos, face paint, beads, and hair ribbons in school colors, and almost everyone will be in some sort of team gear. And I mean everyone—from your seventy-five-year-old grandpa in a team sweater vest, to your mom in a cute fitted T-shirt, to your roommate in a woman's jersey, with face paint, beads, and the team name written across her butt. The fanfare is so overdone at college games that you really can't be too over-the-top when it comes to supporting your school. No matter how all out you go on the team wear, there will be somebody more overdone than you. I've seen men in full body paint and overalls. Doesn't get much worse than that.

General game rules still apply: Skip the gray team T-shirt especially during hot games (gray shows the most sweat). Also, stiletto high heels are a no-no unless you are in certain parts of the Deep South (see below). For shoes, NFL rules apply, with sneakers a top choice in case you get stepped on or spilled on. At the beginning of the season, it will still be warm in most parts of the country, as college football starts earlier than the NFL. Although your feet will get dirty, most students and tailgaters will be in comfortable flip-flops and sandals when it's still warm. This is a college game, so more laid-back attire will be prevalent. But the fall season creeps in quickly, and by midseason boots, scarves, and jackets may be necessary.

Kelly Petersen, a fashionista who has worked for Shopbop. com, one of the most fashionable retail sites on the Web, went to the University of Wisconsin and knows a thing or two about her Badgers playing in the fall in the Midwest. "The most important aspect of being comfortable at a game is keeping warm," says Petersen. "If you want to look hot and stay warm, wear a wedged fur- or faux-fur-lined boot. Autumn in Wisconsin is rainy and cold. Make sure that you have your waterproof mascara, and the weather will keep your cheeks rosy pink all by itself."

For a nationally televised night game, I will wear a little more makeup, jeans, and a wedge or boot with my jeans long, so it doesn't look like I'm wearing heels. Unless you are still in college, skip the team jewelry and temp tattoos as makeup. It's possible to look great while cheering for your team without looking like a teenager. Going to a college game is about having fun and wishing you were still in college, rather than dressing like you still *are* in college.

Campus stores and team Web sites started carrying tees, tanks, and jerseys cut for a woman's figure when most of the other sports did, but recently retailers like Victoria's Secret— the Pink line—and luxury denim brand Chip & Pepper got in on the action and now offer lightweight and soft T-shirts and sweatshirts with a vintage college feel. So if you attended college ten or twenty years ago, your cute fitted tee can look as if you had it back in college, but it won't smell as if you did.

In the South, where football is religion, Saturdays are holy days. That may explain why the girls dress up for the football games and tailgates—it's as if they're dressing for church. It's all about tradition, and southern girls traditionally want to dress like ladies. It's putting forth your "Saturday best." At schools like Ole Miss, Auburn, and Georgia, it is common to see women in dresses of all lengths, but usually knee-length. They will pair them with sky-high stiletto heels, wide-brimmed hats, and pearls (although a few girls have told me they always bring flip-flops when it's warm, just in case the heels get to be too much). These girls also wear full makeup to the games. They look gorgeous, and although they probably aren't the most comfortable people there, it is tradition, and that is all that matters to them and to the rest of the 100,000 people cheering on their school.

COLLEGE BASKETBALL

NCAA basketball is a very popular sport and not just among students. Although players can go to the pros or the NBA Development League practically straight from high school, college basketball is still a breeding ground for NBA talent. And there is plenty of ground to cover because there are more than twice as many Division I teams in NCAA basketball as in NCAA football.

Like college football fans, fans of college basketball have a real connection to the team they support. They aren't just fans because they live near a particular team. A deep-rooted love for an alma mater can go back generations. Because college sports loses its players every four years, the love fans feel for their college team is different from the love for pro teams. Once a player is a success in college football or basketball, the player will always be remembered by the fans of that school, even if the player does not fare well in the pros.

There are 347 schools and thirty-two conferences in Division I basketball. There are also six Independents. That means a lot of schools and a lot of talent. By comparison there are only twelve Division I college football conferences.

The season usually begins in November, with major conference play (the important games) beginning in January. Fans sometimes don't start watching until conference play begins. At some schools, basketball is the most popular sport, like at the University of North Carolina and Duke University. At Duke, students line up months in advance to get a coveted spot in the

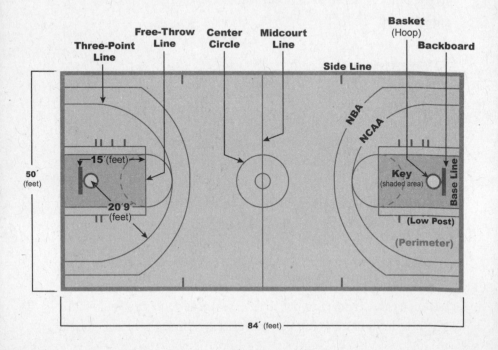

student section (more on this later). The schools that are really big in college basketball aren't necessarily the same schools that are big in college football. There are some notable exceptions, like Florida, UCLA, and Ohio State, but traditionally, the successful, well-known schools that you hear about during basketball season are different from what you hear about during football season.

Teams play around thirty games, although some play more and some play less. It all depends on what conference your team plays in and what division. It's best to check your team's Web page for the most up-to-date information on the team's schedule.

COLLEGE BASKETBALL VERSUS THE NBA

Although the NBA derived from college basketball, there are significant rule differences between the two.

- The NBA plays four twelve-minute quarters. College basketball plays **two twenty-minute halves.**
- The three-point line in college basketball is closer to the basket than the NBA line is (see graphic).
- The college basketball **shot clock is thirty-five seconds,** while the NBA shot clock is twenty-four seconds.
- The width of the "paint," or lane, is twelve feet in college basketball, narrower than the NBA's sixteen feet.
- In the NBA, players foul out on their sixth foul. In college basketball, a player is gone when he reaches **five fouls.**
- In college basketball, a team goes into penalty after the seventh team foul. In the NBA it's on the fifth team foul. Also, in college basketball, on team fouls seven through

ten, the other team shoots a **one-and-one**. That means a player shoots one free throw. If he makes it, he gets another. If he misses, the ball is live (up for grabs) and teams go for the rebound. After the tenth team foul, the free-throw shooting goes to an automatic two shots, and the one-and-ones are over.

• Besides the opening tip, there are no jump balls in college basketball. Possession disputes go to whichever team has the possession arrow in its favor at that time.

MARCH MADNESS

The NCAA Men's Division I basketball championship is known as March Madness or the Dance, and it is anticipated yearly not only by college basketball fans but by millions of office workers excited about that year's office pool. The tournament takes place mostly in March every year.

The "championship" isn't just a game; it is a single-elimination (lose and you are out) tournament that began in 1939 with a starting field of eight teams. The tournament as we know it today (with sixty-four teams) began in 1985. In 2001, however, a sixty-fifth team was introduced. The sixty-five teams that play all qualify during their regular seasons. The number 64 and 65 seeds play first in the "play-in game" to determine who the final 64th seed will really be. This is because the real tournament has only 64 spots. This game is usually held on the Tuesday before the tournament begins.

About half of the field earns an automatic bid to the tournament by winning their conference tournaments at the end of the regular season. The rest of the teams are selected by the NCAA Selection Committee. This committee also determines where

March Madness Bracket

all of the teams are seeded in the bracket. Teams are split into four regions and then seeded 1 through 16, with a number 1 seed being the highest and 16 being the lowest. A team seeded 16 is very lucky to make the tournament and was most likely on the "bubble" on whether or not it would get in. The selection show, popularly called "Selection Sunday," is nationally televised so that the entire country (with cable TV) can see which teams make it to the tournament. The cameras show teams sitting in their locker room or somewhere else, usually on campus, all awaiting their call and watching the same program we are to see where they will be seeded or if they will even get in.

The Madness Begins

The four regions are the East, South, West, and Midwest. Each region is its own mini tournament. It is important to note that the names of the regions are misleading. Just because it says "East" doesn't mean that the teams will actually be from the East. A Virginia team could be in the "South" and an Atlanta team could be in the "Midwest." This is also because the entire tournament must be on "neutral" ground, and teams are prohibited from playing on their own court. They may play in their hometown or home city, but not home court. This may seem confusing, but it's the way the NCAA sorts it out.

The regional play takes place at separate locations, and the games go on simultaneously. I think this is where the term "March Madness" comes into play. The tournament *is* madness, with sixty-four teams all playing over the course of just a few days. It's also the last month of winter, when many northern fans are feeling seasonal depression. The term was actually first coined in 1939 by a talented sportswriter and high-school basketball official in Illinois named H. V. Porter. He used it in reference to high-school basketball tournaments. The term picked up steam throughout the decades and was eventually trademarked by the NCAA in conjunction with the Illinois High School Association in the 1990s.

The field dwindles as the first two rounds are played on the opening weekend of the tournament. The regional brackets are split into "pods," and these first two rounds are played at eight different sites around the country. After the first two rounds, the regional semifinals are played the second weekend of the tournament; the regional semis are popularly known as the **Sweet Sixteen.** The winners move on to the regional finals, known as the **Elite Eight**. The winners of those advance to the **Final Four.** The Final Four may be the most popular part of the tournament because some of the best games happen then rather than in the championship. It's possible to have a one-versus-two matchup in the Final Four and a two-versus-five matchup in the Championship Game. It all depends on how the tournament goes throughout the country. The two winners of the Final Four go on the **Championship Game**.

The Final Four is held in Indianapolis, Indiana, every five years because that is where the NCAA is located. The rest of the time the tournament changes locations.

It is tradition for the four winning teams of regional play (the Final Four) and the winner of the Championship Game to cut down the net from the arena. They literally climb a ladder placed on the court and use scissors to cut the net. The tradition starts with the seniors; then the juniors take a turn, and so on. The players cut a piece of the net to take with them to commemorate the event. Traditionally, the head coach goes last and takes the rest of the net with him.

The term "**Cinderella story**" in sports really comes into play most with college basketball. The same popular fairy tale that we all know and love is used often in sports. A "Cinderella" team is a team that makes it a lot further along in a tournament (or does better in any sport) than anyone would have thought. A Cinderella team is usually a low seed and gets a lot of attention from the media and fans because of the "David versus Goliath" type of story. The media takes the fairy-tale concept even further. When the Cinderella team loses in the end, terms like "the clock has struck midnight" or the team has "turned back into a pumpkin" pop up in sports columns across the country. It happens almost every year.

There have only been two Cinderella stories in college basketball where Cinderella did not turn back into the maid. The 1983 North Carolina State Wolf Pack were seeded sixth (in 1983 the seeds went only to twelve); the team North Carolina State played in the Championship Game, the University of Houston Cougars, were heavily favored and a number-one seed in the tournament. The Cougars were a nationally popular team that had two future NBA stars, Hakeem Olajuwon and Clyde Drexler. The upset became college basketball's first real Cinderella story. The second was two years later: In 1985, the Villanova Wildcats were an eighth-seeded team who defeated the top-seeded Georgetown Hoyas to take the championship. As of 2009, an eighth-seeded team is the lowest to ever win it all. There have been many notable Cinderellas that didn't win it all. Fans always want to see a Cinderella in the tournament, and sometimes years without one can seem dull to the average fan.

Gambling

In 2006 the *Seattle Times* reported that the FBI said at least $2.4 billion will be bet by Americans on the NCAA tournament. There have been countless articles on antigambling Web sites and in parenting magazines to try to curb America's gambling addiction, even if it is just social bets on college sports.

It is all illegal, but betting on sports, especially college sports, is nevertheless widespread. Offices around the country have "pools," and brackets are easily downloadable from the Internet. A lot of office managers I spoke to say they offer the pools to boost worker camaraderie through competition and fun. At my first internship, for a pro hockey team, we did an office pool. Everyone put in $10 or $20 and filled out their brackets. I had my brother do mine. After losing the first few games, I came back and won every game left and ended up winning the whole thing. The men and higher-ups weren't too pleased that a high-maintenance-looking young female won their office pool. I got many e-mails asking if I chose my picks "based on how pretty the uniforms are." I never told anyone that my brother filled out the form, and I haven't played again.

Betting on sports is a billion-dollar business that has been around for more than a century, and it is not going away anytime soon. If you do choose to bet on the tournament (or any game in any sport, for that matter), do your research and make responsible choices, preferably not based on uniform colors.

The NIT

The National Invitational Tournament (NIT) is another postseason tournament run by the NCAA that is also held in March and April, and it intensifies March Madness. The tournament actually began in 1938, but due to the success of the NCAA Division I basketball championship, and since the top teams go to that tournament, the NIT has become more of an afterthought. But NIT officials will argue that since thirty or so of the bids are automatic for the other tournament, some better teams end up in the NIT.

Although the NIT is nationally broadcast it really is seen as a "consolation prize" for not going to the Big Dance. Nicknames include the "Not Invited Tournament," the "Not Important Tournament," and the "Not In Tournament," and sometimes "NIT" will be chanted by fans of other schools mocking a school's bid to that tournament.

Sometimes notable teams do play in the NIT. After the University of Florida won back-to-back national championships at the Big Dance in 2006 and 2007, they didn't make the tournament the following year and went to the NIT. Some coaches will use it as a way to give younger players a chance to play on the national stage and get some big-game experience.

RIVALS

College basketball rivalries are intense. There are teams and fans that have despised each other for decades. The rivalries listed below are ones that even the most casual fan should know about. Even during rebuilding years, when the two teams play each other it is more than just a game; it's an all-out bloodbath. For seniors on either team, defeating their rival can be their greatest college feat. Here are the biggest rivalries in college basketball:

Duke University Versus the University of North Carolina: Duke University and the University of North Carolina are both college basketball royalty. So it is no surprise that this rivalry is considered *the* rivalry, meaning the greatest of all time. The "Tobacco Road" rivalry (named after the tobacco-producing region where the schools are located) stems from many factors. The first is location. Less than twenty miles separate the two campuses. Some parts of the campuses are only eight miles apart. Students, teachers, and employees of both schools live in the same neighborhoods, go to the same restaurants, and share the same dry cleaners. It is a surreal 365-day-a-year rivalry. Families, neighbors, and friends can be separated by the rivalry because the traditions go back generations. Both schools became college basketball powerhouses early on (they have been playing each other since 1920) and compete in the same conference. Duke and North Carolina are usually competing for the ACC championship, and when they play each other, it is a nationally televised event, with Fortune 500 companies spending millions to advertise during their regular-season games (they play twice a year). They have played each other more than 130 times.

Krzyzewskiville

Some schools do not offer tickets to the basketball games for students. The students get to go on a first-come, first-served basis, meaning, wait in line and hope to get in. Duke has taken it to a whole other level. Krzyzewskiville (K-Ville for short) is named after longtime Duke head coach Mike Krzyzewski (see "College Basketball Coaching Legends," below). It's an area of grass outside Duke's Cameron Indoor Stadium, where the team plays. The students camp out before games to be let in. The doors open an hour and a half before game time. The Duke-UNC game is a "tenting" game, meaning students set up tents and wait in the hopes of getting in. But this isn't a night or two camping out. Groups of up to twelve students set up tents and stay there for months. Yes, months. Most tents start popping up around Christmastime, and come January it is officially "tenting season." The game is usually in February. The student government has specific rules about the tenting: One person must be there during the day, and eight people must be in a group at night. Student government representatives check to make sure people are following rules; those who aren't are moved to the back of the line. It is strict, crazy, and a Duke rite of passage for all students to do at least once. Since 2000, K-Ville has been laid with grass to make tenting easier, and it is also equipped with Wi-Fi for students so they do not forget about their studies.

The University of Louisville Versus the University of Kentucky: The Battle of the Bluegrass State is always a big deal for basketball-crazy Kentucky. But this rivalry stems from more than competing schools. Rick Pitino (see "College Basketball Coaching Legends," next page) coached for many years at

Kentucky and had great success there. He now coaches at Louisville. Both schools are national powerhouses and usually have successful programs. Decades ago, the two teams' head coaches hated each other so much that the schools did not play each other between 1959 and 1983. Then the NCAA forced it to happen by having the two teams play in the tournament in 1983. The next year, the game dubbed the "Dream Game" was back on the schedule even though these two teams are in different conferences.

The University of Missouri Versus the University of Kansas: The states of Kansas and Missouri have been fighting since the Civil War. The passion and hatred dates back more than a century, and it's not just the fans that want in on the rivalry. Players and coaches are also very serious about it. Legend says that a former coach of one school refused desperately needed medical attention unless he could go back to his own state. Another legend says that a former coach of one school wouldn't let his players eat or let the bus driver get gas in the other state because he didn't want to contribute to that state's economy. Really. When these two schools play, the game is popularly called the "Border War" or the "Border Showdown." The two teams have been playing each other since 1907 and have played more than 260 times.

COLLEGE BASKETBALL COACHING LEGENDS

John Wooden is one of only three people to be elected to the Basketball Hall of Fame as a coach and a player. He won ten NCAA national championships in twelve years, including seven in a row while head coach of the UCLA Bruins. No other school has more championships than UCLA. He led the Bruins to four undefeated seasons, something that has never been duplicated. At ninety-eight years old he continues to lecture and serves as head coach emeritus at UCLA.

Bob Knight is well known for his almost thirty years coaching the Indiana Hoosiers. He won three NCAA national championships and won the Big Ten Coach of the Year six times. He also led the Hoosiers to an undefeated season (32–0). In 1984 he coached the USA Olympic Team to a gold medal. Knight is even more famous for his temper and an almost military rule over his game. His teams were never sanctioned by the NCAA (something rare nowadays), and he is well known for running "clean" programs. His firing from Indiana was controversial. A player accused Knight of choking him, and a few years later another said Knight grabbed his arm. While some allegations have not been proven, others were caught on tape. The Indiana administration adopted a "zero-tolerance" policy, and Knight was ousted.

Mike Krzyzewski (Sha-CHEF-ski), known as Coach K, started as an assistant at Indiana under Bob Knight and started coaching the Duke Blue Devils in 1980; he still coaches there. He coached the 2008 Summer Olympic team to a gold medal. He turned Duke into a basketball powerhouse, winning three NCAA national championships and eleven ACC titles so far in his tenure. He is a member of the Basketball Hall of Fame and has led Duke to twenty-four tournament berths in twenty-five years, including twenty-four in a row (as of the beginning of the 2009 season).

Rick Pitino has been coaching for more than twenty-five years. He has coached at six different colleges and is most famous for his time at Kentucky, where he led the college basketball powerhouse to a national championship and five SEC tournament championships. He has been coaching at Kentucky's rival, Louisville, since 2001. He is the only coach in NCAA history to lead three different schools to the Final Four. Pitino had three brief coaching stints in the NBA, twice with the New York Knicks (one as an assistant, one as a head coach) and once with the Boston Celtics. He returned to college coaching after his time with the Celtics.

THE GAME EXPERIENCE

College basketball fashion is different from NBA fashion. Although college games are played at indoor arenas just like the pro games, it is a much more casual environment. Most arenas are on campus, so traditional college attire will be prevalent. Team T-shirts and jerseys will be worn by most fans, and at some schools the fans go wild. Body paint, wigs, and other extravagances will be everywhere.

It's hard to go wrong in layered team-colored T-shirts and jeans at a college game. A college basketball game will seem more intimate than an NBA game, and much more casual. The NBA can be dressy if you want it to be; a college basketball game is not.

College arenas are usually smaller than NBA arenas. Some have capacities of only 6,000 or 7,000; but others, like Kentucky's Rupp Arena, can seat up to 23,000, which is like an NBA arena. It's very important to check your tickets or a map of the arena before going to the game to familiarize yourself with the locations of the closest restrooms and concessions. That way you won't miss most of the game by walking around aimlessly looking for things. Because the game is played in halves and not quarters, the game seems to go by much more quickly than an NBA game.

In college basketball, the game time is different than in the pros. Each team is allowed four seventy-five-second time-outs and two thirty-second time-outs per game that is *not* televised. For televised games, each team gets one sixty-second time-out and four thirty-second time-outs, and there are also four "media" time-outs, popularly known as TV time-outs. Any player on the court or the coach can call a time-out.

Because college basketball is played in two twenty-minute halves and not in quarters, leaving the seats becomes a game of cat and mouse. Halftime is fifteen minutes but that will be the most crowded time to leave, since there are no other major breaks. In order to beat the rush, it is best to leave your seat about halfway through each half. Yes, you will miss some of the game, but it is better than waiting in a line that lasts longer than halftime because everyone else in the arena has also left his or her seat.

The fans at college basketball games will probably be much rowdier than NBA fans. The "student sections" will be loud and have the craziest fans. Some of these fans taunt opposing players and coaches, sometimes with no mercy. Fans have been sanctioned in the past for some of their antics. If you do not want to partake, it is best to find seats away from the student section. It's also important to note that because many college campuses are "dry" campuses, if the arena is on campus, there will not be any alcohol served at the game. This is, of course, different from NBA arenas, where the beer and other alcoholic drinks are plentiful.

6

The World's Games

Tennis and golf are different from most other sports because they are both individual sports. Instead of thirty players on one team it's just one man or woman out there. There are really two challenges for each player: the battle with the other player and the battle inside his or her own head. Tennis and golf are also international sports. Yes, baseball and hockey have Canadian teams and travel there to play, but tennis and golf incorporate international players and locations into their everyday tournaments. Games are played in many different countries across the world. Roger Federer is Swiss but plays in many tournaments on American soil. Phil Mickelson is American and plays in Great Britain frequently. Unlike soccer, where the U.S. team travels together and plays in world tournaments as Team USA, tennis and golf have regular seasons and structure, and because these are individually played sports, in reality, country doesn't matter. Many tennis and golf fans may not realize that their favorite player isn't from the United States.

Unlike team sports, where athletes have contracts with certain teams, these sports are all about the individual, who earns money by how well he or she plays. Purses are set up for golf tournaments with the players each taking a share depending on how well they do. The winners of major tennis and golf tournaments can take home a million dollars just from winning one tournament. On top of money earned from playing, many tennis and golf stars have lucrative endorsement deals with various companies, boosting their earnings far higher than many other athletes'. Many of the top earners in the world of sports come from tennis or golf.

TENNIS

THE GAME

There are two sides of a tennis court on each side of the net: the deuce court (the right side) and the advantage court (the left side). Tennis is played in two ways: singles (one-on-one) and doubles (two-on-two). In singles tennis, there are two players standing on opposite ends of the court. One is the server and the other is the receiver. The server tosses the ball in the air and hits it into the opponent's court. The ball must land in the opponent's front court on the deuce side, diagonal from where the

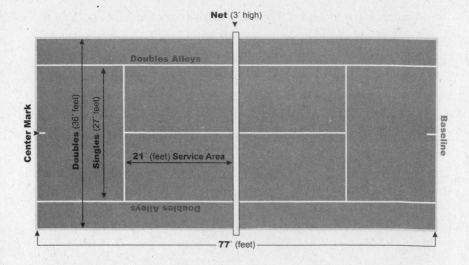

Net (3′ high)

Doubles Alleys

Center Mark

Doubles (36′ feet)

Singles (27′ feet)

21′ (feet) Service Area

Doubles Alleys

Baseline

77′ (feet)

server starts. If the ball doesn't bounce in that box (called the service court) it is a fault. Or if the ball goes in the net it's a fault. A **fault** is a warning. Another reason for a fault is if the server's foot touches the baseline before the server hits the ball. The server gets one fault as a freebie. If he commits two faults in a row (a double fault), the point is awarded to the other player.

The only major differences between singles tennis and doubles tennis are the amount of court that is in play and the number of players on the court. In singles, the outer columns on the court are out-of-bounds and the game in one-on-one. In doubles, the whole court is in play, and one person plays by the net while the other is in the back near the baseline. Doubles is two-on-two.

Love-15-30-40

In tennis love means nothing. Literally. "Love" means zero, nil, nada. The points go as follows:

The first point gives the player 15. The server always shouts out the score before serving, so if he/she got the first point, it would be 15 to love, shouted just as "**15-love**." If both players have 15, it is called **15-all**. The server always shouts his score first.

The next point is 30, so if the server makes the next point, he shouts, "**30-15**." The next point is 40. If the player with 40 gets the next point, he wins the game. If both players get 40, it's called **deuce**. In tennis you have to win by two. Once the score goes to deuce, the next point is called **advantage**. If the player with advantage wins the next point, he wins the game; if not, it goes back to deuce. The simplest way to learn this is to watch a match on television. It will make a lot more sense to read this and watch the action at the same time.

THE BREAKDOWN

If the server wins the first point, the score is 15-love.

If the server gets the next point the score is now 30-love.

Then let's say the receiver gets the next point; it's now 30-15.

Then the receiver gets another point—the score becomes 30-all.

The server gets the next point; the score is 40-30.

If the server scores the next point, she is the winner of the match. If the receiver gets the next point the score is now 40–all, which is called deuce.

If the next point goes to the server, it's called advantage. If the server wins the next point she wins the match. If the receiver gets the next point it goes back to deuce.

The two players switch sides of the court on odd-numbered games. A coin toss establishes who serves first. The winner of the coin toss chooses to either serve or receive, and then the loser of the coin toss chooses which side to start on. The players switch serves every game, meaning that each player gets to serve every other game to make it fair.

In major tournament play it's the umpire (who sits in a high chair on the side of the court) who calls out the score before serve.

The Courts

Most tennis courts are made of one of three surfaces:

Hard court: This type of court is a mix of asphalt and concrete. It is the most popular surface because it needs the least amount of maintenance. The speeds are said to be midway between those of a grass court and a clay court.

Grass: These courts are the rarest in today's society because they are very high-maintenance. They need to be mowed and watered often and take the most amount of time to dry after a rainstorm. Grass courts are said to be the fastest surfaces in tennis.

Clay: There are two kinds of clay: red and green. Clay courts are said to be the slowest surfaces for playing and are very high-maintenance as well. These luxe courts are most popular in Europe and Latin America. The courts need to be watered and rolled regularly.

Match Point

In most tennis play, the first person to win two sets wins the match. A set is completed when six games are won. However, it must be won by two games, so often the winner has to win seven games instead of six. For example, if one player has won six games and the other five, the player with six must win one more to make it 7–5.

In major tournament play, the men must win three sets to win the match. Women must win two sets.

When a player is about to win the whole match it is called match point. In major tournament play, the announcer will say "game-set-match" and then the player's last name after the winning point is made.

If the set goes to six games each (6–6) a tiebreak is played. A tiebreak is when each player serves once for one point, and then each player serves twice. Then they switch. The first player to win seven points but be up by two wins the tie-break. That set would then be scored as 7–6 in favor of the winner.

The ATP and WTA

The Association of Tennis Professionals (ATP) is the governing body for professional men's tennis and is also responsible for the weekly rankings of players. For professional women's tennis, the governing body is called the Women's Tennis Association (WTA).

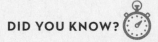

DID YOU KNOW?

Players are required to shake hands at the net after their match is completed.

THE GRAND SLAMS

The four major tournaments during the professional tennis season are called the grand slams or the majors. All grand slam events hold both men's and women's singles and doubles matches. The four grand slams are considered the highest level of playing in the world, on par with the Olympics, where tennis is an Olympic sport.

Australian Open: Played in January, the Australian Open is the first major tournament of the year. The Australian Open is played at Melbourne Park and is played on hard courts.

The French Open: Held in Paris over two weeks in the spring (late May to early June), the French Open is the only major played on clay. Clay is said to be a slower playing surface, and because of this, the French Open is said to be the most physically demanding tennis tournament in the world.

Wimbledon: Widely considered the most prestigious tennis tournament in the world, Wimbledon is the oldest and the only major tournament played on grass. Located in the London suburb of Wimbledon, the tournament is about two weeks long in the summer (late June to early July). Wimbledon also has a strict dress code and requires competitors to wear all-white attire.

U.S. Open: This late-summer tournament is held for two weeks in late August and early September—the weeks before and after Labor Day—in Queens, New York City. The courts are all lit, so night play and television coverage can be in prime time. The courts are a kind of hard court called DecoTurf, which is said to be a bit faster than regular hard court.

DID YOU KNOW?

Although it isn't considered a grand slam event, the Davis Cup is a very popular tournament. It's a country-versus-country event, and the world's sixteen best national teams compete in a round-robin format (see "Tennis Terms to Know"). It's a men-only event. The women's equivalent is called the Federation Cup.

NOTEWORTHY RETIRED PLAYERS

Chris Evert: Evert won eighteen grand slam titles including a record seven at the French Open. She was ranked number one in the world seven years in a row. Known for her blond hair and feminine persona, Evert was rumored to date many famous men including Burt Reynolds. In the 1970s she was romantically linked with famous and talented tennis professional Jimmy Connors, but they broke up before their wedding date. Evert runs a tennis academy in Florida and teaches tennis at area schools.

Martina Navratilova: Navratilova won eighteen grand slam singles titles (eleven were consecutive) and thirty-one grand slam doubles titles. She was arguably the greatest female tennis player of all time. Navratilova famously came out to the public in the early 1980s about her sexual orientation and has written books on tennis and fitness, and has even written fiction. She is a U.S. and Czech dual citizen who continues to play tennis in charity tournaments and other events.

Steffi Graf: Graf won twenty-two grand slam singles titles and won all four majors at least four times. She is the only tennis player to win all four grand slams and an Olympic gold medal in the same year (1988). Considered one of the greatest tennis players of the twentieth century, Graf is married to another tennis legend, Andre Agassi (see below), and one can only assume what sport their offspring will play (and play well).

Billie Jean King: She won twelve grand slam singles titles and sixteen doubles grand slam titles. But despite her competitive tennis achievements, King is most famous for the historic "Battle of the Sexes" match that took place in 1973 in front of more than 30,000 people in Houston, Texas, and more than an estimated 50 million on television in thirty-seven countries. Former Wimbledon men's champion Bobby Riggs, a well-known male chauvinist who was in his fifties, claimed that women's tennis was inferior to men's tennis and that even a man in his fifties could defeat the top-ranked women players. King took on the challenge and defeated Riggs 6–4, 6–3, 6–3.

Arthur Ashe: Ashe was the first African American to win a grand slam tournament and the only one to win a men's singles title at three grand slam events (Australian Open, U.S. Open, and Wimbledon). He is also famous for his social activism and promoting racial peace and civil rights throughout the world. He had a genetic history of heart disease and had two heart surgeries, despite his high fitness level. He contracted HIV from a blood transfusion during surgery and died in 1993 due to AIDS complications. The stadium where the U.S. Open is played is now called Arthur Ashe Stadium.

Pete Sampras: He won fourteen grand slam titles and was also popular in the 1990s due to his fierce (and fun) rivalry with Andre Agassi. Sampras won a record seven Wimbledon titles and a record eight consecutive grand slam tournaments.

He is considered one of the greatest tennis players of all time. Sampras is married to actress Bridgette Wilson (who has starred in films with Adam Sandler and Jennifer Lopez).

Andre Agassi: Also considered one of the greatest tennis players of all time, Agassi won eight grand slam singles titles. He is well known for his huge personality and reveled in the fame and fortune that came with playing pro tennis. His good looks and charm secured him many endorsement deals. His charisma is what some consider the sole reason for tennis's increase in popularity in the 1990s. He won an Olympic gold medal and had one of the best serve returns in the game. He and his wife, Steffi Graf, are very active in charity work and philanthropy.

John McEnroe: McEnroe won seven grand slam singles titles and nine doubles titles. His larger-than-life personality and on- and off-the-court antics made him famous with non–tennis fans and tennis fans alike. He is well known for his tantrums. You-Tube has videos dedicated to McEnroe's most famous rages. The British press nicknamed him "Super Brat," and Nike featured him in an ad campaign in the late 1970s called "Rebel Without a Cause." He has played himself in several movies (two are Adam Sandler movies). He is currently involved in philanthropy and is a tennis commentator in the booth for most of the grand slam tournaments (U.S. coverage). He also was famously married to (and divorced from) Oscar winner Tatum O'Neal and is currently married to musician Patty Smyth.

Honorable Mentions: Bjorn Borg, Jimmy Connors, Ivan Lendl, Boris Becker.

WHO TO KNOW NOW

The Williams Sisters: The Williams sisters are the two most famous and recognizable players in women's tennis today. What they have done for the game is unprecedented. I believe they are the greatest female athletes of all time. They have played each other so far (as of 2009) in eight grand slam finals and in more than twenty matches total. The all-Williams sisters finals are like a soap opera. Writers could not have written the drama any better. They have also competed together in ten grand slam doubles matches and have won them all, as well as two Olympic gold medals. They are so fantastic that each deserves her own spot on the list.

Serena Williams: As of September 2009, Serena had won eleven grand slam singles titles and ten grand slam doubles titles. She held all four grand slam titles simultaneously before having major surgery in 2003. Determined not to let it ruin her career, she stormed back and is still one of the best players in the world today, if not of all time. Her backhand (see "Tennis Terms to Know") is one of the best in the game, and her serve has topped out at the second-fastest speed ever. Serena is a partial owner of the NFL's Miami Dolphins and is involved in numerous charities. She is also a fashion designer and has a popular line of tennis and workout wear for Nike. She is well known for her choice of outfits on the court and has raised quite a few eyebrows around the world.

Venus Williams: Just a year older than Serena, Venus Williams is also one of the best players in the game. Venus has won seven grand slam singles titles so far in her career and ten doubles titles (with her sister). She also has three Olympic gold medals, two in doubles (with Serena) and one in singles play. Venus is also a designer and owns an interior design company in Florida.

Maria Sharapova: Although Sharapova has three grand slam titles (Wimbledon in 2004, the U.S. Open in 2006, and the Australian Open in 2008), she is better known for her modeling and endorsement deals. The striking Russian beauty has modeled in some high-profile shoots including the *Sports Illustrated* swimsuit issue.

Roger Federer: The Swiss tennis sensation has won fifteen grand slams; though he is still playing, he is considered by many to be the greatest tennis player of all time. He reached ten consecutive grand slam finals (a record). He also holds the record for the most consecutive weeks ranked number one in the world (237).

Andy Roddick: North America's highest-ranked player has won only one grand slam final (the U.S. Open in 2003) so far but still has had an illustrious career. He is well known for some heartbreaking losses in grand slam finals including a recent thriller against Roger Federer at Wimbledon in 2009. Roddick holds the record for the fastest serve ever, recorded at 155 mph. The hunky blond married a *Sports Illustrated* swimsuit model in 2009 and prior to that famously dated actress-singer Mandy Moore.

Rafael Nadal: The Spanish tennis heartthrob has won six grand slam titles so far and an Olympic gold medal in singles play in 2008. He and Roger Federer have developed a major rivalry, playing each other in seven grand slam finals so far. Their breathtaking match at the Wimbledon finals in 2008 is said to be the greatest tennis match of all time by many tennis professionals, commentators, and critics.

DID YOU KNOW?

Tennis balls were originally white and stayed that way for more than a hundred years. It wasn't until 1972 that the yellow balls we know today were used in matches. Research showed that the yellow ball was easier to see on television. Wimbledon continued to use the white balls until switching to yellow in 1986.

GOING TO A TENNIS MATCH

Marlena Hall knows a thing or two about tennis. She played competitively in college and teaches the game at a Florida high school. She is also the public relations and media manager at the Delray Beach International Tennis Championships. Here are her tips for having the best tennis experience possible. Hall covers everything from what to wear to decorum so there are no surprises when attending a tennis match.

Bring a Decent-sized Handbag

"In my opinion, a versatile (dress it up or down) and fashionable tote (medium to large size) is optimal. And size is key. A big, bulky bag would be uncomfortable and would be heavy on your lap, plus it would take up a lot of leg space on the floor. A small clutch is convenient; however, it would provide you with only enough room for a credit card, an ID, your ticket, maybe a lip gloss, and a Sharpie pen for autograph signing. Where would you put the autographed tennis ball or T-shirt, sponsor souvenirs, and tournament program? Be prepared to walk out of a tennis event with more things than you walked in with."

Apparel Changes Depending on If It Is a Day Event or a Night Event

"A daytime session ticket is usually ten A.M. to five P.M. and a nighttime session is usually five P.M. to last call. Depending on where you are and what time of year it is, your apparel choice will depend on the temperature, especially for an outdoor event. There will be many people wearing polo T-shirts, shorts, and jeans at the daytime session. But the nighttime session transforms into a 'see-and-be-seen' catwalk. Consider changing the daytime shorts or cargo pants to dark denim jeans. Or throw on a cute cardigan or scarf over the summer cotton dress you wore during the day. Take the light-colored spaghetti-strap tank top you had on earlier and add a blazer.

"Because you never know who you might meet at a tennis event, dress to impress. Tennis tournaments now are making a move to become all-encompassing events with live music, great food and drinks, fashion, celebrity sightings, and even cheerleaders. Multipurpose footwear just doesn't cut it anymore. Dressy but comfortable stylish sneakers or fashionista flats will work well at a tennis tournament. Look for versatile shoes that will allow you to participate in the 'Fast Serve' contest but will also help you get your groove on on the dance floor. Flip-flops aren't tops on my list, as most don't come with the support of a fastened back. All that walking and talking, browsing and carousing, will beg for some comfort and support. So leave those three-inch-and-up heels at home. The most common tennis game wear is a cross between concert attire and casual to mildly dressy dining wear."

The Bathrooms Will Most Likely Be Clean and New

"Bathrooms differ from event to event. You can expect that the bathrooms at a tennis tournament will be stocked with soap and towels, and they will most likely not be portable."

There Is a Lot More Going On Than Just Tennis

"When purchasing a ticket for a tournament, ask the ticket office or look on the tournament's Web site and investigate what kinds of functions the tournament hosts, whether on site or off, during the tournament and leading up to it. Yes, you might have to shell out a couple more bucks than your admittance ticket requires, but you'll experience an opportunity to see and interact with tournament players, CEOs, sponsor representatives, and other business types at various hospitality functions.

"I'd also recommend taking advantage of all of the tents and sponsor booths around the site. Most have something to offer that you can take home as a souvenir, like pens, T-shirts, koozies, food samples, raffles for cruises, racquets, autographed and framed posters, etc. This is where having a large tote would come into play."

Be Aware of Proper Fan Behavior

"Like at many sporting and nonsporting events, ushers are there to greet you and help you get to your seats. But in tennis they are trained to act like the guards at Buckingham Palace when a point is in play. Until the players switch sides on the odd games, don't even think of getting past the usher. On court, the players can hear and see every twitch and turn. If fans were allowed to come and go, moving in and out of their seats to get another drink or use the restrooms, a player would get easily distracted and publicly annoyed. The best time to leave would be at the end of a set, or simply leave at the changeover and watch the matches from the outside stadium television screens until it's time to get back in. During serves the announcer will say, 'Quiet please,' and you can hear a pin drop."

But Tennis Has Evolved a Bit

"Tennis is no longer a conservative and all-too-polite, quiet sport. Feel free to get a little rowdy. Unlike at team sports, a tennis spectator has the unique opportunity to 'feel' what the player is feeling vicariously from the sidelines. Clapping and cheering and 'oohs' and 'ahhs' can really make a difference in the third tiebreak of a match. It can be the visual and auditory elixir that a player needs to revive him- or herself. Energy is infectious."

TENNIS TERMS TO KNOW

Ace: A serve that is not touched by the receiver. Usually a powerful, great serve.

Backhand: Hitting the ball on the backside of the racquet at the opposite side of the body. A right-handed player hits a backhand on the left side of his body; a left-hander, on the right side.

Break: To win a game as the receiver, meaning to "break" serve.

Break point: The point before a **break** would occur, for example, 30-40 or 40-advantage.

Fault: A serve that does not place the ball where it should be.

Forehand: The most common, powerful, and natural stroke. A right-handed player hits the ball with the racqet on the right side of her body; a left-hander, with the racquet on the left side.

Mixed doubles: When a doubles match is played with a man and a woman on each side of the court.

Round robin: A tournament where the players are split up into groups of three or four. They all play each other, and then the top one or two advance to the next round.

Volley: A forehand or backhand shot executed before the ball bounces in the court.

GOLF

First, the urban legend that the word "golf" is an acronym for "gentlemen only, ladies forbidden" is simply not true. However, there were many (and there still are a few) golf clubs around the world that were "men only" clubs.

Like tennis, golf is a popular recreational sport played by the everyday man and woman. The point of golf is simple: Hit the ball in the hole. Simple, right? Well, if you have ever tried to take a swing at a golf ball, you know that nothing is ever that simple. You may be a putt-putt champion, but things change more than a bit once you get out on a course.

The goal of golf is to use clubs (tools for hitting the golf ball) to put the ball in the hole using as few strokes as possible while combating various obstacles on the course like water hazards (ponds, usually man-made), bunkers (sand traps), and rough (tall grass that will slow down or even stop a ball in its tracks).

There are four main kinds of clubs. They are woods, putters, irons, and hybrids. Putters are used to "putt" or roll the ball into the hole. Woods are used for long-range drives. Irons are generally used on more difficult surfaces like the rough. Hybrids are a combination of a wood and an iron.

THE COURSE

Most golf courses have eighteen holes. Some courses have nine holes that can be played twice to make the full round of golf. A **round** is playing eighteen holes. No two golf courses are exactly alike. Designing golf courses is a lucrative business. Golf courses are a billion-dollar industry. There are landscape architects, maintenance crews, and other personnel that work on golf only. There are golf colleges in the U.S. that specialize in learning how to run a golf course, from growing the grass properly to maintenance to management.

Each hole has a teeing area, where there are usually three marked spots: one for men, one for women, and a tournament or championship tee. Each has a different distance to the hole. When **teeing off**, a player can either put the ball directly on the ground or place it on a tee, which is a little piece of plastic that sticks in the ground. The tee slightly elevates the ball off of the ground.

The **fairway** and the **rough** are the middle ground between the teeing area and the hole. After a golfer tees off, the ball will most likely end up in one of these two areas. It is more advantageous to have the ball land on the fairway because the grass is cut short and is perfect for driving the ball toward the hole. The rough has longer grass, so it's harder to hit the ball cleanly.

The **green** is the small area surrounding the hole where putts are made. On all other areas of the course the ball is hit in the air. But on the green the ball stays on the ground and is putted into the hole. The grass is cut very short and smooth so the ball can roll evenly.

PAR

Every hole on a golf course is classified by its par. **Par** is the number of strokes a skilled golfer would take to put the ball in the hole. For example, if a hole is called a par 3, a golfer should have the ball in the hole on his third stroke. Most holes are a par 3, par 4, or par 5. There are some par-6 and par-7 holes around the world but they are very rare.

Usually championship-caliber courses are around a par 72, meaning that if you added up par for all of the holes the total number would be 72.

Scoring

The key in golf is to have the least number of strokes. The golfer wants to have a low number. A score of -11 (11 under par) is much better than -3 (3 under par).

The most common form of professional golf played is called stroke play. In stroke play, a golfer's score on each hole is tallied to make a final score at the end.

If a hole is a par 5, but the golfer gets in in three shots, it's called an eagle. The golfer just made 2 under par. Here are the common golf scoring terms:

An **ace** is a hole in one.

−2 is called an **eagle,** two strokes under par.

−1 is called a **birdie,** one stroke under par.

+1 is called a **bogey,** one stroke over par.

+2 is called a **double bogey,** two strokes over par.

The most commonly heard terms are birdies and bogeys.

Handicap

A handicap is leverage given to an amateur golfer while playing the course. It is a numerical measure of a golfer's ability. The lower the handicap, the better the golfer. The handicap is the number of strokes above par a golfer usually scores for a round. The golfer's handicap is subtracted from his or her final score at the end. This way, if a golfer who averages a 95 is competing with someone who averages a 72, a fair and competitive game can be played.

THE MAJORS

The four most prestigious professional golf tournaments are called "the majors" and are played in spring and summer. Three of the four are played in the U.S.

The Masters is the first major tournament of the year, held in April. The Masters is played at Augusta National Golf Club in Georgia and is the only major that is played at the same location every year. The winner of the Masters gets a signature green jacket.

The **U.S. Open** is held in June. An "open" championship is one where, technically, any golfer can play, either by invitation or by qualifying at one of the qualifying events held before the tournament. The U.S. Open's location changes yearly.

The British Open (called the Open Championship in most other countries) is played in July and is held at one of seven different locations in Great Britain.

The PGA Championship is played in late August. (Although recent contests have not started until September due to scheduling conflicts, it is traditionally played exactly four weekends after the British Open.) The PGA Championship is held at different distinguished golf courses around the country.

WHO TO KNOW

Arnold Palmer is considered one of the greatest golfers of all time. He began along with Jack Nicklaus (see below) during the beginning of the television age of golf. With the first televised events taking place, Palmer helped bring the game into the mainstream and became one of its most popular players. He won seven majors during his career. He currently focuses on humanitarian efforts. He is also well known for his namesake drink (half iced tea, half lemonade), called Arnold Palmer Tee.

Jack Nicklaus is also considered one of the greatest golfers of all time. He won eighteen majors during his long career. He currently owns one of the largest golf course design companies in the world, and his award-winning courses are considered some of the best in the world. He has also written many books on golf, golf instruction, and life as a pro golfer.

Tiger Woods has transcended golf and entered mainstream culture. He is bigger than the game, and everyone in the country knows his name. Even if you have never seen a golf tournament, you have definitely heard of Tiger Woods. He is arguably the greatest player ever to play the game. As of 2009 he had already won fourteen majors, and he was the youngest player to ever win the grand slam of golf—winning all four majors in the same calendar year. He is also the only person (so far) to be named *Sports Illustrated*'s Sportsman of the Year more than once. His endorsements reach far and wide, and his name is far more recognizable than any other golfer's, if not any other athlete's in the world.

Golf rankings change so frequently that it is hard to list current players to know. This is because one year a few golfers dominate, but the next year different players are on top. **Phil Mickelson** (known as "Lefty") was once famous for being the "best golfer who had never won a major," but he finally won his first in 2004, and as of 2009 he had won three. **Sergio Garcia,** a young Spanish player, is now known as the best golfer without a major championship win. He is a golf heartthrob with legions of young girls as fans. Golf's "bad boy" is **John Daly**. He is better known for his off-the-course antics and his questionable on-the-course clothing choices (Google "John Daly pants" and see what cringeworthy pictures come up). Some sportswriters have joked that you can see his pants from space. There are many other notable players, but because the rankings change so quickly, someone popular today can be yesterday's news tomorrow.

GOING TO A GOLF TOURNAMENT

The first thing I learned at the very first golf tournament I attended was that it is not for the prissy. Long walks, hot sun, and Porta Pottis are usually not my idea of a fun day. But a golf tournament can be worth it if you like the sport and know how to deal with the elements. I previously worked in public relations in the golf industry and have been to many events. Here is what you need to know:

Wear Comfortable Shoes!

Sneakers are the best footwear at a golf tournament. Comfortable sandals are also acceptable, but no heels (you are walking on grass, hello!). Very comfortable low wedges are acceptable too, but sneakers are best, even if they're not the most flattering footwear. This is because you will be walking. A lot. Sometimes the walk from the parking area to the course is longer than the entire course. Many times the parking areas will be so far away from the action that trolleys are there to take spectators to and from their cars. And the average golf course is almost four miles long from hole to hole—not considering the twists and turns, which make it even longer.

Know What to Bring

Going to a golf tournament entails a long day, so the girlie girl will definitely want a hairbrush and makeup and maybe blotting sheets or powder. But besides money and makeup, spectators really aren't allowed much else. All golf tournaments ban cell phones, cameras, and food and beverages. You will be turned back if security finds a cell phone or camera, so leave the gadgets at home or in the car. Although most of us can hardly imagine going a whole day without our cell phones, that is the rule, and in order to attend you must comply.

Preppy Is Always Chic

Golf tournaments are a sea of khaki and polos. Pants or capris in a light cotton material and any khaki color are recommended. Khaki skirts and shorts are also recommended, but nothing too short. The classic preppy look is appropriate at golf tournaments because golf is always associated with country clubs and proper etiquette. Knee-length cotton dresses are also appropriate. Denim, short shorts, and skirts and tank tops are frowned upon. Shoulders must traditionally be covered at golf tournaments, hence the sea of polos. If your outfit is deemed inappropriate you will be turned away.

There Will Be a Lot of Men There

Typically the crowd at a golf tournament is mostly men. Lots of club professionals (golfers who teach at courses) and corporate professionals attend these events.

The Only Bathrooms Will Be Porta Pottis

Don't be too frightened. Many times they are new high-tech systems and are scattered throughout the course, but while you are on the course, Porta Pottis are the only bathrooms. You will not want to walk all the way back to the clubhouse to use the restrooms throughout the day.

Food and Beverage Tents Will Be Set Up Throughout the Grounds

Bring cash for the food and beverage tents. Walking back to the clubhouse is too far during the tournament, so these tents are typically set up throughout the course. Some are nicer than others.

There are a few different ways to enjoy a golf tournament. Here are the three most typical scenarios:

Typical Day 1: "Stalking" Specific Players

Many times people are there to see certain individuals. Get a tee time sheet so that you can be there when your favorite golfer tees off (hits the ball on the first hole). If you want to see multiple players (Tiger Woods, Phil Mickelson, etc.) you may want to stay at the same hole to see them all tee off.

Typical Day 2: Find a Seat and Stick with It

If you want to see every player pass by, find a nice relaxing spot on the course. There will usually be bleachers set up at some par 3s and at the final holes. Arrive early to grab your seat, as they are first-come, first-served and they fill up quickly! If you are lucky enough to get a bleacher seat, you may want to stay there the whole day and leave the seats in shifts. If your whole party leaves, chances are the seats will be gone before you get back.

Typical Day 3: Watch in Style

Corporate tents are really the way to go if you can get into one through a company or charity purchase. The tents are usually very nice and offer air-conditioning and full-service food and beverages. They are also usually set up at a great location on the course so you can see every golfer pass at one point during the day.

GOLF TERMS TO KNOW

Approach: A shot intended to land the ball on the **green**.

Back nine: The last nine holes of the course.

Fairway: The area of the course between the tee and the **green**.

Green: The area where putts are played.

Hazards: A bunker or a permanent water fixture such as a pond.

Laying up: Choosing to hit the ball shorter than you can in order to avoid a **hazard**.

Par: The standard score for a hole and for the entire course.

Putting green: An area close to the clubhouse used for practicing putts.

Rough: The tall, rough grass that borders the **fairway**.

Teeing ground: The area where a player drives the ball or tees off.

MAJOR LEAGUE SOCCER (MLS)

Soccer is the world's most popular sport. One of the few countries where it isn't the most popular is the United States. The proper name for soccer is association football. "Soccer" is a nickname that was created in England. The reason we use "soccer" and not "football" is because we have our own football, which was originally based on the old rules of association football (soccer).

The regular season runs from March through October. The playoffs start at the end of October and run through November. The MLS Cup (the championship) is played in late November and aired on ESPN.

U.S. Soccer is the governing body for international play for the U.S. teams. The U.S. women's team and the U.S men's team compete in international tournaments. Many MLS players are also on the U.S men's team.

The Fédération Internationale de Football Association (FIFA) is the international governing body of the most famous soccer tournament in the world, the FIFA World Cup. The World Cup is held every four years, and qualifying for the event is held in the three years prior to the event. Thirty-two nations make the final tournament. As of 2009, Brazil has the most World Cup wins with five.

FIFA also hosts a Women's World Cup tournament.

The top professional league in North America is called Major League Soccer (MLS). The league is split into two conferences.

WESTERN CONFERENCE	EASTERN CONFERENCE
Chivas USA	Chicago Fire
Colorado Rapids	Columbus Crew
FC Dallas	D.C. United
Houston Dynamo	Kansas City Wizards
Los Angeles Galaxy	New York Red Bulls
Real Salt Lake	New England Revolution
San Jose Earthquakes	Toronto FC
Seattle Sounders FC	Philadelphia (2010)
Portland (2011)	
Vancouver (2011)	

Soccer is a big part of the Olympics on both the men's and women's side as well.

NASCAR

National Association for Stock Car Auto Racing (NASCAR) fans are some of the most passionate and educated about their sport in the country. The proof is in the more than 100,000 people that show up for (and sell out) every major race. That is the largest turnout of fans for any sport in the U.S.

The highest level of competition in NASCAR is the Sprint Cup Series. "The Chase" for the Sprint Cup narrows the field

BEST TENNIS, GOLF, SOCCER, AND NASCAR MOVIES

Happy Gilmore **(1996)**. The always hilarious Adam Sandler plays Happy Gilmore, a wanna-be hockey player with a great slap shot. His grandmother is about to lose her home because she didn't pay her taxes for many years. Happy joins the PGA Tour after winning a contest for his amazing driving abilities (as in driving the golf ball when teeing off—see "Golf") in order to make money to win the house back. The movie is charming and funny but it's the scene-stealing Bob Barker who makes this movie a classic and must-see.

Caddyshack **(1980)**. This movie is on many critics' all-time-best lists and not just in the sports category. The story centers on a working-class character who works as a caddy at an upscale country club in order to make money for college and the hilarious antics that go on there. The quality of actors and comedians makes this flick stand out from all others. Chevy Chase, Rodney Dangerfield, and Bill Murray (whose scenes are laugh-out-loud hilarious) all star in the film, although Chase and Murray have only one scene together. Rumor had it that the two were still fighting from their *Saturday Night Live* days. The film is now a cult classic but original reviews weren't very positive.

Pat and Mike **(1952)**. Truth is, I can't find one quality tennis movie. A couple have been attempted (*Wimbledon, Match Point*) but neither was fantastic enough for me. *Pat and Mike* may be an old film, but it stars Katharine Hepburn as a tennis and golf pro and Spencer Tracy as her manager. Seeing the two longtime real-life lovers on screen together is magical, especially considering that they hid it so well from the public eye. You can almost see the fireworks and tension between them.

Bend It Like Beckham **(2002).** There are many great soccer documentaries but this indie fictional film was a sleeper hit that won the 2003 ESPY for Best Sports Movie and was also nominated for Best Musical or Comedy at the Golden Globes. A young Indian girl in a very religious family rebels against her parents and culture in order to play on a women's soccer team. The movie centers on the girl and her struggle to keep her family and teammates happy all while trying to find herself and decide where she will go to college the following year. The title comes from soccer celebrity David Beckham's ability to score by bending (curving) the ball around defenders. Beckham does not appear in the film (although he was okay with the idea) due to schedule conflicts; a look-alike is used at the end.

Days of Thunder **(1990).** Starring Tom Cruise and Nicole Kidman, this movie revolves around Cruise's character, who is a young, hotshot rookie looking to make it big in NASCAR. Kidman plays a brain surgeon (yes, a brain surgeon) and his love interest. This big-budget production was produced by Jerry Bruckheimer and in classic Bruckheimer fashion contains lots of explosions and pyrotechnics. The movie itself does showcase NASCAR and the passion behind the sport.

Honorable Mentions: *Tin Cup* (1996); *Talladega Nights: The Ballad of Ricky Bobby* (2006).

of drivers to the twelve with the most points; they then continue on to see who can win the cup.

More Fortune 500 companies sponsor NASCAR events than any other sport. Sponsoring and branding are very visible and important in NASCAR. The NFL is the only sport to have higher television ratings.

I, however, do not know much about NASCAR and am still learning the sport. So trying to write and teach about NASCAR in this book would be doing a disservice to the sport and its fans. There are many books and Web sites dedicated to teaching new fans about NASCAR. For more information, start with NASCAR.com.

Note: While NASCAR is only in the United States, auto racing takes place around the world, in Europe, Asia, and Australia.

7

Quick Guide: The Girlie Girl's Cheat Sheet for Information on the Fly

RANDOM FACT

Games from all four major pro sports (baseball, basketball, football, and hockey) last, on average, three to three and a half hours. Playoff and championship games will be longer due to commercials and in-game entertainment.

MAJOR LEAGUE BASEBALL (MLB) CHEAT SHEET

There are **nine** innings in a game. There are two halves to every inning. The top half is when the visiting team bats and the bottom half is when the home team bats.

There are also **nine** starters that play the **nine** positions in the field and fill the **nine** spots in the lineup (the batting order).

Three **strikes** is an out, called a **strikeout**.

Four **balls** is a **walk** and the batter goes to first base.

There are three **outs** in an inning.

The team with the most runs at the end of nine innings wins the game. But if the home team is winning when it comes time for them to bat in the bottom of the ninth, the game is over and they don't need their "**last ups**."

If the score is tied after nine full innings, the game goes to **extra innings**.

Once a player is taken out of the game for any reason, he is out for the rest of the game.

Most games are played outdoors. Night games usually start around seven P.M. and day games usually start around one P.M.

Alcoholic beverages are not served after the **seventh-inning stretch**—which occurs between the halves of the seventh inning.

The **hot stove** is a term that involves off-season trades, sign-ings, and other deals. It comes from the old days and invokes an image of fans sitting around a "hot stove" discussing the off-season rumors and acquisitions.

When reading player "stats" (statistics) on television or in a newspaper, if it says a player is **0-for-1**, it means that out of one try, the player did not get on base and was called out for what-ever reason. If the box score says **3-for-4**, it means that out of four at bats, three were successful with either a hit or a home run.

Do wear flats. Flip-flops will be comfy, but your feet will probably get filthy. Update the casual look by wearing sandals, ballerina flats, or city sneakers. If you wear only heels, stick with a wedge for some added height.

Do remember that baseball is a casual game. It's played in summer, and midseason games will most likely be hot. Shorts, casual cotton sundresses, T-shirts, and tanks will fill the stands.

Do remember that the baseball season is long. Early and late in the season will require a jacket or sweater. In northern climates, bring a lightweight cardigan or wrap even to midsummer games.

Do bring whatever size bag you like. But remember that the floor will not be clean and there may be no place to put your bag. I keep my bag (I prefer large bags) stuffed between my lower back and the seat back.

Do wear summer makeup, like tinted moisturizer with SPF (for day games), and bring blotting sheets and/or powder to combat summer stickiness and shine.

Don't wear stilettos or superhigh heels of any kind to a baseball game. Even in the luxury boxes you will feel uncomfortable. If you must wear a heel, stick with a wedge or summer espadrille.

Don't wear anything too short or too tight. You will be sitting most of the game.

Don't be embarrassed about wearing or bringing a rain poncho. You will be glad you have one when the occasional summer shower hits.

> ## INJURIES
>
> When a player gets injured, the name of "where" they go differs from sport to sport.
>
> Baseball: Called the **DL**: the disabled list.
>
> Hockey, basketball, and football: Called the **IR**, injured reserve.

COMMONLY HEARD MEDICAL TERMS IN SPORTS

Torn ACL: The ACL is a ligament that stabilizes the knee. When someone has a torn ACL he often says his knee "gave out." After surgery, rehab can take up to a year. The player is probably out for the entire season.

Tommy John surgery: When a ligament in the elbow is replaced with a tendon from somewhere else in the body. The surgery is named after former Los Angeles Dodgers pitcher Tommy John, who was the first person to successfully have the surgery.

Concussions: A concussion is usually caused by a big blow to the head and most commonly occurs in football and hockey. Concussions can be minor or major, but they do affect how a person's brain works. They can usually be healed by rest. Doctors are still debating and researching the long-term consequences of too many concussions.

Rotator cuff: A rotator-cuff injury is damage to the muscle and tendons in the shoulder. This injury can heal on its own with rest.

. . .

NATIONAL FOOTBALL LEAGUE (NFL) CHEAT SHEET

The game is made up of four fifteen-minute **quarters** separated by a twelve-minute **halftime**.

The first two quarters are called the **first half**. The second two are called the **second half**.

Each team gets three **time-outs** per half.

The **quarterback** (QB) is the leader on the field; he either throws the ball or hands it off to a **running back**.

The offense gets four **downs** (tries) to advance the ball ten yards.

A **first down** is after a team gets ten yards, and so, a fresh set of downs.

If the offense gets into the other team's **end zone**, they score a **touchdown**.

A **touchdown** is worth six points. After the touchdown the offense goes for the **point after** or **extra point**, worth one point. Usually a team completes this and gets a total of seven points for a touchdown.

If the offense can't get into the end zone after three downs but is close, they try to kick the ball through the **goalposts**. This is called a **field goal**.

A **field goal** is worth three points.

Even if you have no idea what the penalty is, the referee will point his arm in the direction of the team that the penalty is against.

Do remember that football is all-weather and to dress appropriately. The game is played in blizzards and tropical storms. The only time a game is delayed or canceled is for severe lightning or if there is a threat to life.

Do be aware that for most of the country, a heavy jacket, boots, gloves, a hat, and a scarf are appropriate, especially for mid- to late-season games.

Do tailgate. It's half the experience. Arrive early and be prepared to leave late. Football stadiums are some of the largest in the country. More than sixty thousand cars all leaving at once can be hectic. Be patient.

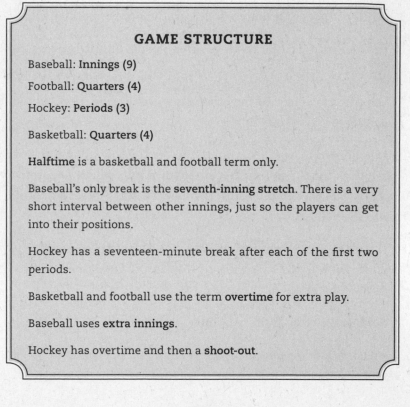

GAME STRUCTURE

Baseball: **Innings (9)**

Football: **Quarters (4)**

Hockey: **Periods (3)**

Basketball: **Quarters (4)**

Halftime is a basketball and football term only.

Baseball's only break is the **seventh-inning stretch**. There is a very short interval between other innings, just so the players can get into their positions.

Hockey has a seventeen-minute break after each of the first two periods.

Basketball and football use the term **overtime** for extra play.

Baseball uses **extra innings**.

Hockey has overtime and then a **shoot-out**.

WHERE THEY PLAY

Hockey: rink, arena

Football: stadium, gridiron

Baseball: park, field, stadium

Basketball: court, hardwood, arena

Do wear flats. If you must wear a heel, you can get away with a wedge boot or sandal (depending on the weather), but city sneakers or flat boots will be the most appropriate and comfortable.

Do invest in some team gear. The slim-fitting, cut-for-a-woman's-figure jerseys they sell on team Web sites are a flattering and sexy way to attend the game but still fit in with the boys.

Don't wear stilettos or high heels; they will be uncomfortable and dangerous. The narrow stairs and narrower seating rows beg for a stable shoe. Football is usually played outdoors (except for a few domed stadiums) and football is one of the more casual sports. Why would you want to ruin your pricey heels?

Don't wear a long coat. Although a coat will most likely be necessary, a full-length or three-quarter-length coat will be uncomfortable for sitting in stadium seats. Opt for a shorter coat that ends at the waist or hips.

. . .

NATIONAL BASKETBALL ASSOCIATION (NBA) CHEAT SHEET

Basketball games are made up of four twelve-minute **quarters** separated by a fifteen-minute **halftime** in between the second and third quarters.

The offense (the side with the ball) has twenty-four seconds to take a shot that at least touches the rim or backboard.

A **rebound** is when a player gets the ball immediately after a missed shot.

Each player is allowed five fouls. On the sixth he must leave the game. A **foul** is contact that disrupts the game or play.

Five players on each team are on the court at a time: two **guards**, two **forwards**, and a **center**.

The players play both offense and defense.

Free throws are worth one point.

A shot from behind the painted arc (the **three-point line**) is worth three points. All other shots are worth two points.

Defense is usually either **zone** (when the players cover a specific area) or **man-to-man** (when the players cover a specific player).

"**Swish**" is the same as "**nothing but net.**" When a basket is made it hits only the net and makes a *swish* noise.

"**And one!**" is shouted when a player makes a basket and is fouled on the play, resulting in a free throw following the basket.

Players must **dribble** the ball in order to walk or run with it. They are allowed only two steps without dribbling.

A **travel** is when a player takes too many steps without **dribbling**.

Do wear heels if you wish. Basketball is the dressiest sport of all the majors. Games are played in indoor temperature-controlled arenas that are cleaner and often newer than other sports stadiums.

Do feel free to dress a little nicer than you would for other sports. Jeans, blouses, and boots will fill the stands. People will be in everything from team jerseys to suits to sweat suits.

Do wear your regular makeup routine.

Don't wear flip-flops. Basketball isn't a cutoffs and flip-flop environment. If you prefer flats then sandals, ballerina flats, or city sneakers are perfect.

Don't go too dressy. Although basketball is the most fashionable sport, save the club outfits for, well, the clubs. Office/business attire is perfect for a basketball game.

. . .

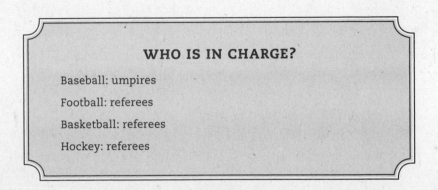

WHO IS IN CHARGE?

Baseball: umpires

Football: referees

Basketball: referees

Hockey: referees

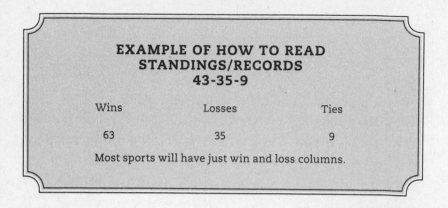

**EXAMPLE OF HOW TO READ
STANDINGS/RECORDS
43-35-9**

Wins	Losses	Ties
63	35	9

Most sports will have just win and loss columns.

SPORTS BUSINESS TERMS

Free agency: The rules vary among sports, but generally a free agent is a player who is free to pursue options from other teams and test the open market. His contract has expired and he is eligible to sign with another team. An unrestricted free agent is just that, unrestricted. A restricted free agent means that the player can entertain offers, but his last team has some rights in the transaction, usually related to some form of compensation.

Salary caps: A salary cap is a limit that teams can spend on player salaries. This can be on a per-player basis or on the entire roster or, in most cases, both.

- NBA: In basketball, the salary cap is a "soft cap," meaning teams can exceed the salary cap in order to retain the rights to a player who has already been on the team. The NBA has a salary cap for both total roster and individual players.
- NFL: In pro football, the salary cap is a "hard cap," meaning no team can go over the cap. Ever. If violated,

fines of up to $5 million can be imposed as well as a loss of draft picks. There is also a "hard floor," meaning a minimum amount that a team must pay its players. This keeps competition equal. Some say it is the reason for the popularity of the NFL: It has a "level playing field."

- NHL: The NHL has a hard salary cap for teams and for individual players. This was implemented after the lockout during the 2004-5 season. The cap changes yearly, as it does with most sports, based on inflation and adjustments to revenues each season.

Baseball is the only sport without a salary cap. That's why the New York Yankees can have a payroll of $200 million and the Florida Marlins can have a payroll of $30 million, yet both teams compete in major league baseball against major league talent. Some superstars are paid more individually than entire small-market teams. Baseball has a **luxury tax**, which is a fee that teams with payrolls higher than a determined amount pay to the league.

RANDOM FACT

Just as the NCAA Division I Tournament's finalists are called the Final Four, NCAA hockey calls its finalists the Frozen Four.

CONVERSATION STARTERS

Baseball: What do you think of the DH rule? Should Pete Rose be in the Hall of Fame? Who are the top three baseball players of all time?

Football: What is your favorite team and why? (Since football is so popular, everyone has a team.) Do you prefer college over pro football? Sudden-death overtime . . . yes or no?

Basketball: Magic or Bird? Russell or Chamberlain? Can defense really win games? Do you think players should be able to go to the NBA straight from high school?

Hockey: How bad did the lockout (2004–5) affect the game and its fans? Do you think it can come back? What do you think about the shoot-out rules?

Below are topics I'd stay away from unless you are extremely knowledgeable about the subject and don't mind a good fight:

- Steroids and other performance-enhancing drugs
- Player arrests/personal problems off the playing field
- Controversial/missed calls

NATIONAL HOCKEY LEAGUE (NHL) CHEAT SHEET

NHL games have **three twenty-minute periods**.

There is about a seventeen-minute break in between periods to resurface the ice.

RANDOM FACT

All basketball and hockey games are played indoors unless there is a special promotion going on. Most baseball and football games are outdoors.

SERIES PLAY

Best of five: First team to win three games wins the series. Games four and five are "if necessary."

Best of seven: First team to win four games wins the series. Games five through seven are "if necessary."

In **baseball**, a seven-game series follows a **2-3-2** format. The home team plays two at home, then the away team plays three at its home, and then the series goes back to the home team if necessary for the final two games.

In **basketball**, a seven-game playoff series is played with a **2-2-1-1-1** format. The home team plays two games on its court and then the away team plays two games on its court. Then it goes back to the home team for one game, the away team for one game, and then the final game will be played on the home team's court. But the **NBA Finals** (the championship series) is played with a **2-3-2** format.

In **hockey,** a seven-game playoff series is in a **2-2-1-1-1** format.

Football is the only sport of the majors that does not play a series during the playoffs. Football is one and done, meaning win and you are in, lose and you go home.

Note: Turn to the chapter about the sport you're watching to find out how home-field advantage is determined.

The machine you see "cleaning" the ice between periods is an ice resurfacer, generally called a **Zamboni**.

There are six players on the ice for each team at a time: a **goalie**, a **center**, two **wings**, and two **defensemen**.

SEASONS

Winter: Football, hockey, basketball, college basketball

Spring: Basketball, hockey, baseball

Summer: Baseball

Fall: Baseball, college football, football, college basketball

A **power play** is when one team has more skaters than the other team. This occurs when the other team was issued a penalty and has a player sitting in the **penalty box**. A power play is usually five skaters against four.

Icing is when the puck crosses at least two red lines before being touched. This is called so that a team can't just slap the puck away to get it out of their zone. If icing occurs, the puck comes back into the defending zone of the team that caused the icing.

Three stars are awarded at the end of a hockey game. They go to the three best performances in that particular game.

Do bring a jacket, sweater, or wrap. Ice equals cold. The arenas are chilly so the ice doesn't melt.

Do wear a heel if you want to, especially on a boot, since it is so cold in hockey arenas.

Do wear cute jeans, boots, and a sweater to a game if you wish, but note that hockey is the sport with the most team jerseys in the stands. Many people will be wearing hockey jerseys, so if you are a big fan, invest in one.

Don't wear flip-flops, shorts, or skirts without tights or leggings. It is cold. Even a bra with some padding is a good idea.

Don't forget that there are three periods and ample time in between the periods to leave the seats. There is no specific halftime.

ACKNOWLEDGMENTS

Thank you . . .

To my mom. Thank you for everything you are and everything you do. Thank you for your love and support during this long, difficult process. You are truly an inspiration to me and the strongest woman I know. I love you more.

To my brother David, the smartest sports guy I know. Thank you for going to games with me for almost three decades and putting up with my persistent questions, my overanalyzing of everything, and the occasional shoe mishap. Also thanks for always waiting for me outside the bathroom in crowded stadiums. Thank you for having my back when I almost got you into a few fights in rival parking lots (not my finest moments) and for always being there to answer every sports question I ask. And P.S.: Foul ball incident? The guy was sitting next to me!

To my best friend, "Andrea." If you'd never shouted, "Intersection!" at a football game more than a decade ago, this book would never have happened.

To the Gutierrez sisters, Carolina and Maritza, because your questions and willingness to learn the games sparked my love for teaching others.

To Mediabistro.com: Without your courses I would never have gotten the ball rolling on this project.

ACKNOWLEDGMENTS

To Ryan Fischer-Harbage for teaching my first Mediabistro night class (nonfiction proposal writing) and taking me into your agency.

To Nicole Robson, my agent, for showing me how this is done and working hard to see it through.

To Susan Shapiro for teaching that very first "Secrets to Selling Your First Book" six-hour Sunday seminar. I believe I still owe you dinner.

To Michelle Richter, my editor at St. Martin's Press, an extraordinary and talented writer and editor. Your patience is very much appreciated, and your willingness to work with me to make the best project possible is amazing. I am forever grateful.

To Lenny Camacho, the best kickball pitcher on the planet, not to mention a fabulous artist who is responsible for all of the artwork in this book, including the cover gal.

To Adam Goldberger, an amazing copy editor whose meticulous work and attention to detail are greatly appreciated.

To Jack Falla, Boston University journalism professor and book author, who passed away before this book was printed. In your office hours, while I was showing you my clips (back in 2004), you said that if I could find a way to combine my sports clips with my fashion and beauty clips, then I would have my own niche. You lit the creative spark that started this whole process, and I wish you could have seen the completed work.

To the Boston Red Sox, New England Patriots, Boston Celtics, Boston Bruins, Florida Gators, Florida Marlins, Miami Heat, and Florida Panthers because without all of you I'd have no one to cheer for! Thank you for being there to fuel my sports addiction and passion for the games, and the history and the beauty in sports.

REFERENCES AND SUGGESTED READING

The sources below not only helped me write this book, but are excellent tools for any sports fan to learn more about the games. I recommend visiting these Web sites and reading these books and magazines to build upon your now vast sports knowledge.

Web sites

Bleacherreport.com (for aspiring sports journalists)

CBSsports.com

ESPN.go.com

Foxsports.com

MLB.com

NBA.com

NFL.com

NHL.com

Opensports.com

Sportsillustrated.cnn.com

Magazines

ESPN The Magazine

Golf

Golf Digest

Sports Illustrated

Sporting News

Street and Smith's Sports Business Journal

Tennis

Books

Bissinger, H. G. *Friday Night Lights*. New York: Addison-Wesley, 1990.

Davidson, John. *Hockey for Dummies*. New York: Wiley Publishing, 2000.

Falla, Jack. *Home Ice*. Tampa, Fla.: McGregor Publishing, 2001.

———. *Open Ice*. New York: Wiley Publishing, 2008.

Formosa, Dan, and Paul Hamburger. *Baseball Field Guide*. New York: Thunder's Mouth Press, 2006.

Garcia, Nina. *The Little Black Book of Style*. New York: HarperCollins, 2007.

Kinsella, W. P. *Shoeless Joe*. New York: Houghton Mifflin, 1982.

Lewis, Michael. *Moneyball*. New York: W. W. Norton, 2003.

Linett, Andrea, and Kim France. *The Lucky Shopping Manual*. New York: Gotham, 2003.

Lovinger, Jay, ed. *The Gospel According to ESPN*. New York: Hyperion, 2002.

Malamud, Bernard. *The Natural*. New York: Harcourt, Brace, 1952.

Morgan, Joe. *Baseball for Dummies*. New York: Wiley Publishing, 2006.

National Baseball Hall of Fame and National Geographic. *Baseball as America*. Washington, D.C.: National Geographic, 2002.

Oliver, Jon. *Basketball Fundamentals*. Champaign, Ill.: Human Kinetics Publishers, 2006.

Phelps, Richard. *Basketball for Dummies*. New York: Wiley Publishing, 2000.

Stover, Lauren. *The Bombshell Manual of Style*. New York: Hyperion, 2001.

Sullivan, George. *All About Football*. New York: Putnam, 1987.

——, ed. *Football Rules Illustrated*. New York: Simon & Schuster, 1981.

Theisman, Joe. *The Complete Idiot's Guide to Football*. New York: Penguin Group, 2001.